ITEMS ATT … TS
MIGH …

- **A Traditional Crib—**It may seem unimaginable, but you actually might not need this expensive, space-wasting "babycage" unless you plan to modify it to set up a sidecar-type family bed using a crib.

- **Bottles—**It is assumed that every baby will, at one time or another, drink from a bottle and that every new parent needs to have at least a couple on hand. Not true! You shouldn't offer your breastfed baby a bottle in the early weeks lest she become nipple confused. And if you can avoid being away from your baby at feeding times until she is six or seven months old, there is no need for her to *ever* have an artificial nipple in her mouth.

- **A Baby Carriage/Stroller—**Think how disorienting it must be for a tiny baby to be rolled around in a box on wheels after having spent the past nine months curled up snugly inside his or her mama. Although western parents seem to have a love affair with the stroller, attachment parenting asks that you limit its use and instead actually carry your baby and toddler.

Find out more ways to raise a happier, healthier child in

ATTACHMENT PARENTING

Attachment Parenting

Instinctive Care for Your Baby and Young Child

Katie Allison Granju

with **BETSY KENNEDY**, R.N., M.S.N.

Introduction by William Sears, M.D.

POCKET BOOKS

New York London Toronto Sydney Singapore

Publisher's Note
Please be aware that the phone numbers and web site addresses included in this book are up-to-date as of publication, but they may be subject to change.

An *Original* Publication of POCKET BOOKS

POCKET BOOKS, a division of Simon & Schuster Inc.
1230 Avenue of the Americas, New York, NY 10020

ISBN: 0-671-02762-X

First Pocket Books trade paperback printing August 1999

10 9 8 7 6 5 4

Cover design by Rod Hernandez
Cover photo © Barnaby Hall/Photonica
Book design by Alma Orenstein

Printed in the U.S.A.

Permissions

"Sleeping with Baby, December" by Kelly Averill-Savino, copyright © 1999 by Kelly Averill-Savino; reprinted with permission. Excerpts from *The Baby Book: Everything You Need to Know About Your Baby—From Birth to Age Two* by William M. Sears, M.D., and Martha Sears (Little, Brown & Co., 1993), copyright © 1993 by William M. Sears, M.D., and Martha Sears; reprinted with permission. Excerpts from *Our Babies, Ourselves: How Biology and Culture Shape the Way We Parent* by Meredith F. Small (Doubleday, 1998), copyright © 1998 by Meredith F. Small; reprinted with permission. Excerpts from *The Vital Touch: How Intimate Contact with Your Baby Leads to Happier, Healthier Development* by Sharon Heller (Henry Holt and Co., Inc., 1997), copyright © 1997 by Sharon Heller; reprinted with permission. Excerpts from *So That's What They're For!: Breastfeeding Basics* by Janet Tamaro-Natt (Adams Media Corp., 1996), copyright © 1996, 1998 by Janet Tamaro; reprinted with permission. David Servan-Schreiber, M.D., Ph.D., quotes printed with permission. "Ten Things That Every Expectant Parent Needs to Know About Breastfeeding," essay by J. Rachael Hamlet, copyright © 1995 by J. Rachael Hamlet; reprinted with permission. "Breastfeeding Myths," essay by Jack Newman, M.D., F.R.C.P.C.; reprinted by permission. Katherine Dettwyler, Ph.D., Associate Professor of Anthropology and Nutrition, Texas A&M University; quotes printed with permission. "Breastfeeding & the Law," essay by Elizabeth Baldwin, J.D.; reprinted with permission. Quotes from "Rethinking Healthy Infant Sleep," by Dr. James McKenna, copyright © 1995 by James McKenna; reprinted with permission.

For my grandmother, NANCY ORR ANDERSON,
who tenderly rocked me, held me, and loved me, and
who gave me her gift of language

And in memory of KADIN SCOTT WILLIAM LONG,
who taught parents all over the world some
life-changing lessons

ACKNOWLEDGMENTS

I would like to thank my own parents, who modeled attachment parenting for me long before there was a name for it. I also want to thank Kimi Abernathy for showing me how a real mama does it! My sister, Betsy, has seen me through both the best and worst days of my life as a parent and I look forward to watching her attachment parent my beloved niece, Eleanor. Although my brother Robert has teased me unmercifully about my "lactomania," he has also served as cheering section and careful editor. Dale Rosenberg, Amy Scott, and Lisa Cabus also merit mention as editors and sounding boards extraordinaire. Thank you to those people who helped me by caring lovingly for my children so that I could work on the book: Bill and Karen Pyle, Buck and Suzanne Rogers, Karen and Jenna Nolt, and the folks at The Episcopal School of Knoxville. Special appreciation goes to my inimitable in-laws, Jean-Pierre and Barbara, without whom I could never take care of my family, much less write anything! Spike Gillespie also has my slavish appreciation. As she knows, without her guidance, this book would not exist. I would also like to thank my agent, Elizabeth Kaplan and my editor, Nancy Miller, as well as assistant editor, Kim Kanner, all of whom have made my maiden voyage as an author an extremely satisfying one.

And then there are the APMOMS, an incredible group of attachment parenting mamas from whom I continue to learn every single day. Mothers need other mothers in their life and I am lucky to have this bunch. Thank you to Cecilia, Janice, Meg, Heidi, Dawn, Joylyn, Peggy, Laura, Jeannie, Lori, Alison, Robin,

Pauline, Rachael, Melissa, Paula, Carolyn, Andrea, Maury, Susan, and Darcy. I also want to offer my public gratitude to the scores of attachment parents who allowed me to listen in (and sometimes quote them!) during their Internet conversations, as well as those who took the time to fill out my lengthy survey on attachment parenting.

Writing the book involved utilizing the expertise and collective knowledge of numerous helpful experts. Jan Barger, IBCLC provided invaluable assistance with the chapters on breastfeeding. Her unparalleled professional background and understanding of parents and babies added greatly to my understanding of human lactation. Kathy Dettwyler's input was also crucial to me, especially in writing about extended breastfeeding and weaning. Thanks also go to Rachael Hamlet, Lisa Marasco, Rich Buhler, Norma Jane Bumgarner, Dr. Jack Newman, Elizabeth Baldwin, Meredith F. Small, Martha Sears, Diane Weissinger, Kathleen Auerbach, Kelly Averill-Savino, Sharon Heller, Dia Michels, James McKenna, Drs. Klaus and Kennell, Robert Wright, and others for allowing me to reprint some of their brilliant insights in order to make my own points. My deep gratitude goes to the very generous Dr. William Sears for writing the introduction. And of course, I couldn't have written the book without my collaborator (and dear friend since the first day of seventh grade), Betsy Babb Kennedy.

Lastly, I want to say thank you to Chris, my husband, friend and the best attachment father imaginable to our three exceptional little people, Henry, Jane, and Elliot.

CONTENTS

"Sleeping with Baby, December"
by Kelly Averill-Savino **xvii**
Introduction by William Sears, M.D. **xix**

1. What Is Attachment Parenting? **1**
Why Is It Called Attachment Parenting? 3
What's in the Attachment Parenting Toolkit? 4
Attachment Parenting: The Rest of the Story 6
The Very Best Attachment Parenting Resources 10

2. The Pregnant Parent's Guide to Planning for Attachment **19**
Working Through Personal Issues: Dumping Your Own Attachment-Inhibiting Baggage 20
How Were *You* Parented? 20
The Very Best Resources for Moving Past Your Own Childhood and Becoming an Attachment Parent 22
Second Time Parents, First Time Attachment Parents 23
Your Personal Touch-O-Meter 24
When You and Your Partner Disagree 26
(Not) Shopping for Baby: Why Attachment Parents Don't Need All That Baby Gear 27
Items You Will Definitely Want 28
Items You Might Need or Enjoy Having 32
Items You Might Not Need (or at least should consider carefully before acquiring) 36

The Very Best Attachment Parenting Retail Resources 39
Planning to Breastfeed . . . Instead of Planning to *Try* to Breastfeed 43
Ten Things That Every Expectant Parent Needs to Know About Breastfeeding 45
Doctor Shopping: Choosing Your Baby's Health Care Provider 51
The Very Best Children's Health Care Guides 56

3. Attachment Parenting Your Newborn 57
Your Birth Setting 58
The Baby-Friendly Hospital Initiative 62
Baby Arrives! 63
Rooming In: Because New Parents Need Their Babies and New Babies Need Their Parents 70
Gentle Care for Your Newborn 74
Consider *Not* Circumcising Your Baby 75
The Very Best Resources for Learning More About Circumcision 78
Bonding After a Cesarean Birth 79
Have Your Partner Present for Your C-section 79
Breastfeed Your Baby as Soon as Possible After Birth 80
Enlist Help with Rooming In 80
Stay with Your Baby If She Can't Stay with You (When Your New Baby Needs Special Care) 81
Tricia's Tried and True Tips for Attachment Parenting Your Hospitalized Preemie 83

4. Making the Breast vs. Bottle Choice 89
Breastfeeding Isn't "Better"; It's Just Normal: A New Way of Thinking About Infant Feeding Choices 90
The Breast-Bottle Decision and Your Baby's Health 91
There's Just Something About Breastmilk. . . . 94
So What About Infant Formula? 95

The Breast-Bottle Decision and *Your* Health 100
"But I Wasn't Breastfed and I'm Just Fine!" 101
Wow! Why Don't Doctors Tell You This Stuff?! 102
The Role of Infant Formula Manufacturers 106
The Story of the "WHO Code" 110
Become a Lactivist!: The Very Best Resources for Learning More About Breastfeeding Advocacy 111
Chapter Endnotes, including medical research on infant feeding issues 114

5. Breastfeeding: Much More Than Food **122**
Breastfeeding and Attachment: Your Biological Connection with Your Nursling 123
Breastfeeding and the Pleasure Principle 125
How Does Your Baby Experience Breastfeeding? 127
Supply and Demand: You and Your Baby in Sync 128
Why Do So Many Women Believe That They "Don't Have Enough Milk" for Their Babies? 129
How Can I Be Sure My Breastfed Baby Is Getting Enough Milk? 133
Cloth Diapering 134
The Very Best Resources for Cloth-Diapering Parents 136
Learning How to Breastfeed 136
The Very Best Resources for Learning *How* to Breastfeed 138
What Is La Leche League? 141
When Breastfeeding Is a Challenge 144
Breastfeeding and Guilt 146
Slaying the Most Common Breastfeeding Myths 150
Breastfeeding Multiples: One Mother's Experience 158
Cue-feeding: Breastfeeding Success, Attachment, and Convenience . . . All Rolled into One 161
The Problem with Parent-Directed Schedule-Feeding 166
The Difference Between Breastfeeding and *Nursing* Your Child 169

Breastfeeding in Public 171
The Breastfeeding Father 174
Nursing Your Bottle-Fed Baby 176

6. Attachment Parenting All Through the Night 181
Desperately Seeking Sleep . . . and Finding It Right in Your Own Bed 182
How Humans Sleep 184
The Many Benefits of Family Sleep Sharing 185
The Family Bed: A How-To Manual 189
Safety and the Family Bed 191
Sleeping with Your Baby May Prevent SIDS 193
Questions About the Family Bed 196
Infant Sleep: What's "Normal"? 199
Sleeping Through the Night: Don't Rush It (Yes, you read that correctly!) 201
Nighttime Parenting 203
Gentle Weaning from the Family Bed: One Family's Story 206
Sleep Problems 207
The Very Best Resources for Solving Your Child's Sleep Problems 209
Please, Please, *Please* Don't "Ferberize" Your Baby 210
But Do the "Cry It Out" Techniques "Work"? 214

7. The Working Parent's Guide to Attachment Parenting 219
Your Baby's Need for You and Your Decision Whether or Not to Work 220
To Work or Not to Work? That Is the Question 223
Keep Your Options (and Your Mind) Open! 225
Working Parent/Attachment Parent 226
Breastfeeding and the Working Mother 229
Breastfeeding on the Job: The Basics 231

Creating a Breastfeeding-Friendly Workplace 237
The Very Best Resources for Working, Breastfeeding Mothers 241
The Attachment Parent's Guide to Childcare 245
The Attachment Parenting–Friendly Caregiver 246
Creating Community for Your Child 248
The Critical Importance of Consistency in Caregiving 249
Child-Caregiver Ratio 250
Attachment Grandparenting 252
Don't Settle 253
The Very Best Childcare Resources for Attachment Parents 254
Money, Money, Money 255
Paradigm Busting: New Ways to Work for Attachment Parents 257

8. To Have and to Hold 265
Baby-Carrying Around the Globe 267
Why Don't We Carry and Hold Our Babies? 268
Our Untouched Babies 268
Artificial Baby-Containers 270
Can a Baby Be Held or Carried "Too Much"? 272
The Many Benefits of Wearing Your Baby 274
Which Baby Carrier Is Right for You? 278
Safety Tips for Baby-Wearing Parents 288

9. Breastfeeding Past the First Year 290
I've Never Seen a Nursing Toddler; Is It "Normal" to Breastfeed Past the First Year? 291
Breastfeeding Duration Around the World 293
A Natural Duration for Breastfeeding? 294
The Growing Popularity of Sustained Breastfeeding 296
Sustained Breastfeeding and Your Child's Health 298
Sustained Breastfeeding and Your Health 299

Mothering Your Older Nursling 300
What's It Really Like to Breastfeed Past the First Year? 302
Dealing with the Opinions of Others 303
The Very Best Resources for Parents of Older Nurslings 306
Nursing Through Pregnancy 307
Tandem Nursing 309
Weaning: Upward and Onward! 311

SLEEPING WITH BABY, DECEMBER

Steam rises, here and north of here,
from a hundred holes in the snow,
from a hundred warm stone caves
where sister bear curls dreaming against the cold
around a cub who grumbles, stirs
the way you do against my belly,
under this thick, white blanket.

In the walls of here and everywhere
in fluffy nests of shredded work gloves,
leaves, insulation,
mouse mother's white belly curves
like the crescent moon around her naked brood,
containing their blindness.
Think of it: in attic boxes, basement drawers,
warm fur and the tiny miracle of mouse milk.

Even in deepest sleep I cannot put you down.
I know from instinct
that birth takes months; a push from womb
to cradleboard, hammock, sling.
Woman rises, sore, from birthing,
returns to the work of life. Hands free
for gathering, digging in dirt, kneading bread,
she walks unhindered, patting the sling
like a pregnant belly, shifting familiar weight.

Baby remembers the tight, dark warmth,
the comfort of heartsounds, rides rocked
in her walk, awash in the waves of her breathing
like before.

At night, in the furs and quilts,
in hammocks and sleeping mats, pioneer rope beds,
in wigwams, grass huts, soddies,
they slept as we sleep now
heart to heart.

Before you were born
I listened for you all night, curled on my side around your squirming.
Now your breathing comforts me back; you wake
and nurse, rooting, grunting like a lion cub,
smelling of warmth and milk.
When newborn nightmares furrow your brow,
(what fear from deep and long ago?)
Push that quivering bottom lip, you stiffen, reach out, touch . . .
mama
and that face erases, small pond after a rain.

I try to imagine why you should be
in the next room, alone, on that wide caged mattress
where predators drool and prowl,
where instinct (your only compass) says unheld is unsafe.

Alone, crying that wail of the dropped and falling,
the howl of the foundling,
orphan left on forest floor,
on glacial ridge, in desert sand,
alone.

Kelly Averill-Savino, 1995

INTRODUCTION

by William Sears, M.D.

When I first began using the term "attachment parenting" nearly twenty years ago, I felt ridiculous giving a name to a style of baby care that parents would naturally practice if they followed their own intuition rather than listening to the advice of others. Attachment parenting is a high-touch, responsive style of baby care that brings out the best in both baby and parents. It is a style of parenting that my wife Martha and I have practiced with our own eight children and have refined after years of on-the-job training. The five features of this style of parenting are what we call the "baby B's": birth bonding, breastfeeding, bedsharing (sleeping with your baby), babywearing (carrying your baby in a sling), and belief in the signal value of your baby's cry. Not all parents will be able to practice all five of these parenting practices all of the time, as there may be medical or lifestyle circumstances that prevent it. Yet you can regard these as starter tips—attachment tools to help you and your baby get connected. When expectant parents come into my office for prenatal counseling, I tell them that my main goal is to help them become an expert in their own baby, because no one else will. These attachment parenting tools help new parents to become experts in their own baby.

Over the past twenty-seven years in pediatric practice, I have counseled thousands of parents on how to practice attachment parenting and have had the opportunity to see the long-term beneficial effects of this style of parenting on babies, parents, and the family. Here is what I have observed:

Attachment parents develop confidence. They start out using the basic tools of attachment parenting, but soon feel confident and free enough to branch out. They find what works for them rather than succumbing to the norms of their neighborhood. During well-baby checkups, I often ask new parents, "Is it working?" I advise parents to periodically take inventory of what works with their parenting and discard what doesn't. For example, some babies initially sleep better in bed with their parents, but become restless later on, necessitating a change in sleeping arrangements. I advise parents that there is no right or wrong place for babies to sleep. Wherever all family members get the best night's sleep is the right arrangement for that family.

Attachment parents also seem to enjoy parenting more. Because of the strong early connection with their babies, attachment parents orchestrate their lifestyles and working schedules to include their baby.

Over the years, as I have followed more and more attachment parents, I have noticed one other quality that distinguishes attachment parents and their children: "sensitivity." Attachment-parented infants grow up to become "kids who care." They are compassionate when other children cry and are quickly there to offer comfort. As teenagers, they are bothered by social injustices and do something to correct them. Because of their inner sensitivity, they are willing to swim upstream against the current.

Additionally, I have noticed that attachment-parented children are easier to discipline. Attachment parents are intuitively able to see situations from their child's viewpoint. In return, the connected child desires to please his parents, so discipline becomes easier. Attachment parents and their children trust one another, and trust is the basis of parental authority. Because attachment parents are better able to convey what behavior is expected of their children, their children are better able to understand those expectations.

Sometimes, parents are criticized for practicing this style of parenting. They may be told that attachment parenting will produce spoiled and clingy children. In my experience as a pediatrician and father of eight, however, just the opposite is true. Attachment parenting promotes independence. Because the child trusts his parents and has such a healthy self-image, the child naturally becomes more self-confident and independent.

I like to think of attached baby care as a wonderful parenting pill. If you give your child proper doses of attachment parenting during the early years, you have a greater chance of turning out to be confident, competent, sensitive, and connected to others. Yet, even the best medicines have a warning on the package insert. For attachment parenting, this insert might read, "Overdose may lead to mother burnout." For this reason, healthy attachment parenting means responding appropriately to your child's needs—knowing when to say "yes" and when to say "no." Even in our family, we have to work hard to achieve this balance. With each one of our children I have had to occasionally remind my wife, Martha, to take care of herself in addition to meeting the needs of our babies. One day I put a note up on the bathroom mirror that read, "Each day, remember that what our baby needs most is a happy, rested mother."

If this is your first exposure to attachment parenting, the early months with your baby may sound like one big give-a-thon: parents give and baby takes. Yet, healthy attachment parenting involves mutual giving. Parents give to baby and baby gives back to them. A classic example of this mutual giving is breastfeeding. Mother gives to baby nature's most perfect milk. In turn, the nursing baby stimulates maternal and intuition building hormones that flow to the mother. As a result of this mutual giving, babies and parents grow together.

Finally, as you and your baby become more strongly connected through attachment parenting, you may wonder if he will ever ease into independence. He will. Keep in mind that the time in your arms, at your breast, and in your bed is a very short time in the total life of your child, yet the memories of love and parental responsiveness last a lifetime.

CHAPTER 1

What Is Attachment Parenting?

✦ **"From all we know, every primate baby is designed to be physically attached to someone who will feed, protect and care for it, and teach it about being human—they have been adapted over millions of years to expect nothing less."**

—*Anthropologist Meredith F. Small, From* Our Babies, Ourselves

NEW PARENTHOOD CAN BE PRETTY OVERWHELMING. EAGER TO provide the best possible care for the little person you have created, you may find yourself calling your pediatrician's office frequently with questions about how best to interact with your baby. Maybe you have turned to one of the scores of childcare experts whose works crowd the bookshelves, magazine racks, and airwaves in search of information regarding your many parenting concerns. Perhaps you have picked up this book looking for further instructions and step-by-step advice on "what to expect" or how to become "babywise."

If so, you will be disappointed. Why? Because the parenting book you now hold in your hands is fundamentally different from the others you may have seen. It isn't going to tell you exactly how often you should nurse your baby, or how many hours he should sleep each night because *we don't know you, your child, or your family.* Our philosophy is that you yourself—in partnership with your child—are the real "parenting experts" when it comes to your own family, even if you don't realize it yet. What, then, does this book offer in place of the usual laundry list of parenting "do's and "don'ts"? We are going to introduce you to a wonderfully adaptable parenting *style* that really works for today's families. Christened "attachment parenting" by bestselling pediatrician and father of eight, Dr. William Sears, this philosophy embraces gentle, common sensical, cross-cultural, and time-tested parenting practices. While you will likely find that the information in *Attachment Parenting* is in many ways quite different from much of the childcare guidance you may have read before, you will also discover that it is supported by a growing body of solid scientific research, as well as recommendations by specialists in a wide variety of disciplines related to family life.

> ▶ *"In my view, a healthy family is one in which there is a recognition of needs and, even if they can't all be met, they are acknowledged."*
>
> —RICH BUHLER

In writing this book, we have listened to hundreds of today's parents from every background and walk of life tell us how and why attachment parenting works for their families. As you read what we have learned from them, you will discover that attachment parenting, so radically different from the conventional parenting wisdom with which many of us were raised (and which still permeates most of today's childcare guidance), offers you the tools to confidently and successfully nurture your child in a highly respectful way that also maximizes your own enjoyment and fulfillment as a parent. We hope that you will read this book with an open mind and the understanding that you can and should adapt the information we will be presenting so that it is most relevant to your life. The ways in which these ideas take root and blossom within your own family is up to you and your child—the parenting experts. Welcome to the growing community of attachment parenting!

Why Is It Called Attachment Parenting?

> ✦ **"There is no such thing as a baby; there is a baby and someone."**
>
> —*British psychoanalyst D.W. Winnicott*

This parenting style is called attachment parenting in recognition of both the beauty and the critical importance of a secure attachment between parent and young child. Many of the ideas and practices to which you will be introduced in this book—such as long-term breastfeeding and sleeping with your baby—easily and naturally assist in the development of this crucial love-bond. Numerous studies—as well as common sense and personal experience—tell us that the early relationships that babies and young children form with their parents play a pivotal role in the development of the adults they will later become. The attachment parenting style produces securely attached children, not to mention confidently responsive parents. When mothers and fathers stay physically close to their babies and learn to intuit their unique cues, babies are assured that they are being heard and understood. As a result, they are encouraged to continue trying to communicate with their parents. This delicate give and take teaches your child that she can trust you, and it empowers you in the knowledge that you truly understand her needs. Attachment parenting is a gift you give to your child that will serve her well in all her subsequent relationships.

What's in the Attachment Parenting Toolkit?

Although the precise way in which these concepts work will vary from family to family, the following practices are the core nurturing tools for attachment parents. We will be exploring them in great depth as you make your way through the book, but here is a brief introduction to the "basics" of attachment parenting:

1. Bond with your baby in the early days.

The first hours and days that parents and baby spend together constitute a unique "sensitive period" during which both are exceptionally open to falling in love with one another. A gentle birth, followed by close, relaxed physical contact with your new baby provides the best context in which to get attachment parenting off to a great start. With supportive caregiving for the new mother, you have the ideal setting for a group of individuals to begin the process of becoming a family.

2. Breastfeed your baby.

Breastfeeding is a centerpiece of the attachment parenting style. For starters, it's one of the most important things you can do as a parent to safeguard your child's health. But breastfeeding is about much more than nutrition. In fact, the nursing relationship is like no other in the human experience. For both baby and mother, breastfeeding enhances their interaction with and enjoyment of one another. Attachment parenting encourages "cue-feeding" (sometimes called "breastfeeding on demand"), as opposed to parent-directed scheduled feeding. With cue-feeding, parents trust babies themselves to know when and how much they need to nurse. In addition, many attachment parents breastfeed far past the first year and respect their nursling's own unique timetable for weaning. Throughout the following chapters, you will be introduced to the very best in resources for nursing families—at the bookstore, on the Internet, and in your own community—all from the attachment parenting perspective.

3. Practice responsive caregiving.

Parents who are in close physical contact with their babies and young children and who remain open to their cues find that they are better able to figure out the "how" of parenting. On the other hand, parents who have been convinced that they should let their babies "cry it out" or only nurse for nourishment (as opposed to comfort) can often feel out of sync with their young children. When you allow yourself to get to know your own baby's special cues and routines you will feel more connected and comfortable with him. While it's true that this process of getting in tune with your child comes more easily for some parents than for others, consistently responsive caregiving eases the way for *every* parent-child pair.

4. Sleep with or very near your baby or young child.

Although "family bedding" is the cultural norm over much of the planet, it has misguidedly become something of a taboo in modern, western parenthood. However, parents who sleep with their babies and young children nestled nearby enjoy both restful nights and enhanced family closeness. Additionally, properly prepared family bedding is safer for babies than being left alone in a crib down the hall.

5. Carry, hold, or "wear" your baby.

In many cultures all over the world, parents believe that it is beneficial to keep their little ones safe and healthy by carrying them close to their own body in some type of soft, cloth carrier. Of course, many other mammals also carry their "velcro babies" close to the warmth of their bodies until their offspring are ready to venture forth on their own. Attachment parents utilize one or more of the various types of modern baby carriers—as a cloth sling frontpack or backpack—in order to "wear" their children. This allows busy parents more freedom to get things done while still offering their little ones the physical closeness that they need. Research has confirmed that carried babies cry less and are more content than others.

6. Respect your child as an individual right from the start.

Although many parents today push their babies and very young children to become "independent" as quickly as possible, attachment parents respect each child's own special timetable for growing out of their early (and healthy) dependency needs. Children who are allowed to enter each new developmental stage *as they become ready,* as opposed to when parents deem it "time" to wean, sleep through the night, or stay alone without parents, are ultimately *more* self-confident and independent as older children and adults. You can't force a flower to bloom before it's ready. Trying to do so will only damage the petals.

> ✦ **"Every stage in a child's life is there for a purpose. If we can respect and respond to her needs fully during each stage of her life, she can be done with that stage and move on."**
>
> —NAOMI ALDORT, FAMILY COUNSELOR AND WRITER

Attachment Parenting: The Rest of the Story

> ✦ **". . . you may be thinking that attachment parenting is all giving, giving, giving. Well, to a certain extent, that is true. Mothers are givers and babies are**

takers—that is a realistic expectation of a mother-baby relationship. The baby's ability to give back will come later. Better takers usually become better givers."

—DR. WILLIAM SEARS

Now that you have an understanding of the basics of attachment parenting, you may be left with some questions about how this parenting style actually works with real parents just like you. Here are some points to remember:

1. Attachment parenting is flexible.

The basic philosophy and practices of this style of parenting can mesh with a wide variety of family configurations and lifestyles. Married, single, adoptive, foster, working, and at-home parents all find attachment parenting to be a wonderful way to nurture their children and grow as parents. Attachment parenting is also adaptable to your child's unique temperament. Mothers and fathers of fussy, high-need children usually discover it to be an especially good fit.

2. Attachment parenting is about mothering . . . and fathering.

Although attachment parenting does emphasize the seminal role that mothers have in breastfeeding their babies, this doesn't leave fathers out. A willing, involved father or other partner has many important roles in attachment parenting a baby. So, as you read this book, assume that, with the exception of actually putting baby to breast, the attachment parenting concepts and practices that we describe will work well for both men and women.

3. Attachment parenting doesn't turn mothers and fathers into "martyrs."

Initially, the parenting style we advocate may sound tiring or overwhelming. The idea of spending so much time simply being with our children—in our arms, at our breasts and in our beds—

may seem daunting. This is because most of us come to parenthood steeped in the sterile, detached, put-the-baby-down-with-a-propped-bottle parenting culture with which we were raised. But babies and young children thrive better—and develop into healthier adults—with the attachment parenting style. A great deal of the much-discussed burden of guilt that modern parents seem to carry around comes from the fact that deep down, perhaps unconsciously, we know this. We sense that—no matter what some parenting expert has told us—we *should* hold our babies more, *should* be there for them during the night, and *should* nurse them when they simply need our loving touch. This internal struggle between what we intuitively know our young children need and how we have been told we should behave toward them really exhausts parents. On the other hand, parenting in a way that we can be sure meets our children's needs is actually very liberating. As Dr. William Sears has said, "There is great comfort in feeling connected to your baby. Attachment parenting is the best way we know to get connected."

4. Attachment parenting can be "the easy way" for busy, modern parents.

Parenting is hard work, no doubt about it. And parents should adapt their lives to their children rather than expecting a baby to fit conveniently into an already overscheduled adult life. However, in many ways, attachment parenting allows parents to more easily combine caring for a baby or young child with continuing to enjoy their "old" life. For example, by "wearing" your baby in a sling, you can simply take him along when you go shopping, to a restaurant or even to work. By sleeping with your baby, you avoid much of the legendary sleeplessness of new parenthood, thus allowing you to be more alert and productive during the day. Breastfeeding offers you the spontaneity to get out of the house quickly, easily and without the advance planning of packing (and then lugging around) bottles, sterile water, formula, pacifiers, etc.

You will discover many other ways in which attachment parenting can make your life easier as you read through the chapters ahead.

5. Attachment parenting is family-centered, not child-centered.

Perhaps you worry that caring for your child in this way will place your child "in control." This isn't the case. Although most parents naturally find that their beloved children are indeed the center of their world in many ways, attachment parenting takes everyone in the family's needs into consideration. Other parenting styles emphasize parents' needs over baby's or occasionally, vice-versa. With attachment parenting, parents and children find their needs in cooperation with one another, thus creating a family-centered lifestyle. A key benefit of this responsive style of caregiving is that both parents and their children feel that they are getting their "cup filled," as some parents say. Children feel whole and secure, while parents feel more relaxed and confident. When the inevitable stresses and strains of daily family life come calling, everyone is better equipped to deal with them . . . together.

6. Attachment parenting assists with your gentle guidance (aka: discipline) of your child.

Meeting your child's needs through attachment parenting doesn't "spoil" her; it allows your child's natural independence, self-control, and ability to delay gratification to develop. When babies and young children feel secure and nurtured, they have less cause to engage in behaviors that many parents find annoying, such as whining, crying, and clinging. When you feel bonded with your baby and you have learned to read her cues, you are better able to respond to what she is trying to tell you through her various behaviors.

Perhaps the most important thing to remember about attachment parenting is that it is much more than the sum of its parts. It isn't just a simple list of parenting tools. Some women who breastfeed do not practice attachment parenting, while many parents who have never used a baby sling do. Attachment parenting is a way of thinking about your child and your relationship with her. It is a belief that your child is to be trusted, and that she knows what she needs at each developmental stage. It is a willingness to be truly present for your child, both physically and emotionally. It is a respect for the value of your role as parent and for the sensitive bond that the two of you share. Experienced attachment parents who have seen their children through early childhood and beyond describe this gentle nurturing style as a completely fulfilling way of life.

The Very Best Attachment Parenting Resources

BOOKS (IN ADDITION TO THIS ONE, OF COURSE!)

Our Babies, Ourselves: How Biology and Culture Shape the Way We Parent. Small, Meredith F. New York: Doubleday, 1998.

Bonding: Building the Foundations of Secure Attachment and Independence. Klaus, Marshall, H., Phyllis H. Klaus, and John H. Kennell. Reading, MA: Addison-Wesley, 1995.

The Discipline Book: Everything You Need to Know to Have a Better-Behaved Child—From Birth to Age Ten. Sears, William M., and Martha Sears. New York: Little, Brown & Co., 1995.

The Vital Touch: How Intimate Contact with Your Baby Leads to Happier, Healthier Development. Heller, Sharon. New York: Henry Holt and Co., Inc., 1997.

Giving the Love That Heals: A Guide for Parents. Hendrix, Harville, and Helen Hunt. New York: Pocket Books, 1997.

Untouched: The Need for Genuine Affection in an Impersonal World. Caplan, Mariana. Prescott, AZ: Hohm Pr., 1998.

The Baby Book: Everything You Need to Know About Your Baby—From Birth to Age Two. Sears, William M., and Martha Sears. New York: Little, Brown & Co., 1993.

Children First: What Our Society Must Do—And Is Not Doing—For Our Children Today. Leach, Penelope. New York: Alfred A. Knopf, Inc, 1995.

Growing Together: A Parent's Guide to Baby's First Year. Sears, William. Schaumburg, IL: La Leche League, Intl., 1997.

The Continuum Concept. Liedloff, Jean. Reading, MA: Addison-Wesley, 1985.

The Complete Book of Christian Parenting & Child Care: A Medical & Moral Guide to Raising Children. Sears, William M., and Martha Sears. Nashville: Broadman & Holman Publishers, 1997.

Twenty-Five Things Every New Mother Should Know. Sears, Martha, and William Sears. Edited by Linda Ziedrich. Boston: Harvard Common Press, 1995.

A Secure Base. Bowlby, John. New York: Basic Books, 1990.

A Ride on Mother's Back: A Day of Baby-Carrying Around the World. Bernhard, Emery. San Diego: Harcourt Brace Children's Books, 1996.

PERIODICALS

Mothering Magazine

Mothering Magazine
P.O. Box 1690
Santa Fe, NM 87504

Phone: (505) 984–8116

Subscriptions: (800) 984–8116

Mothering *is the best and best known magazine for families who are interested in attachment parenting concepts. Describing itself as "the natural family living magazine,"* Mothering *tackles parenting topics—from breastfeeding your toddler to cloth diapering to family bedding—in a thoughtful, thought provoking way.*

Breast & Belly

P.O. Box 395

Dover, NH 03821

Breast & Belly *is a magazine of birth stories, gentle parenting, and breastfeeding advocacy.*

Hip Mama

P.O. Box 9097

Oakland, CA 94613

Phone: (510) 597–1610

http://www.hipmama.com

Hip Mama *is the most provocative parenting magazine in existence. Unlike many other parenting periodicals,* Hip Mama *doesn't leave out nontraditional and low income reader families.*

Compleat Mother

P.O. Box 2009

Minot, North Dakota 58702

http://www.compleatmother.com

Compleat Mother *provides readers with support and information for the attachment style of parenting. Its views tend toward the radical.*

New Beginnings

La Leche League International

1400 N. Meacham Rd.

P.O. Box 4079

Schaumburg, IL 60168–4079
http://www.lalecheleague.org

New Beginnings *is the official magazine from La Leche League International, the world's foremost breastfeeding support volunteer organization. In the magazine you will find articles relating to every aspect of La Leche League's philosophy of "mothering through breastfeeding."*

The Mother Is Me
64 Voorhis Road
Lincoln Park, NJ 07035
http://www.motherisme.com
E-mail: Colleen@kjsl.com

The Mother Is Me *is an innovative feminist quarterly chronicling both the extraordinary and the everyday experience of mothering.*

ORGANIZATIONS

La Leche League International
1400 N. Meacham Rd.
P.O. Box 4079
Schaumburg, IL 60168–4079
http://www.lalecheleague.org

La Leche League provides mother-to-mother support for breastfeeding families (see the expanded discussion of La Leche League on page 141).

I Am Your Child Foundation
P.O. Box 15605
Beverly Hills, CA 90209
http://www.iamyourchild.org

This exciting organization has a goal of making sure that all parents are aware how critical the first three years of their children's lives are. They have a strong emphasis on encouraging responsive parenting.

Northwest Attachment Parenting (NAP)
P.O. Box 2433
Port Orchard, WA 98366
E-mail: info@northwest-ap.org

NAP is a grassroots, nonprofit organization offering a growing number of attachment parenting support groups around the country, a newsletter, and attachment oriented mentoring and parenting classes for young parents.

Attachment Parenting International (API)

1508 Clairmont Place

Nashville, Tennessee 37215

Phone or Fax: (615) 298–4334

http://advicom.net/~parkers

E-mail: ATTParents@aol.com

With the slogan "peaceful parenting for a peaceful world," API works to educate the public about the importance of parent-child attachment. API offers local attachment parenting support groups, an educational web site, a speaker's bureau, and more.

Apple Tree Family Ministries

P.O. Box 2083

Artesia, CA 90702-2083

Phone or Fax: (888) 925–0149

E-mail: ATFM@aol.com

Apple Tree Family Ministries provides family life education from a Christian Biblical perspective. They offer books and study materials, training and certification for Christian childbirth educators, and one-on-one support on issues ranging from marriage to childbirth and early parenting. Their approach incorporates attachment parenting principles. Dr. William and Martha Sears are members of their board and recommend their materials.

The Liedloff Continuum Network

P.O. Box 1634

Sausalito, CA 94966

http://continuum–concept.org

E-mail: editor@continuum–concept.org

Jean Liedloff, an American writer, spent several years living among a group of South American Indians, an experience which led her to write her book, The Continuum Concept. *After observing the way in which this traditional culture raised their children, she became an advocate of attachment style parenting. Through her organization you can learn more about her views and connect with other "continuum" parents from around the world.*

INTERNET E-MAIL LISTS

PARENT–L

The Parent–l List is a forum for discussing issues related to parenting the nursing baby or child. The topics for discussion vary widely, and include subjects related to life with a nursing toddler or baby, nursing during pregnancy, tandem nursing, societal attitudes towards breastfeeding, weaning, and any other related topics. To subscribe to parent–l, send the following command in the body of an e-mail message to: parent–l–request "subscribe parent–l" (no quotes).

The Attachment Parenting List

This list provides a gentle introduction to the attachment parenting style. You will find many expectant, new, and experienced parents here who can answer your questions and share your daily parenting joys and challenges. To subscribe, go to: http://www.onelist.com/subscribe.cgi/Attachment-Parenting

APWORKS

APW is for parents who combine a career with attachment parenting. If you are interested in issues such as working and breastfeeding or finding attachment parenting–friendly caregivers, this list is the right place for you! To subscribe, go to the APW web page at: http://www2.cybernex.net/~gene/ap-works.html

FEM-AP

This is a list for feminist attachment parents. You can subscribe by sending mail to: listproc @listproc.bgsv.edu containing the line "subscribe Fem-APMas YOUR FULL NAME" (no quotes)

SAH-AP

The SAH-AP mailing list is a support and learning forum for moms or dads who make attachment style parenting a way of life. Many are stay-at-home parents. To subscribe send the command "subscribe" (no quotes) to: sah-ap-request@kjsl.com

PGAP

For parents interested in natural pregnancy and birth and attachment parenting. To subscribe, send an email to: pgap-request@kjsl.com *and in the body of the message, put* "SUBSCRIBE" (no quotes)

WOH2SAH-AP

A support group for attachment parenting working mothers contemplating a move to stay-at-home mothering. To subscribe send the command "subscribe woh2sah-ap" (no quotes) *to:* majordomo@nursingbaby.com

RES-PAR

A list for attachment parents (of children past babyhood) who wish to continue to raise their kids in a respectful, gentle way. Send the command "subscribe res-par firstname lastname" (no quotes) *to:* listproc@listproc.bgsu.edu

APS

Alternative Parenting Styles is for anyone who does not fit in with "mainstream" parents. Can be anything from unschooling, to vegetarian kids, attachment parenting, living off the land, etc. Send an e-mail message reading "subscribe APS" (no quotes) to majordomo@nurtured.com

PARENTING AS MINISTRY (PAM)

A list for Christian attachment parents. You can subscribe automatically at the web page: http://www.mailing-list.net/redrhino

NAP-LIST

A discussion list for attachment parents offered by Northwest Attachment Parenting. To subscribe, send email to naplist-request@mylist.net *and in the body of the message, put* "subscribe" (no quotes)

INTERNET WEB SITES

There are literally hundreds of attachment parenting oriented Web sites on the Internet today and the number grows each month. Here are a few of the best to get you started:

The Nurturing Parent
http://www.splatterwerx.com/tnp

The Attachment Parent
http://www.attachmentparent.com

Wears the Baby
http://www.wearsthebaby.com

The Breastfeeding and Parenting Resources Page
http://www.prairienet.org/community/health/laleche/other.html

Laura's Parenting Page
http://www.kjsl.com/~thisbe/parenting.html

The Nursing Baby
http://www.nursingbaby.com

Kelly's Attachment Parenting Page
http://www.geocities.com/Heartland/Prairie/3490/parenting.html

The No-Spanking Page
http://www.neverhitachild.org

The Natural Child Project
http://www.naturalchild.com

The Attachment Parenting WebRing Homepage
http://www.members.tripod.com/~JudyArnall/ring.html

The Willendorf Pages
http://wg.rnet.com/willie/WILLIE.html

The Kidz Are People Too Page
http://www.geocities.com/Heartland/8148

Bestfed.com
http://www.bestfed.com

Nurtured.Com
http://www.nurtured.com

The Nature of Nurturing
http://www.seldomfar.com/nurturing/index.html

Attachment Parenting at Suite 101
http://www.suite101.com/welcome.cfm/attachment–parenting

The Natural Parenting WebRing Homepage
http://www.kjsl.com/webring

CHAPTER 2

The Pregnant Parent's Guide to Planning for Attachment

✦ **"Accepting that babies are sometimes a burden, and then trying to parent in a style that does not interrupt the natural parent-infant dyad but does make a life a little easier, is the challenge we all face. Most often, this means trusting the parental instinct—that is, common sense, which also evolved as a guide. And babies, too, help out with their reaching out, their goofy smiles, and their crying and fussing to let us know if we are on the right track."**

—*Anthropologist Meredith F. Small*

Working Through Personal Issues: Dumping Your Own Attachment-Inhibiting Baggage

IF YOU HAVE THE FORESIGHT TO BE LEARNING ABOUT THE BENEfits of attachment parenting *before* welcoming your baby, you can begin dealing with personal issues in ways that can facilitate your ability to connect and bond with your little one once he arrives, setting your own emotional stage for attachment parenting. Although it is certainly possible for a parent to address the following issues at any time, giving them some attention and thought prior to birth is wise.

How Were *You* Parented?

All of us come to parenting with a history. The way we ourselves were parented can have a profound effect—often the *most* profound effect—on the way we mother and father our own children. Boldly and honestly facing your own parented past frees you up to construct your unique parenting future. Perhaps you were lucky as a child and were breastfed, carried frequently, and allowed to sleep with your parents when you felt the need. More likely, however, you were bottle-fed artificial baby milk on a strict schedule, placed to sleep alone in a crib down the hall, and allowed to "cry it out" when you resisted bedtime. If you spent your entire childhood listening to your parents tell you to get back in your own bed, it may feel strange to think of *purposely* bringing your baby to bed with you. If your grandmother has always opined that "babies need to cry to exercise their lungs," you may feel uncomfortable at the thought of quickly responding to your child's cues before she even begins to fuss. If your entire family still talks incredulously about the time "that woman began breastfeeding her baby *right there in the restaurant!,"* you may be hesitant to consider casually breastfeeding your child in public.

In fact, as you learn about attachment parenting and realize how radically different it is from the way most of us have been—and for the most part, still are—raised, the whole concept may strike you as vaguely insulting to your own parents. You might wonder if they will feel that you are passing judgment on them by practicing attachment parenting with their grandchildren when they didn't do it with you. First of all, it isn't your responsibility to validate or invalidate anyone else's parenting choices with your own. Your task is a simpler one: to parent your children in your own best way. Secondly, your parents shouldn't be held completely responsible for any detachment promoting parenting practices they utilized. They may have had all the best intentions and were only doing what the physicians and experts of the day advised them to. Even the revolutionary Dr. Spock, parenting guru to most of our parents and many of our grandparents, advised readers to "harden their hearts" against babies' "manipulative behaviors" such as vomiting after being left to cry themselves to sleep! So, forgive your parents if that feels right to you . . . or at least try to move past your own childhood so that you can create a healthy attachment with your new baby.

> ▶ *"Attachment parenting my children has been a very healing experience for me and my mother. Through most of my adult life, I felt angry at her for something I could never express. Now I know that I felt like she never really mothered me in the way that I wanted to be mothered. I never remember being held or rocked or cuddled as a child. As she has watched me breastfeed the kids into early childhood and give them all the hugs I can, day and night, she has slowly opened up to me about how hard it was for her to follow her pediatrician's advice not to pick us up too much or respond to us when we cried. He told her that she*

would ruin us if she did. I think she feels very cheated now, although she is turning into a wonderful attachment grandparent!"

—MARIANNE, MOTHER OF THREE

▶ *"Whenever my mother is with me and my son, she feels the need to defend her own parenting even though I have never said one word to her about the way I was raised as compared to the way we are raising Sam. When she sees me nursing Sam, she tells me how she never had enough milk and when I wear him in the sling, she says that she never could have carried a toddler because of her bad back. This can be very tiresome but I have realized that she feels some sadness about her own mothering and talking about it helps her."*

—JANET, MOTHER OF A ONE YEAR OLD

▶ *"I was actually afraid to have a child because I was afraid I wouldn't be able to parent differently than my own father, who was completely hands-off. I'm glad I worked through these feelings before we had our kids."*

—MARK, FATHER OF TWO

The Very Best Resources for Moving Past Your Own Childhood and Becoming an Attachment Parent

BOOKS

Becoming the Parent You Want to Be: A Sourcebook of Strategies for the First Five Years. Davis, Laura, and Janis Keyser. New York: Broadway Books, 1997.

For Your Own Good: Hidden Cruelty in Child-Rearing and the Roots of Violence. Miller, Alice. New York: Noonday Books, 1990.

INTERNET E-MAIL LISTS

Mothers As Survivors (MAS) *was created for parents who are practicing attachment parenting in the belief that this will assist them in breaking the cycle of violence, addiction, or other harmful behaviors in their own lives. To subscribe, send an e-mail to* MAS-request@kjsl.com *and in the body of the message, put* "subscribe" (no quotes)

WEB SITES

The Mothers as Survivors Web Page
http://www.netwalk.com/~moomin/MAS

ORGANIZATIONS

Parents Anonymous
675 W. Foothill Boulevard, Suite 220
Claremont, California 91711-3475
Phone (909) 621-6184 • Fax (909) 625-6304
http://www.parentsanonymous-natl.org

Hundreds of local Parents Anonymous chapters assist mothers and fathers who are struggling to become better, more effective, more empathic parents for their own children.

Second Time Parents, First Time Attachment Parents

Many people adopt attachment parenting only after they have already seen one or more older children through their early years with a different childrearing style. Perhaps you bottle-fed your first baby but now realize how important it is that you breastfeed your second. Maybe your preschooler went everywhere in a stroller but you would like to try a sling with your new baby. You may be concerned, however, that it wouldn't be "fair" to your older child to begin attachment parenting with the younger sibling you are now expecting. Stop worrying! Although some attachment parenting practices are exclusive to or especially useful during infancy and toddlerhood, others are applicable to children of any age. You can't go back and breastfeed a child who was bottle-fed as a baby, but you can certainly increase your physical snuggle time with an older child and respond more attentively to his cues. And your older child will reap the great benefits of watching you breastfeed, carry and sleep with his sibling. This will become the parenting model he will inherit to offer to your grandchildren. It's never too late to begin attachment parenting.

> ► *"I wanted to breastfeed my first son but I made all the classic breastfeeding 'mistakes' and he was soon weaned to formula by one month of age. I felt a great deal of guilt about this. He was constantly sick as a baby and toddler and has had terrible allergies. Instead of dwelling on my guilt, I became utterly determined to breastfeed my second child and I prepared myself completely by reading, talking to other breastfeeding moms, and attending La Leche League meetings. I have gone on to breastfeed my younger daughter and son without a single bottle. I have explained to my older son that he wasn't breastfed because I still had a lot to learn as a mama. Despite this, after seeing his little sister and brother nursing, breastfeeding is his idea of normal and this is a great consolation to me."*
>
> — KATIE, MOTHER OF THREE

Your Personal Touch-O-Meter

Attachment parenting is a touch-intensive family style. Breastfeeding, sleep-sharing, skin-to-skin snuggling and frequent baby-holding all involve your being a very hands-on parent. A number of scientific studies have now proven that babies and children literally *require* physical touching in order to thrive and grow. And the warmth of a parent's loving touch is something that we remember all our lives.

> ✦ **"The arms of the sensitive mother invite. When the world looms too large, too loud, too bright, too cold, the infant knows that she will be enveloped in a warm, protective embrace. This gives the baby a clear message: 'You are safe. You are loved. You are loveable.' And so the infant relaxes, secure against the world."**
>
> —*Sharon Heller, Ph.D.*

But it may be that you yourself didn't receive enough physical touch as a child. Or perhaps you received inappropriate touching from adults or the message that your body was somehow "bad." Starting parenthood with unhealthy feelings about your own body or your baby's can make it difficult to relax and get physical with your little one. As a result, you might miss out on some of the most amazing pleasures of parenthood: a lazy afternoon of lying in bed naked with your sweet-smelling newborn, a bath with your toddler, or the ability to nourish your child anywhere, anytime by offering your breast without hesitation. If the thought of intimate physical closeness with your child troubles you in any way, now is the time to try to work through your own body issues so that you don't risk passing them on to your child.

> ▶ *"Before my wife had our children, I was really freaked out at the thought of her breastfeeding them. For one thing, as a typical American guy, that isn't what I was raised to think of breasts as being for. And secondly, I felt proprietary. I wasn't comfortable with the idea of someone other than me maybe catching a glimpse of her breasts while she was nursing. But her relaxed attitude, plus the information she*

kept giving me about how important breastfeeding is, slowly changed my views. Now I feel proud of our parenting when she breastfeeds our eighteen month old at a party or something."

—GARY, FATHER OF TWO

▶ *"As a sexual abuse survivor, it took a lot of work with a therapist and within myself before I was able to let go and really touch my children. I was worried that I would do something wrong. Ultimately I decided that my abuser wasn't going to be given the opportunity to affect my kids' childhoods too."*

—LORA, MOTHER OF TWO

When You and Your Partner Disagree

Perhaps you've made the decision that gentle, instinctual parenting is for you but your partner isn't so sure. In fact, it's possible that he vehemently disagrees with you about one or more aspects of attachment parenting. This is often the case when the partner in question didn't receive enough loving touch and nurturing as a child. What to do? As with many situations in life, actions speak louder than words. You can go about the business of caring for your baby with attachment promoting practices and let him learn by watching. It's pretty hard to argue in favor of bottle-feeding once you have observed the special communication between a nursing mother and her child. When it comes to attachment parenting practices that require the active cooperation of both parents, like a family bed, education may be key. Talk with your partner about the science behind bringing your child into your bed (see our chapter on sleep) and explain how it can help to ease the legendary sleeplessness of new parenthood. And once your child can actually *tell* your partner her preferences, through behavior or words, encourage your partner to take your child's expressed feelings into acount in making childrearing decisions.

> ▶ *"I read voraciously when I was pregnant with Andy and I soon stumbled onto* The Womanly Art of Breastfeeding *from La Leche League. As I read about this very different style of parenting, I knew right away that this was how I wanted to raise my children. John wasn't so sure. He worried that what I was describing would spoil the baby. We have had to do a lot of talking over the past two years but John now can see that Andy is anything but spoiled. Instead, attachment parenting has given us a secure little boy and an extra close family."*
>
> *—Lisa, mother of a two year old*

(Not) Shopping for Baby: Why Attachment Parents Don't Need All That Baby Gear

Never before have parents had access to so much baby *stuff*. In addition to the usual department, boutique and discount stores carrying baby equipment, we have now witnessed the emergence of warehouse-sized "baby superstores" packed full to the ceiling with every imaginable gadget for the new parent. From a variety of elaborate cribs, to forty different types of bottles and nipples, to the combination stroller/carseat/cradle/carriers that do everything but give birth for you, parents are left with the impression that there must be an awful lot of equipment that you simply *must* have in order to properly welcome and care for a baby. And then there is the matter of the nursery. One of the first questions asked of expectant parents is what "theme" they will be using to decorate the baby's room. Will it be Beatrix Potter? Classic Pooh? Laura Ashley? What you should recognize when considering what to buy is that you yourself, and not a plastic device or a beautiful cherry crib, will provide the physical environment in which your young child will spend most of his time. Many experienced parents ultimately find that a lot of this mostly plastic baby gear is useless and can place unnecessary barriers between parent and child. Not to worry, however, you don't have to miss out on all the fun of preparing your nest for the new baby. If you feel that you would really enjoy decorating a nursery, do so with the intention of using it as a room for toys, clothes, and possibly a changing table, not as a place where your baby will be left alone for long periods of time. And in addition to the usual baby blankets, diaper pails, and sleepers that every new parent needs, there are some items in particular that attachment parents will want to have on hand. Several of the attachment parenting retail catalogs even have gift registries, so you can sign up for shower and baby gifts that you can really use.

Items You Will Definitely Want:

- **A Baby Carrier:** A wonderful way to get and stay close to your baby and toddler is by transporting him on your body in a carrier. Later in the book, we'll discuss the various types of carriers in more detail. In doing your pre-baby shopping, you might want to skip ahead to the chapter on wearing your baby ("To Have and To Hold") so that you can decide what type (or types) of baby carrier you would like to use.

> ▶ *"If I had to give new parents a recommendation for one truly essential piece of baby equipment, it would have to be the baby sling. I simply couldn't get along without mine!!"*
>
> —LYNN, *MOTHER OF TWO*

- **Clothes to Make Breastfeeding Easy:** One of the cardinal rules of motherhood for attachment parents is that you have to have fast and easy access to your breasts! Because young infants in particular do not usually nurse at predictable times and because you will want to keep your baby close and respond to her cues with ease, you need to be able to breastfeed comfortably in whatever clothes you might be wearing. Breastfeeding mothers today have the benefit of a number of retailers that offer a wide variety of clothing with easy, discreet breastfeeding access, allowing you to feed your baby in any setting, from a black tie dinner to a board meeting to worship services. On the other hand, it is absolutely *not* necessary to go out and buy an entire new wardrobe in order to breastfeed your baby. Most breastfeeding mothers invest in (or sew themselves) a couple of items of "nursingwear" such as one dressy dress and maybe a swimsuit. (Yes! There are attractive nursing swimsuits so that you don't have to undress poolside to feed your child.) Otherwise they wear "regular" clothes that work for breastfeeding. Any two-piece outfit, from a sweater and jeans, to a silk blouse and power suit, will allow a mother to lift her top and feed her baby. Although unbuttoning a shirt or dress from the top down in order to nurse can be more of a hassle and less discreet, button-up items will work too. Overalls and jumpers that allow you to let down a strap to nurse are big favorites with breastfeeding mothers as well. It is likely that you already have a closet full of clothing that will work just fine for breastfeeding, but you'll want to take an inventory of your needs before the baby arrives.

In addition to clothing with nursing access, you will probably also want two to four nursing bras. Small breasted women may choose to go braless for breastfeeding (and some larger breasted women may as well), and a few nursing mothers make do with standard bras, but most nursing mothers enjoy having a well-fitting, supportive bra that allows them to easily let down a flap and feed their baby. As they are with nursing clothing, breastfeeding mothers today are blessed with a plethora of good nursing bra options, from discount store brands costing under ten dollars to specialty catalog editions that can cost up to $35. When buying a bra, look for cotton cups that will breathe, one-handed nursing flap access and adjustability so that the bra will fit as your breasts swell in the early postpartum period and then slowly decrease in size during your nursing years. The customer service departments of the catalogs listed in the resources section of this book, or at your local maternity store, should be able to help you get fitted for a comfortable nursing bra.

► *"Until I got the hang of nursing in public, it was a great comfort to me to have some nursing clothes that I had bought that allowed me to feed Emily without anyone even noticing what I was doing. After a couple of months I was much more relaxed and confident and I began to feed her wherever I was, but in the beginning, those nursing clothes helped a lot."*

—DORIE, MOTHER OF A TEN MONTH OLD

► *"I don't make any effort whatsoever to be discreet when I nurse because if anyone has a problem with me nursing my baby, well, that's their own issue. Even so, I enjoy nursing clothes because they allow me to easily meet my child's need to eat without a lot of messing with buttons or straps."*

—MONICA, MOTHER OF TWO

• **Breast Pads:** During the first few weeks or months of breastfeeding, your breasts will sometimes leak milk. This usually happens when you are thinking about your baby or when you are feeding on one side and the other breast leaks at the same time. The amount of leakage varies a lot from woman to woman (and even from baby to baby in the same mother) and often stops altogether after breastfeeding is well established. In the meantime, many breastfeeding mothers find it comfortable to place what is called a breast pad inside their bra over the nipple to absorb any leakage. Breast pads are small and round and are either disposable or washable, re-usable cotton. Be sure to have some on hand for your first weeks at home with your baby. You can get them at any baby store, pharmacy or from a catalog.

• **A Prepared Family Bed:** In the upcoming chapter on sleep, we will discuss the many ways you can happily sleep with your child right from the start. Before your baby's first night in your home, however, you will want to learn all about family bedding and decide what type of sleeping arrangement will work best in your household. Most of these require some basic preparation on your part in order to create a safe, comfortable family sleep space. A waterbed, for example, is *always* incompatible with sharing sleep with an infant, so if you have one, you would want to replace it with something more appropriate. Jump ahead to the chapter on sleep and start planning your own family bed.

• **A Carseat:** Happily, a carseat is now standard equipment for any conscientious new parent, and there are many, many styles of carseat from which to choose. While making your decision, you should obviously consider safety record (check the Internet, *Consumer Reports* and your state's highway patrol safety office for recommendations), ease of use, and the way the seat fits in your model of car. You should never buy a used carseat for your child, as it may have been involved in a prior accident that damaged the frame or straps in a way that isn't visible to the casual observer. As critically important as carseats are for safety on the roads, however, they have unfortunately become popular for a less healthy use: as a plastic substitute for holding and carrying babies. Many modern babies spend much of their day being schlepped around in these "baby buckets." With the advent of "all-in-one" carseat/stroller combos, as well as shopping carts that allow carseats to be attached while adults shop, parents can easily overuse the carseat as a carrier. So, when choosing your carseat, think of it only in terms of a safety seat for use in the car, not as a means of transporting your child at other times.

► *"Although we occasionally carry Jenny into the house from the car in her carseat so that we don't have to wake her up, we try to avoid carrying her around in it all the time. I see babies in the mall and at the doctor's office lately, all being carried around strapped in their carseat instead of being held by their mothers and fathers. It looks very strange and artificial to me. Don't these folks want to touch their babies? And don't they know that their babies want to be touched?"*

—*ANABEL, MOTHER OF A SEVEN MONTH OLD*

Items You Might Need or Enjoy Having:

• **A Breastpump:** Breastpumps are a wonderful modern invention that allow nursing mothers to pump and store their own milk for use at times when the mother herself cannot offer the breast. Utilized by mothers who have jobs that take them away from their nursling at feeding times, mothers with babies who are hospitalized and unable to feed at the breast yet, adoptive mothers who wish to induce lactation, and others, breastpumps can sometimes play a valuable role in the breastfeeding experience. There are a number of types and models of breastpumps available today and we will discuss them at length in the chapter on combining attachment parenting with outside employment. When you're deciding what type of breastpump you need, first be sure that you really need one at all. Many nursing mothers will never need to use a breastpump. If you do not plan to work outside the home, if you won't be returning to work until around your child's first birthday, or if you have a job that will allow you to be with your child during feeding times, you probably won't need one. Because attachment parents recognize that breastfeeding offers much more to a child than just the (admittedly critically important) breastmilk itself, bottle-feeding breastmilk runs a distant second to nursing when both options are available. Generally speaking, it is best *not* to pump your milk for someone else to feed your baby unless you absolutely must. Bottle-feeding breastmilk, although much healthier for a child than formula-feeding, still involves the *other* drawbacks of bottle-feeding (see the chapter entitled "Breastfeeding: Much More Than Food"). The same is true of pumping your milk so that you yourself can feed it to your child. Unfortunately, many women today seem to be unnecessarily pumping and bottle-feeding in lieu of actually nursing their babies. Unless you are absolutely certain that you will have a need for a breastpump, it may be best not to have one in the house in the early weeks of breastfeeding. It might just prove too tempting when you are suffering from postpartum adjustments or if you are finding breastfeeding a bit challenging to instead pump your milk and feed it to your baby in a bottle. Well-meaning but uninformed relatives or friends might see the breastpump and encourage you to use it so that they can offer a bottle. This could lead to *nipple confusion** in your baby, and you might find yourself headed down the slippery slope toward unplanned weaning.

If you believe that you will need a breastpump and have questions about finding or using one, contact your local La Leche League Leader or a *Board Certified* lactation consultant (IBCLC) and discuss it with her. She can assist you in deciding whether you should have a pump on hand and if so, she can help you choose the best type, and teach you how to use it. Whatever you do, don't go out and buy a pump manufactured by any company that also produces infant formulas. These pumps are of notoriously poor quality and will likely only lead to discomfort and problems for you. Many observers doubt that this situation is a coincidence,

---

* Nipple confusion, sometimes also called "nipple preference" is when your breastfed baby begins to prefer the easier and very different physiologic sucking motion required to draw milk out of an artificial nipple as opposed to your breasts. This is a leading cause of premature weaning from the breast.

since a woman who is able to successfully pump her milk for her child won't have a need to spend money on artificial breastmilk substitutes.

• **A Postpartum Doula:** Okay, so a doula isn't an *item*, but she is something you might want to shop for and line up before birth. Doulas are usually women who work as labor support helpers during birth, but there is also a growing number of women who offer their services to postpartum women. A good postpartum doula takes care of *you* so that you can take care of your baby. She can assist as you get started breastfeeding, which is especially helpful if your own female relatives and friends did not breastfeed and can't offer any guidance, and talk you through any baby care concerns you might have. She can also help out around the house by answering the phone, doing laundry, cooking, and cleaning. It is possible that your own mother, sister, or grandmother can serve as your doula after birth, but be sure that the person you have helping you is supportive of attachment parenting so that you aren't dealing with criticism ("You're holding that baby too much; you'll never get him on a schedule at this rate!") while you are trying to rest and get to know your newborn. Because the cost of a postpartum doula can be outside many families' budgets, several friends, or maybe your parents, might want to chip in and pay for doula services as a gift for you. Many larger metropolitan areas have doula services listed in the yellow pages or you might be able to get some references through a local birthing center or midwife. You can also find a doula in your area by contacting:

Doulas of North America (DONA)
http://www.dona.com
E-mail: askdona@aol.com

• **A Rocking Chair (or glider):** A rocking chair is a wonderful way to spend time with your nursling. It may prove to be one of your favorite nursing spots, particularly in the early months. Look for a really, really comfortable chair. Although an antique wooden rocker might appeal to your good taste, it also may dig into your back and creep across the floor as you rock. You want a chair with a comfy back and arms that will allow you to assume a relaxed nursing position. Make sure the chair is the right size for you so that you can rise smoothly from a sitting position without waking your child. An oversized chair that will allow you to nurse or snuggle two children at once may be useful if you have or are expecting to have several little people in your family at the same time.

- **A Footstool or Ottoman:** While nursing in your rocker (or elsewhere), it can be very comfortable to put your feet up on a footstool. Retailers catering to nursing mothers often sell "nursing stools," and many glider rockers come with a matching ottoman. Some mothers choose to purchase a combination rocker recliner that has an attached flip-up footrest. Alternatively, you may already have an old footstool or even a box around the house that will work quite nicely.
- **A "Nursing Pillow":** Nursing mothers have long known that in the early months of nursing, a well-placed pillow can help to position the baby at the breast. Today, several types of pillows made specifically for this purpose are on the market. These nursing pillows rest on a mother's lap and wrap around her waist, providing a secure spot for the new baby to rest and eat. Although this is an item that you will probably only use for a few months, many first time nursing mothers in particular find it a worthwhile investment. New mothers who have had a c-section find that pillows offer extra comfort for their tender bellies, and breastfeeding mothers of twins and triplets often rave about these pillows because they help with positioning one baby at each breast. You can get nursing pillows at baby supply stores and in catalogs. But remember, the pillow off your bed may work just fine for this purpose.

▶ *"I used to put one baby on each side of the wraparound nursing pillow and this way I was able to nurse them both at the same time very comfortably and easily. A mother of triplets recommended that I buy the pillow and it was one of the best baby things that I had."*

—NANCYE, *MOTHER OF THREE YEAR OLD TWINS*

Items You Might Not Need (or at least should consider carefully before acquiring):

• **A Traditional Crib:** That's right, a crib. It may seem unimaginable to consider a baby without a crib, but you actually might not need this expensive, space wasting "babycage" unless you plan to modify it to set up a sidecar-type family bed using the crib (see chapter on sleep).

▶ *"The crib we bought for Zak is now used as a clean laundry hamper in the basement!"*

—JIMMY, *FATHER OF AN ELEVEN MONTH OLD*

• **Bottles:** Bottles, like cribs, are another one of those universal symbols of modern babyhood that we take for granted. It is usually assumed that every baby will, at one time or another, drink from a bottle and that every new parent needs to have at least a couple on hand. Not true! Even if you will need to bottle-feed your pumped breastmilk after you return to work, you shouldn't offer your breastfed baby a bottle in the early weeks lest she become nipple confused. And if you can avoid being away from your baby at feeding times until he is six or seven months old, there may be no need for him to *ever* have an artificial nipple in his mouth. Many fully breastfed babies progress straight to a sippy cup (even as they continue to nurse into the toddler years and beyond). Having bottles in the house during the sometimes challenging period it takes to become a successful nursing couple is a real risk factor for breastfeeding problems. If the bottles are there, someone in the household may be tempted to use them unnecessarily. So, let your friends and family know that your baby is fully breastfed and that—for now at least—your house is a "bottle free zone." Tell them that you don't want or expect to receive any bottles or nipples for gifts. If for any reason you actually do need a bottle for your baby, you can go out and get it after breastfeeding is well established.

- **Pacifiers:** It seems that everyone has an opinion on pacifiers, including babies. Some love 'em and some wouldn't touch 'em with a ten-foot pole. Because attachment parented babies are breastfed on cue, including for comfort sucking, they usually won't want or need a pacifier. And as with any artificial nipple, pacifiers used in the early weeks can undermine breastfeeding in some babies. Pacifiers may serve a useful role in attachment parenting a bottle-fed baby because bottle-feeding doesn't allow for comfort sucking, a basic human need in the early years.
- **Infant Formula:** Many pregnant mothers are convinced by misinformed doctors, friends and relatives that, even if they plan to breastfeed, they should have some formula on hand in the house "just in case" breastfeeding doesn't work out. Nothing could be more untrue. Lactation professionals have observed the differences between new mothers who go home from the hospital armed with formula samples and those who do not and have found that the "just in case" formula samples are a clear risk factor for breastfeeding problems. As with other substitutes for actually putting baby to breast (like pumps, bottles, etc), if the formula is there, you or a family member will very likely be tempted to use it unnecessarily, possibly setting mother and baby down the road to premature weaning. Formula companies have long been aware

of this phenomenon and it is for this reason that they give away millions and millions of dollars in free samples to new mothers every year. This is a well-thought-out marketing ploy; these huge corporations certainly don't give their product away out of the goodness of their hearts. If your hospital or birth center attempts to send you home with any "free" formula (and most will, even if they know you are breastfeeding), politely hand the stuff back to your doctor, nurse, or midwife when she comes to sign you out. If the formula companies themselves begin sending cases of free formula to your front door—and they probably will. Your OB, midwife, maternity shop, parenting magazine, or hospital will have given them your name and address—mark the boxes "return to sender" and hand them back to the delivery person. (Some women are more comfortable accepting the formula samples and then donating them to a local women's shelter for women who are already bottle-feeding.)

- **A Baby Carriage/Stroller:** Think how disorienting it must be for a tiny baby to be rolled around in a box on wheels after having spent the past nine months curled up snugly inside her mama. This is why many infants resist being transported in a carriage, yet love being carried on their parents' body in a cloth carrier or backpack. Although western parents have something of a love affair with the stroller, attachment parenting asks that you limit its use and instead actually carry your baby and toddler. Many parents decide that they really don't need a baby carriage at all. If you do decide to buy one, follow your child's cues as to whether she is enjoying or merely tolerating strolling. Many babies don't like to be strolled until they can sit up and look around. And as mentioned previously, give especially careful consideration to any use of the newer stroller/carseat/carrier/swing combos that now allow a child to be rolled from site to site without ever being touched or held.

The Very Best Attachment Parenting Retail Resources

Attachments
Phone: (800) 873–5023
http://www.attachmentscatalog.com

The original attachment parenting catalog, offering slings, homebirth items, art and photography celebrating breastfeeding, breastfeeding dolls for big siblings, attachment parenting books for children and adults, and much more.

Wears The Baby
Phone: (800) 527–8985
http://www.wearsthebaby.com

Distributes slings, kidslings (for carrying dolls), nursingwear, "Don't Ask Me When I'm Going to Wean" T-shirts, free informative newsletter, and many other goodies for attachment parents, nurtured children, and mindful family life.

Little Koala Mother and Baby Catalog
Phone: (800) 950–1239
http://www.littlekoala.com

Nursing clothing and bras, slings, breastpumps, family beds, books on attachment parenting and more.

The Motherwear Catalog
Phone: (800) 950–2500
http://www.motherwear.com

The most complete line of nursingwear to be found. Motherwear's clothes are designed for breastfeeding in public—modestly, easily, and comfortably. Every top, dress, sweater, and nightgown in this catalog has hidden openings that allow you to give your baby easy access to your breasts while keeping discreetly covered. Bras, breastpumps and nursing pillows are available as well.

One Hot Mama
Phone: (800) 217–3750
E-mail: customer@onehotmama.com
http://www.onehotmama.com

With hip, stylish nursing clothes for hot mamas with attitude. Also carries slings, baby shoes, parenting books and more. "Attachment parenting never looked so good!"

The La Leche League International Catalogue
Phone: (847) 519–7730
http://www.lalecheleague.org

This comprehensive catalog features books for children and adults on every aspect of attachment parenting, as well as breastpumps, breastfeeding supplies, art celebrating motherhood, and resources for medical professionals.

Peavine Timeless Essentials
http://www.peavineonline.com
E-mail: peavine@kjsl.com

Featuring an exclusive line of products honoring and supporting attachment parenting, as well as handcrafted soaps made from mother's milk, homebirth baby books and more.

Magic Wardrobe
PO Box 35072
Victoria, BC V8T 5G2
Canada
Phone/Fax: (250) 361–1670
http://www.magic-wardrobe.com
E-mail: <sonia@magic-wardrobe.com>

Beautiful, hand-crafted nursing sweaters.

Mother and Child, etc.
http://www.motherandchildetc.com
E-mail: mother@motherandchild.com

Offering nursing fashions, custom-made, baby slings, nursing necklaces, nursing pillows, and other items. Affordable pricing for the one-income family.

The Nurtured Baby
4004 Keble Drive
Charlotte, NC 28269
Phone: (888) 564–BABY
http://www.nurturedbaby.com
E-mail: Beth@nurturedbaby.com
Nurturing products for your baby and family.

Baby Becoming
Phone: (888) 50STYLE or (888) 507–8953
Fax: (925) 449–1015
http://www.california.com/~edgare/baby_be/home.html
E-mail: gstyle@grandstyle.com
Terrific nursing clothing and bras for large women.

The Baby Lane
Phone: (888) 387–0019 (toll free) or (252) 463–0019
Fax: (252) 463–0018
http://www.thebabylane.com
The Baby Lane features slings, cloth diapers and supplies, as well as other items for parents and parents-to-be.

Peapods Natural Attachment Parenting Products
http://www.peapods.com/index.html
E-mail: millie@peapods.com
Peapods features slings in many fabrics and colors, unique nursingwear, attachment parenting and breastfeeding books, as well as toys.

The Nursing Baby
http://www.nursingbaby.com
E-mail: paulabob@nursingbaby.com
An online attachment parenting community and catalog offering babyslings, nursing apparel, attachment parenting books, breastpumps, kid slings, nursing pads and mattress pads (for the co-sleeping family).

Nestmom Naturals
P.O. Box 646
Smithsburg, MD 21783
Phone: (301) 824–NEST (6378)
http://www.nestmom.com
E-mail: Nestmom@nestmom.com
Nestmom naturals offers attachment parenting slogan T-shirts, uniquely designed nursing clothing, and more.

Earthwise Basics
214 Elliot Street, Suite 2
Brattleboro, VT 05301
Phone: (800) 791–3957 or (802) 254–2235
http://www.earthwisebasics.com
E-mail: service@ediapers.com
Natural toys, cloth diapers and more.

The Attachment Parenting Bookstore
Phone: (831) 476–7537
http://www.mamamoon.com/books.html
E-mail: mamamoon@mamamoon.com
A carefully chosen selection of books and other items for the attachment parenting family.

Bestfed Books
Phone: (215) 887–5662
Fax: (215) 887–4815
http://www.bestfedbooks.com
E-mail: bestfed@phillynet.com
Books with positive images of breastfeeding, the family bed and other attachment parenting traditions.

Slightly Crunchy
37 West Street
Cromwell, CT 06416
Phone: (860) 635–5662 or (877) CRUNCHIES

http://www.slightlycrunchy.com
E-mail: crunchmail@aol.com
Environmentally conscious products that promote attachment parenting.

Duzins
http://www.duzins.com
E-mail: Robyn@duzins.com
A wide variety of natural parenting products, including slings, parenting books and more!

Planning to Breastfeed . . . Instead of Planning to *Try* to Breastfeed

Imagine if, at the beginning of pregnancy, healthy women spoke of "trying to stay pregnant" or of "giving pregnancy a shot." It sounds absurd, but this is exactly the attitude taken by many women at the start of their breastfeeding relationship with their baby. They doubt their ability to nurse their own babies and plan to "try breastfeeding." The great majority of pregnant women *will* safely carry their babies to term. Our healthy bodies are designed to maintain a home for a growing child until the baby is ready to be born. The same is true of breastfeeding. The *vast* majority of mothers are physically able to comfortably and adequately nourish a baby at the breast, occasionally after a bit of supportive guidance in getting started. Despite the fact that the odds are overwhelmingly in her favor, the average woman often questions her actual ability to breastfeed. Living in a bottle-feeding culture, as we do, you may have never actually known anyone who breastfed their baby past a couple of weeks or months. When you have encountered breastfeeding women, they may have felt it necessary to hide themselves away behind blankets or closed doors. And it is likely that you have heard woman after woman tell you how she "didn't have enough milk" or how her baby "weaned himself" before he was even one year old.

In the upcoming chapters on breastfeeding, we will explore both the importance of breastfeeding and the reasons why so many mothers today do not breastfeed their children. We will also offer solutions to some of the more common breastfeeding challenges, and resource information so that you will know how and where to get assistance should you need it after your baby arrives. As an expectant attachment parent, you should develop the mindset that you will breastfeed your baby just as surely as you will give birth. Instead of planning to *try to breastfeed,* you should just *plan to breastfeed.* And whether you are a first time parent or a parent who has bottle-fed an older child, before birth is the best time to learn all that you can about breastfeeding so that you can get off to a smooth start once your baby is in your arms, ready to nurse.

► *"By the time my son was born, I knew more about breastfeeding than my obstetrician (which probably wasn't saying much) and I felt like there was no problem that could arise that I wouldn't know how to tackle. My commitment and preparation really paid off when an emergency c-section and a stay in the NICU made getting started a little trickier than we had anticipated."*

—RHONDA, MOTHER OF A FIFTEEN MONTH OLD

Ten Things That Every Expectant Parent Needs to Know About Breastfeeding

Rachael Hamlet, J.D., Author of The Breastfeeding Advocacy Page

1. Breastfeeding is an important health issue.

Hundreds of medical studies have now been done on the differing health consequences of breastfeeding and formula-feeding. The results are unanimous: every study shows significantly greater instances of illness among artificially fed babies, even where clean water, adequate supplies of formula and modern medical care are available. Some of these illnesses are minor and easily curable and some of them are extremely rare regardless of feeding method. Some of them are fairly common and fairly serious (gastroenteritis and pneumonia, among them). And the impact appears to be life long: several studies have shown a significant influence on adult illness rates (e.g., both pre- and post-menopausal breast cancer are 25% less common among the population of adult women who were breastfed as infants). I want to be absolutely clear that I am NOT saying that all, or even most, formula-fed babies are sick. Nor am I saying that all breastfed babies are healthy. The studies I am pointing to are epidemiological in nature. When researchers look at different feeding methods among populations and compare disease rates among them, they have consistently found higher disease rates among the population that was fed substitutes for human milk. It is therefore worth investing some of your time and energy in breastfeeding. Take some steps before your child is born to increase your chances of success. Be prepared to take steps to solve problems that arise. Make a commitment to do whatever you can manage to do to make breastfeeding work for you and your baby. If, despite your best efforts, breastfeeding does not work out, you will at least have the consolation of knowing that you did your best.

2. Breastfeeding is a learned art.

If you have grown up around breastfeeding women, you probably know enough to breastfeed without expert help. Indeed, those other breastfeeding women in your life are likely to be the best experts you can turn to for help. However, if you have been raised in a bottle-feeding culture (the U.S. and the U.K. being the most pervasive in their bottle-feeding bias), you may have never even glimpsed another woman breastfeeding. If you mistakenly think that breastfeeding is completely instinctive, you may not think it necessary to educate yourself about the process and it may be harder for you to accept the help you may need to get started. If, instead, you go into breastfeeding with the knowledge that it sometimes must be learned, you will be able to arm yourself in advance with the knowledge you need to succeed, and you will know when to accept expert help. Because breastfeeding is a learned art that has been lost to the majority of mothers in a bottle-feeding culture, all mothers should be prepared to deal with potential breastfeeding problems. This does not mean obsessing over every horror story that you hear, but it does mean being aware that problems can occasionally arise, and learning how to find help if they do.

3. The best sources of information on breastfeeding.

La Leche League International, the Nursing Mothers Council, the National Childbirth Trust (U.K.), the Nursing Mothers Association of Australia, and the International Lactation Consultants' Association (ILCA) are the best sources of accurate and helpful information about breastfeeding. If you can afford it, buy a book that covers all of the basics. You may also be able to find helpful books in your local library or borrow them from a local La Leche League group. Additionally, the Internet now hosts an abundance of excellent information on breastfeeding in the form of Web pages, e-mail lists, bulletin boards, and newsgroups.

4. Many breastfeeding problems are caused by medical mismanagement.

Ideally, you should be able to choose health care providers who are educated about and supportive of breastfeeding. But that is not always possible. It is an unfortunate fact that, in addition to educating yourself about breastfeeding, you may have to educate your obstetrician, pediatrician, family practice doctor, midwife, maternity floor nurses, etc., about breastfeeding. You must also be prepared to fend off bad advice and unnecessary procedures that may interfere with breastfeeding. To avoid misunderstandings, it is advisable to set aside some time in your preparation for childbirth to discuss breastfeeding with your health care providers. Make it plain that you are committed to breastfeeding your baby and that you want to remove all unnecessary barriers to breastfeeding. One of the most important issues to discuss is the avoidance of all artificial nipples in the first days of life. Nipple preference (where a breastfeeding baby learns to prefer an artificial nipple to his mother's) is a leading cause of breastfeeding failure, yet routine bottles and pacifiers are still common in some hospital nurseries. It can't hurt to ask your doctors and hospital to sign a document promising not to use artificial nipples, and make sure that document makes its way into your baby's chart. Then, if supplementary feeds are necessary, they can be administered by cup, spoon, dropper, syringe, or tube (you can learn to feed your baby via one of these alternative feeding methods with the advice and assistance of a well-informed health care provider).

Some other important issues you might want to discuss with your doctors are: what effects any labor medications may have on the initiation of breastfeeding, whether cleaning and examination of the baby can be postponed until after the baby has had his first feed, whether rooming in with your baby can be arranged and, if not, will the nursery staff bring your baby to you frequently enough to get breastfeeding started, whether circumcision (if such is your choice) can be postponed until after breastfeeding has been well-established, whether there are trained lactation consultants on staff at the hospital or pediatrician's office, and whether a family history of allergies or illness makes breastfeeding especially important for your baby. You might also ask the doctor how she deals with a mother who is concerned about the adequacy of her supply because her baby is nursing every hour. If she responds that formula supplementation is the first line of treatment for this concern, you will know for sure that you are dealing with an uninformed doctor, and should not rely upon her advice regarding breastfeeding. Remember: unnecessary supplementation is the fastest road to the end of breastfeeding.

5. If it hurts, it is likely that something is wrong.

Breastfeeding is not supposed to hurt. While some women experience discomfort in the first days of nursing, real pain is almost always a sign that something is wrong. Some possible problems that can cause pain and nipple damage are: incorrect latch, incorrect positioning, incorrect sucking, and yeast infection (thrush). These problems can usually be solved, but only if you seek the right kind of help soon enough. If you wait too long, the baby may be hard to retrain, your nipples may be injured, and the joy of breastfeeding may be replaced with dread and misery. And if you seek help from someone who doesn't really know much about breastfeeding, or who doesn't take the time to watch you and your baby nursing, you may be worse off than with no help at all. The best kind of help is a personal visit with an International Board Certified Lactation Consultant (IBCLC). The IBCLC is the only internationally recognized credential showing thorough training and expertise in the diagnosis and treatment of nursing problems. In a personal visit, a lactation consultant can examine your baby and your breasts, observe you and your baby nursing to evaluate latch and positioning, let the baby suck on her finger to evaluate the baby's sucking behavior, listen for the sound of the baby swallowing, talk to you and get a total picture of your nursing relationship. She can then work with you to put together a treatment plan to solve your breastfeeding problems.

Of course, like any health care professional, a lactation consultant will expect to be paid. If that bothers you, try to remember that the formula to feed a baby for the first year of its life will cost about fifteen times more than a visit with a lactation consultant. Not to mention the risk you run of additional medical expenses that may arise because of the greater risk of illness in formula-fed babies. Always check to see if your health insurance plan covers lactation consultants. Many do and if yours doesn't, you may want to convince them that they should.

6. Know the signs of dehydration in a new baby (whether breast or bottle-fed).

Here are the signs: (a) fewer than six very wet diapers per day, (b) significant color or odor to the urine (it should be clear and nearly odorless), (c) dry skin that doesn't spring back immediately after being pinched, (d) sunken fontanel (that's the soft spot at the top of the baby's head). If your baby exhibits any of these symptoms, get immediate medical attention. If you do have to supplement your baby's fluid intake, remember that expressed breastmilk is preferable to any artificial baby milk. If the baby is not exhibiting the symptoms of dehydration, has good color and can be heard swallowing after every couple of sucks, it is unlikely that you are having problems with your supply of milk. Supplementing with formula because of unreasonable fears at this stage can cause breastfeeding failure. The baby's reduced demand will lead to reduced supply and further supplementation, in a downward spiral toward the complete cessation of breastfeeding.

7. You will need support to breastfeed.

Support can come in many forms. The most important support for many mothers comes from the baby's father: if he is fully supportive of breastfeeding, it is much easier for the mother to breastfeed in a bottle-feeding culture. For some mothers, support can be a partner, relative, friend or neighbor who has breastfed, and who acts as a positive model. For some, it is an organized support group, such as La Leche League. For others, it is a lactation consultant or medical professional who provides expert help if difficulties arise. Without support, many mothers will quickly abandon any efforts to breastfeed. Line up phone numbers for a local La Leche League Leader and/or International Board Certified Lactation Consultant (IBCLC) before birth so that you will have them on hand if needed once the baby arrives.

8. Your breasts are functional and their function is feeding babies.

While many of us have grown up believing that our breasts were primarily sexual, the reality is that their sexual function is a cultural construct. The biological reality is that our breasts are for feeding babies. It helps to keep this in mind as you prepare yourself for dealing with people who think there is something indecent about feeding a baby with your breasts. There is absolutely no reason why you should not feed your baby wherever and whenever any bottle-feeding mother would feel comfortable feeding her baby. If the bottle-feeders aren't forced to feed their babies in the bathroom, neither should you be. If you wish to avoid unwanted attention, it is wise to learn how to nurse discreetly and to wear clothing that permits easy access to your breasts without disrobing. But try not to let the fact that you take those measures make you ashamed if someone detects what you are up to. Feeding your baby is not an indecent act no matter where it occurs.

9. Human milk can be provided in mother's absence.

When mother and baby must be separated, expressing and storing human milk is not only possible but relatively easy. With good hand expression technique or a good quality pump, about fifteen minutes of break time twice a day, and a place to express milk in privacy, most mothers can provide all of their babies' need for milk even if they are working full time. If this is your plan, you will need some additional education and preparation regarding expressing and storing your milk.

10. It is normal to breastfeed for two years or more.

Exclusive breastfeeding, in which the baby receives no nourishment other than his or her mother's milk, usually lasts around six months. Somewhere around the second half of the first year, most babies are ready to start eating some other foods. But the transition to a diet that is similar to that of an adult is meant to be gradual, and human milk is a healthy part of a child's diet for some time after the first solids are introduced. Studies by anthropologists and comparative biologists have revealed that the probable natural weaning age (that is, the age at which no more nursing occurs) of the human species is past 2 1/2 years. There is no harm in permitting a child who wants to continue nursing for two years or more to do so. In fact, it is quite common everywhere in the world that bottle-feeding is not the cultural norm. The fact that it is not unusual in our culture for a child of 3 to be drinking milk from a bottle or using a pacifier is a clue that the need to suck is a fundamental human need that does not disappear at six months or one year of age.

To read more of Rachael Hamlet's work, check out "ProMoM": Promotion of Mothers' Milk, Inc. on the Web at http://www.promom.org

Doctor Shopping: Choosing Your Baby's Health Care Provider

Optimally, you will be able to locate a wonderful pediatrician, family practice doctor, or other health care provider (HCP) for your baby before you give birth. However, finding an HCP who is supportive of the attachment parenting style can sometimes take some digging. Both older and younger doctors are unlikely to have had any significant training in lactation science while in medical school and often, the advice they offer parents on the topic of breastfeeding is a mishmash of old breastfeeding myths and information gleaned from "educational material" provided by the infant formula sales reps who haunt their offices. Despite new research supporting family co-sleeping and the growing numbers of parents who are adopting family beds, many medical professionals continue to warn against sharing a bed with your child under any circumstances. And lots of doctors still advise parents to let their babies cry themselves to sleep.

But don't be discouraged; with a little effort, you can probably find an HCP who will support you in your attachment parenting choices. At the very least, you should be able to find a doctor who won't actively oppose your parenting style. Remember, though, that your doctor's role should be to prevent and treat illness, not to tell you how to raise your children.

In searching for an appropriate HCP for your child, the first place to look is with other parents. If you know mothers and fathers who parent their own children in a way that seems right to you, ask them for recommendations for pediatric care in your community. If you see a woman nursing her toddler at the park, or a father carrying his baby in a sling at the mall, don't be shy! Approach them and ask them for advice on choosing a doctor. You will usually find other parents more than happy to talk with you about the pros and cons of their chosen pediatric or family practice. You might also attend a La Leche League meeting or two to talk with members about their views on local doctors. Your midwife, obstetrician, childbirth educator, or doula may have suggestions as well. After you have narrowed your list of potential HCPs down to a manageable size, call each practice and arrange for a "pregnancy interview." This will be an opportunity for you to meet with an HCP and decide whether she is right for your family. Beware the doctor's office that seems annoyed by your request for an interview, or worse yet, has never heard of such a thing. A good HCP knows and welcomes the fact that conscientious parents will give careful consideration to a decision as important as choosing who will partner with them to provide their child's health care.

In evaluating a potential attachment parenting–friendly health care provider, here are a few things you should look for/ask about. Be sure to also come up with your own list of questions and priorities:

1. What is the doctor's favorite popular reference childcare manual?

If it's *The Baby Book* by William and Martha Sears (or this book!), you're in luck. If the doctor mentions *On Becoming Babywise* by Gary Ezzo and Robert Bucknam, M.D., or *When Breastfeeding Isn't an Option* by Peggy Robin, you'll need to keep looking.

2. Take a careful look around the office.

Is the environment kid-friendly? Are there comfortable places to sit and nurse a fussy baby or child? Do you see other nursing mothers?

3. Is the office free of promotional or "educational" literature or products from the companies that produce infant formula (examples could be calendars, notepads, "baby growth charts," informational booklets, or giveaway infant formula)?

An HCP's willingness to offer this free advertising to infant formula companies can be an important indicator of her lack of interest in or knowledge of breastfeeding.

4. Does the office have an Internationally Board Certified Lactation Consultant (IBCLC) on staff or as a referral?

Do they routinely put new mothers in touch with local La Leche League leaders and meetings?

5. What percentage of the HCP's patients are breastfed? Breastfed at six months? Breastfed into toddlerhood?

If you ask a pediatrician whether she is "supportive of breastfeeding," virtually any one will *say* that she is. Questions like the ones listed above are more revealing. Even if a doctor doesn't have hard numbers to give you in response to this question, she should understand your interest in this information and be willing to give you ballpark figures, along with relevant explanations.

► *"At my son's one year checkup, the pediatrician asked me if I was still breastfeeding. I told him yes and that it was going well. He responded by saying that I really should wean soon or I would have a three year old hanging off my breast. His voice and facial expressions obviously implied that this would be distasteful. This reinforced all the other negative attention I was receiving for breastfeeding just through the first year. I should have been feeling good about doing what was best for my child, but instead I left the office feeling lousy."*

—SALLY, MOTHER OF THREE

► *"My pediatrician was wonderful! She was so supportive of my decision to nurse my daughter. She never asked me when I was going to wean, but applauded me, telling me that there would be benefits for my daughter as long as I continued. I nursed my daughter happily until she was two and a half. What a success! I love my pediatrician and recommend her to everyone."*

—SUSAN, MOTHER OF A THREE YEAR OLD

6. Does the HCP have experience supporting breastfeeding mothers who are employed outside the home?

Working, breastfeeding mothers need specialized information and support to meet the challenges of pumping, introducing alternative feeding methods to their breastfed baby, and keeping their milk supply up. You will want to find an HCP who is very familiar with these issues and can offer you the information and advice you may need if you plan to return to outside employment in the year or so after your baby arrives. An excellent choice would probably be a woman HCP who breastfed her own children for at least two years.

7. What is the HCP's position on routine infant circumcision?

Many attachment parents decide against routine circumcision for their sons (see the section on circumcision in the chapter entitled, "Attachment Parenting Your Newborn"). It is important to find an HCP who will support your decision in this matter and who is familiar with the care of a baby boy with an intact penis.

Three excellent resources for starting your search for an attachment parenting–friendly doctor for your baby include:

The La Leche League International Medical Associates Program

La Leche League International
P.O. Box 4079
Schaumburg, Illinois 60168–4079 USA
Phone: (847) 519–7730
Fax: (847) 519–0035
http://www.lalecheleague.org/MedAss.html

Physicians who become LLLI Associates are knowledgeable about LLL's philosphy of "mothering through breastfeeding." Contact La Leche League to find a LLLI Medical Associate in your area.

The Academy of Breastfeeding Medicine

Academy of Breastfeeding Medicine
P.O. Box 15945–284
Lenexa, KS 66285–5945
Phone: (913) 541–9077
E-mail: shime@applmeapro.com

This organization of medical professionals with strong interest or background in the science of human lactation can tell you where you might find a suitable physician.

Promotion of Mother's Milk, Inc (ProMoM)

Promotion of Mother's Milk, Inc. (ProMoM)
P.O. Box 3912
New York, NY 10163
http://www.promom.org

ProMoM, a nonprofit breastfeeding advocacy organization, maintains an ever-growing list of medical professionals across the United States whom parents themselves have recommended. HCPs can also ask to be included on the list. You can access this information by contacting ProMoM or viewing the list on their Web site.

The Very Best Children's Health Care Guides

Take Charge of Your Child's Health: A Guide to Recognizing Symptoms and Treating Minor Illnesses at Home. Wootan, George, M.D. and Sarah Verney. New York: Crown Publishers Inc., 1992.

The Baby Book: Everything You Need to Know About Your Baby—From Birth to Age Two. Sears, William, M. and Martha Sears. New York: Little, Brown and Company, 1993.

How to Raise a Healthy Child in Spite of Your Doctor. Mendelsohn, Robert S., M.D. New York: Ballantine Books, 1987.

The Holistic Pediatrician: A Parent's Comprehensive Guide to Safe and Effective Therapies for the 25 Most Common Childhood Ailments. Kemper, Kathi J. New York: HarperCollins, 1996.

CHAPTER 3

Attachment Parenting Your Newborn

OVER THE LONG MONTHS OF PREGNANCY, YOU HAVE OFTEN tried to imagine what it will feel like the first time you hold your new baby in your arms. For most parents, the reality of that moment when it finally arrives is something they never forget. Awash in raw emotion, you will gaze down into that little face and feel both exhilarated and overwhelmed. Many mothers and fathers literally weep with joy as they meet their new baby face to face for the very first time.

> ► *"It was like meeting someone I already knew from a previous life or something. When we looked into each other's eyes for the first time, it was clear that we already knew one another."*
>
> —*MARTA, MOTHER OF A THREE YEAR OLD*

And this first meeting is no less momentous for your newborn. Researchers have discovered that in the hour or so immediately following birth, healthy newborns enter what is known as a "quiet alert" state, during which they are exceptionally receptive to seeing, smelling, touching and hearing their mothers. Babies who have experienced a gentle, medication free birth are more easily able to enter this highly interactive state. You may be wondering how anyone could describe your tiny bundle as "highly interactive" when at first glance, he seems to be helpless in your arms. In fact, your brand new baby has amazing capabilities to communicate and begin bonding with you if given the chance to use them.

Unfortunately, the concept of postpartum bonding between parents and babies has been widely misrepresented in the media and popular parenting literature. Currently, it seems that we are experiencing a cultural backlash against bonding research, with many pundits displaying a highly dismissive attitude toward the importance of infant-maternal togetherness in the period immediately following birth. However, both research and anecdotal evidence are quite clear: *although the first hours and days that you spend with your baby certainly won't determine the sum total of your later relationship with him, very early parent-child bonding* will *play an important role in building your confidence as a new parent, and in understanding and responding to your child's cues.* A relaxed, gentle, responsive entrance to life outside the womb helps your baby begin to develop the trust that he is loved and listened to as an individual . . . right from the start.

Your Birth Setting

In the past, hospitals, where the vast majority of American babies continue to be born, had many policies and procedures in place that put barriers between mothers and their newborns. Times have changed and some hospitals have made major improvements in this area. Unfortunately, many institutions still have a long way to go. Today, however, informed parents can make most of their own choices regarding how they will interact with their baby during the hours, days, or in a few cases, weeks or beyond, that mother and newborn are in the hospital's care. You should choose your birth setting carefully while you are still pregnant. Don't assume that just because your friend or sister-in-law liked a certain hospital that you will too. Her parenting philosophy may differ markedly from yours. For example, she may have enjoyed having her baby cared for in the nursery by hospital staff as much as possible, while you will want to have your baby in the room with you at all times. Be sure to take a tour of potential birthing facilities, and ask very specific questions about their policies regarding mother-baby care. It will also be helpful if you include your decisions regarding your newborn's hospital care in your birth plan.* Mothers who give birth in a freestanding birth center or in a planned homebirth** won't generally need to worry about rules and regulations coming between them and their babies. For this reason, among many others, both of these options are worthy of

---

*A birth plan is a flexible written outline for the type of birth experience you would like to have. After you prepare it, your birth attendant (doctor, midwife) should sign it and include it in your medical record. You should write it after becoming informed about all your birth choices, preferably through a really great natural childbirth class.

** If you are interested in learning more about the growing homebirth movement or the location of a freestanding birth center in your area, you can contact:

Midwives' Alliance of North America (MANA)
P.O. Box 82227
Phone: (888) 923–MANA (6262) or (316) 267–7236
http://www.MANA.org

National Association of Childbearing Centers (NACC)
3123 Gottschall Road
Perkiomenville, Pennsylvania 18074
Phone: (215) 234–8068
Fax: (215) 234–8829
E-mail: ReachNACC@BirthCenters.org

your serious consideration. These books offer excellent guidance in writing and utilizing a personal birth plan:

The Birth Book: Everything You Need to Know to Have a Safe and Satisfying Birth. Sears, William M. and Martha Sears. New York: Little, Brown & Co., 1994.

A Good Birth, A Safe Birth: Choosing and Having the Childbirth Experience You Want. Korte, Diana, and Roberta Scaer. Edited by Leslie Baker. Boston: Harvard Common Press, 1992.

Gentle Birth Choices: A Guide to Making Informed Decisions. Harper, Barbara. Rochester, VT: Inner Traditions Intl. Ltd., 1994.

The following childbirth education organizations are supportive of a safe, healthy, informed childbirth experience for you and your baby. Contact them to learn more about their philosophy and to locate an instructor in your area:

The Bradley Method of Natural Childbirth
P.O. Box 5224
Sherman Oaks, CA 91413-5224
Phone: (800) 4–A–BIRTH or (818) 788–5224
http://www.bradleybirth.com

The Bradley Method was the pioneer in helping women achieve unmedicated childbirth and in advocating for fathers to become involved in the birth experience. This childbirth education method is one of the most popular, and course graduates have a very high rate of unmedicated birth. The Bradley Method also includes strong emphasis on nutrition, consumer awareness in childbirth choices, and early parent-child bonding.

The International Childbirth Education Association (ICEA)
P.O. Box 20048
Minneapolis, MN 55420
Phone: (612) 854–8660
Fax: (612) 854–8772

ICEA is an organization of over 8,000 members from forty-two countries that unites those who believe in freedom of choice based on knowledge of alternatives in family centered maternity and newborn care.

Birth Works® Childbirth Education

Phone: (888) TO–BIRTH

http://hometown.aol.com/Birthwkscd/bw.html

E-Mail: BirthWksCD@aol.com

Birth Works® embodies a philosophy that develops a woman's self confidence and trust in her innate ability to give birth. The classes are experiential and provide both a physical and emotional preparation for birth. Birth Works® classes are taken by new parents, as well as by parents with prior cesarean or vaginal births.

Association of Labor Assistants and Childbirth Educators (ALACE)

P.O. Box 382724

Cambridge, MA 02238

Phone: (617) 441–2500

E-mail: Alacehq@aol.com

According to ALACE, normal birth today has often come to resemble a mechanized, medical emergency. ALACE childbirth educators and labor assistants provide pregnant women with information and practical alternatives so that they may give birth with confidence, strength and joy.

Association of Christian Childbirth Professionals (ACCP)

P.O. Box 94

New Almaden, CA 95042–0094

http://www.kaleidoskope.com/accp

E-Mail: mjo_bcce@pacbell.net

The ACCP's philosophy is that natural birth is the best, safest and most efficient mode of delivery for the vast majority of babies and mothers. The organization promotes the excellent preparation of expectant parents via comprehensive, consumer-oriented, natural childbirth classes. They further encourage parents to seek out and assemble a birth team who supports these views.

The Baby-Friendly Hospital Initiative

It seems like a simple enough idea: hospitals and birth centers should make it easy for new mothers to successfully breastfeed their babies. But according to the World Health Organization (WHO), most American maternity facilities actually have many policies and procedures that work against breastfeeding. The Baby-Friendly Hospital Initiative (BFHI) was launched in 1991 by the World Health Organization (WHO) and the United Nations Children's Fund (UNICEF) as an effort to increase breastfeeding rates. WHO's medical experts devised a ten-step program for optimal breastfeeding support which hospitals and birthing centers can adopt in order to receive recognition as a "Baby-Friendly" institution. Although thousands of hospitals around the world have now been certified by WHO, fewer than twenty Baby-Friendly hospitals and birth centers currently exist in the United States. Even if the facility in which you plan to give birth isn't certified, you can still look for a birth setting that has adopted as many of WHO's ten steps as possible. And be sure to let your hospital or birth center know that you would like to see them strive toward Baby-Friendly status.

WHO's Ten Steps Toward a Baby-Friendly Birth Setting

1. The institution will have a written breastfeeding policy that is routinely communicated to all health care staff.
2. All health care staff will be trained in the skills necessary to implement this policy.
3. All pregnant women will be informed about the benefits and management of breastfeeding.
4. New mothers will receive appropriate lactation guidance, enabling them to initiate breastfeeding within half an hour of birth.
5. Mothers will receive instruction in how to breastfeed, and how to maintain lactation even if they should be separated from their infants.
6. Newborn infants will be given no food or drink other than breastmilk, unless medically indicated.

7. The hospital or birth center will practice rooming in by allowing mothers and infants to remain together twenty-four hours a day.
8. The medical staff will encourage cue-breastfeeding (as opposed to a feeding schedule).
9. No pacifiers will be given to breastfeeding infants.
10. The hospital or birth center will foster the establishment of breastfeeding support groups and refer mothers to them upon their discharge.

Baby Arrives!

The moment you have anticipated is finally here! After that final push or, in the case of a c-section, as your doctor lifts your baby out of your womb, the person you have created, nurtured, carried, and longed for is ready to meet you. Immediately after birth, even some healthy babies do require a couple of minutes of observation by birth attendants or possibly a bit of oxygen to stabilize, but most can go directly into their parents' arms. And that is where all the choices you make regarding your baby's care can begin building a secure and lifelong parent-child attachment.

• **Warm Your Baby Yourself.** Most hospital birthing rooms include a mechanical "baby warmer." This is a high tech bed on wheels with a heat lamp over it to allow a just born baby to get and stay warm in the period directly following birth. However, your room actually already contains a much more natural and effective baby warmer: you! Newborns do need to have their body temperature kept stable and warm and the best way to accomplish this is to have your partner or birth attendant place your naked newborn onto your own naked abdomen or chest and then cover the baby with a soft, warm blanket or towel. There is no reason why a healthy mother and baby shouldn't be skin to skin directly following birth. In fact, the smell, touch and feel of your own body is exactly what your newborn craves. And since you have waited eagerly for so long to be able to get your hands on your baby, that's exactly what you should be able to do!

• **Request Privacy.** After you and your baby are observed to be medically stable, you may want to ask that your birth attendant(s) and their helpers leave you, your partner and/or other close family members or friends of your choosing alone with your newborn for a period of quiet time together. This is when you can first count those fingers and toes and take a stab at deciding who the baby looks like. It has been observed that women all over the world engage in the same pattern of tentatively touching and stroking their newborns when first given time alone with them. Private time also begins the process of letting you know that this is *your* baby; not the doctor's, the midwife's, the nurses', or the hospital's. This sense of "ownership" for your relationship with your baby is important to your confidence level as a new parent.

✦ **"If kept with her newborn an hour or more following birth, there is a 70% chance that, if blindfolded and marched along a row of babies, the mother will identify her own just by feeling the back of her baby's hands or cheeks. And fathers have this ability too, although they recognize their newborns only by the feel of their baby's hands."**

—*Sharon Heller, Ph.D.* in The Vital Touch: How Intimate Contact with Your Baby Leads to Happier, Healthier Development

▶ *"I couldn't believe it when everyone left the room and it was just us with the baby. We could tell immediately that he recognized and responded to our voices. That made us feel really great after a hard birth."*

—*Lynn, mother of a one week old*

• **Look into Your Baby's Eyes.** Not so long ago, mothers were told by doctors and others that their newborn babies could see very little. Today, however, researchers have discovered that newborns in the quiet alert state are able to distinguish patterns and focus on objects. Not surprisingly, it has been demonstrated that a newborn's favorite object upon which to focus is his mother's face, and particularly her eyes and mouth. Newborn babies *are* rather nearsighted and can see best at a distance of eight to ten inches from their own faces. Perhaps not coincidentally, this is about how far away your face will be from hers when you are breastfeeding. Gazing lovingly into your newborn's eyes as he looks back at you is a wonderful first form of communication between parent and child. Most hospitals require (as per state law) that antibiotic ointment be placed in your newborn's eyes soon after birth. This is to prevent the baby from acquiring any infection she may have come into contact with during childbirth. This medication is known to blur the vision of the newborn for a brief period and make it harder for her to engage in this wonderful early visual interaction. You may want to request that this procedure be delayed until after you have had a period of at least an hour or two to hold and look into the beautiful little eyes you have waited so long to see. And if the trauma of a tough birth or labor pain medication still in his system means that all your new baby wants to do is sleep in your arms, you can still enjoy holding him close and looking at him, even if he's not yet ready to look back.

• **Nurse Your Newborn in the Hour or So After Birth.** Perhaps during your natural childbirth class your instructor showed you one of the amazing films of a newly born baby—after being placed onto his mother's abdomen—slowly inching his way up a naked belly toward his mother's breast. Newborn babies, like other mammals, have an inborn and powerful attraction to what they know will be their source of physical and emotional sustenance outside the womb: their mother's breasts. You can and should offer your healthy newborn the opportunity to breastfeed within the first hour, or even the first few minutes after his entrance into the world. Make it clear to your health care providers that you intend to offer your baby the breast soon after birth. Don't accept the still too common arguments from some misinformed doctors and nurses against early breastfeeding. The 1998 breastfeeding guidelines from the American Academy of Pediatrics state that:

"Breastfeeding should begin as soon as possible after birth, usually within the first hour. Except under special circumstances, the newborn infant should remain with the mother throughout the recovery period. Procedures that may interfere with breastfeeding or traumatize the infant should be avoided or minimized."

Nursing soon after birth offers your protective colostrum* to your vulnerable newborn, as well as stimulating your uterus to contract and expel the placenta, thus slowing postpartum bleeding. Studies have demonstrated that women who put their babies to breast within the first hour after birth are more successful at breastfeeding in the long run. Nature clearly designed both baby and mother to begin nursing almost immediately. However, don't stress out over the way the first few nursings go. Babies who have had a traumatic or medicated birth may be too tired or groggy to actually suck. Your baby may latch on to your breast eagerly, she may merely lick or nuzzle your nipple, or she may nod off as soon as she feels securely snuggled at your breast. The most important

---

*Colostrum is the very first milk that your body signals your breasts to produce. It is an amazing substance, loaded with white blood cells and other potent infection-fighting properties. Colostrum is important for protecting your vulnerable newborn against disease. Farmers have long known that calves, piglets and other mammals who don't receive their mother's colostrum soon after birth are much more likely to become sickly and even die.

thing is to offer the two of you an early introduction to one of the most special of all human relationships: that of mother and nursling child. If for any reason you are unable to breastfeed immediately after birth, make it a priority to put your baby to your breast as soon and as often as your particular circumstances will allow. Babies are hardwired to begin breastfeeding immediately after birth and sometimes a delay can interrupt the natural rhythm between mother and newborn, making it a little harder for breastfeeding newbies to get started. If you find yourself in this situation, call a La Leche League Leader or the board certified lactation consultant (IBCLC) that you lined up before birth.

▶ *"I treasure the video of my daughter's birth when I put her to my breast at only a few minutes old and she began to nurse! I couldn't believe that a baby this young knew just what to do. In the video, I look over at my husband and yell, 'she's nursing!' I was so excited."*

—KATIE, MOTHER OF THREE

- **Ban the bottle and pacifier.**

✦ **"No supplements (water, glucose water, formula, and so forth) should be given to breastfeeding newborns unless a medical indication exists. With sound breastfeeding knowledge and practices, supplements rarely are needed. Supplements and pacifiers should be avoided whenever possible and, if used at all, only after breastfeeding is well established."**

—*THE AMERICAN ACADEMY OF PEDIATRICS' POLICY STATEMENT ON BREASTFEEDING*

There are many reasons why a breastfed newborn should not receive supplemental bottles of infant formula or glucose water during the first hours and days after birth. Even one bottle can carry unwanted consequences. Perhaps most importantly, giving bottles to a newborn who is still learning to breastfeed can cause nipple confusion, which we discussed previously. It's true that a few babies are able to switch easily between breast and bottle from day one. And some are able to learn to take a bottle after breastfeeding is well established (usually between three and six weeks), while others won't ever stand for anything except mama's breast in their mouths. *However, some babies are unable to tolerate any bottle or pacifier use without becoming nipple confused.* For these babies (and unfortunately there is often no way to know if your baby is prone to nipple confusion until it is too late), very early bottle use can spell potential disaster for breastfeeding. Some mothers who have experienced this phenomenon have observed that once their newborn "imprinted" on a bottle or pacifier nipple, he seemed unable to successfully latch on to a breast. Some babies who receive early bottles and develop poor breastfeeding technique end up causing sore breasts and nipples in their mothers. This can lead to more bottle use and a predictable spiral toward unplanned weaning.

Even if you plan to offer bottles at some point, it is strongly recommended that you avoid them in this early newborn period. The same goes for pacifiers. Many breastfeeding families find it very helpful to attach a conspicuous note to their baby's hospital bassinet with the message: *"Our baby is exclusively breastfed. He should not have any bottles or pacifiers at any time without our written consent."* This may seem like overkill, but if you make your wishes known in no uncertain terms, the nursery staff should respect your decision and commitment. If for any reason your baby does receive artificial nipples and you find that it has had a negative impact on your ability to breastfeed, do not delay in getting help from a La Leche League Leader or IBCLC. With the right assistance early enough, you can usually get back on track with breastfeeding your baby.

✦ **". . . hospitals think, at least for the first day or so, 'let's give the mother a rest and have a bottle or two bottles before moving to breastfeeding.' There's lots of evidence to show that even a bottle or two in those first days reduces the likelihood of a mother breastfeeding for a sufficient period by as much as one-third."**

—*Richard Jolly, UNICEF*

As for what might go in a bottle, healthy infants are born with a need for only their mother's colostrum until her milk comes in (usually in one to four days); thus, there are *very* few instances when a just-born baby should need any nourishment other than his mother's breast. Misinformed HCPs will sometimes still convince a tired new mother that her healthy baby *needs* formula or glucose water because he is "hungry" (mothers of larger-than-average babies, as well as smaller-than-average babies, often hear this advice). Unnecessary formula supplementation upsets the delicate, healthy and desirable pH balance in a breastfed baby's bowel. Early exposure to formula also places a baby at higher risk for serious allergy to cow's milk protein or soy protein. Lastly, use of supplements at this stage can throw off the delicate supply and demand system upon which successful breastfeeding develops. If you feel confident in your HCP's recommendation that your newborn does genuinely need nourishment other than your breast, inquire as to the availability of alternative feeding methods such as Haberman™ feeder, Supplemental Nutrition System (SNS), cup-feeding, syringes or finger feeding. A board certified lactation consultant can assist in supplying these methods, which are all preferable to early bottle use in a breastfed baby.

► *"It only took a couple of unnecessary bottles in the early days before my son was screaming for the bottle every time I tried to nurse him. Of course, I hated to see him so unhappy, so I would give up in tears and fix him another bottle. Ultimately, this was what ended breastfeeding for us within a few weeks. Now he is six years old and it's clear that he is a very sensitive person. He was definitely very sensitive to artificial nipple use but there was no way for me to know that back when he was a newborn and I was an inexperienced, tired new mother with family members bugging me to let them bottle-feed the baby."*

—*KATIE, MOTHER OF THREE*

Rooming In: Because New Parents Need Their Babies and New Babies Need Their Parents

We have already offered several ideas for getting off to a good start attachment parenting your brand new baby while still in the hospital. But in order for you to take advantage of early breastfeeding or time alone with your newborn, the two of you must actually *be together*. The practice of allowing a healthy newborn to remain in her mother's room rather than in a separate nursery during the postpartum hospital stay is called "rooming in." Not so long ago, mothers and their newborns were routinely separated at birth and for the length of their time in the hospital. Babies were warehoused in a private, glass-walled nursery and mothers stayed in their own rooms. The two were allowed time together on a regimented schedule determined by hospital staff—usually every four hours except at night when mothers might not see their babies at all. Nurses would bring a new mother her baby at the beginning of a visiting period and return to whisk the baby back to the nursery a short time later. If a mother wanted to see her baby at any other time, she was forced to stand behind the nursery window and wave or tap on the glass as if at the zoo. Needless to say, this arrangement was hard on parents, newborns, and their attempts to bond. As for breastfeeding, this practice of separating mothers and babies usually spelled disaster.

Today, virtually all maternity units advertise the availability of rooming in, allowing parents and their healthy baby to stay together in the same room while in the hospital's care. The importance of rooming in cannot be overstated. It provides the best context for a group of individuals to gel into a new family.

> ✦ **". . . when we enable parents to be together in privacy with their baby for the first hour and throughout their hospital stay, and add supportive caregiving, we establish the environment most conducive to the beginning of the bonding process."**
>
> —*From* Bonding: Building the Foundations of Secure Attachment and Independence *(Addison-Wesley, 1995), by world-renowned bonding researchers* Marshall H. Klaus, M.D. *and* John H. Kennell, M.D.

Some of the most important benefits of rooming in include:

• **Relaxation for tired mother and baby.** No one who has just given birth needs or wants to have to go to a separate area of the hospital to see or beg for access to her baby. Mothers who are separated from their new babies for even brief periods often report feeling ill-at-ease and unsettled—not a very restful state—until their babies are returned to them. This isn't surprising considering the close physical connection they have shared with their baby for the past nine months. And babies who are still adjusting after birth long for quiet comfort in the arms of people who love them; not the bright lights, plastic bassinets and rotating nurses of an institutional nursery. If a new mother is too tired or sore from birth to do much holding or caring for her new baby, she still doesn't have to send him off to the nursery. Her partner, parents, or close friends can all hold the baby while she sleeps soundly, knowing that her baby is nearby. Both mother and baby get more rest with rooming in.

• **A better start to breastfeeding.** As we will discuss more fully in the chapter on breastfeeding, newborns require frequent, free access to their mother's breasts. This is especially important during the period during which mother and nursling are first learning each other's rhythms. Some newborns need to nurse every twenty minutes, if only for a moment or two. Others need to be awakened if they sleep too long without eating. These individual adjustments can be impossible when mother and baby aren't even in the same room. Without frequent sucking stimulation from the newborn, some women find that their milk actually takes longer to come in. Perhaps no factor is more important to getting breastfeeding off to a smooth, productive start than rooming in. Unfortunately, far too many parents who intend to breastfeed get off to a poor start in the first few days in the hospital due to mother-baby separation. As a result, their baby ends up on a bottle.

• **First steps of the mother-baby dance.** Dr. William Sears has noted that rooming in is "especially helpful for women who have trouble jumping right into mothering." The more quickly a mother and baby are able to start learning each other's cues, the more easily they are able to engage in behaviors that bring out the best in one another. For example, a woman who notices that her newborn begins to suck his hands just before starting to cry can pick him and comfort him as soon as that little hand goes in his mouth, thus averting upset for both of them. For his part, the baby is discovering how he can get and keep his mother's attention. This sort of delicate and highly interactive communication simply isn't possible when parents are separated from their new baby.

• **An increased sense of ownership and responsibil-**

ity for the baby on the part of the father. New fathers in particular are often nervous and fearful about actually caring for their newborns. Having their baby taken away to a nursery for care by "professionals" simply magnifies that feeling. Both parents can learn basic babycare tasks (diapering, clipping nails, etc) better from working with caring nurses in their own hospital room than they will from turning their baby over to the nursery staff.

• **More safety for baby.** More often than we would like, we hear about babies who have been "switched at birth." Needless to say, this can't happen when parents are with their babies at all times. Mothers who are with their babies for even a few hours after birth become quite familiar with the look, feel and smell of their own baby.

• **Less chance of infection.** Your baby's risk of unwanted infection will be reduced if she is kept with you. Even the most scrupulously clean hospital nursery harbors the potential for passing illnesses to newborns.

> ▶ *"With my first baby, I felt like a nurse was carrying him away every hour or so for one thing or another. Then they would never bring him back when they said they would and many times, I actually had to go find him by banging on the nursery door. With my second baby, I went to a birth center and the baby was with us every second. This last time we had the baby at home with a midwife and our whole family was asleep together in our bed only a few hours after she was born. This was the best!"*
>
> —*JANIT, MOTHER OF THREE*

Sometimes hospitals that claim to offer rooming in actually have their own definition of the term. In many facilities, babies are taken to the nursery each time a new shift of nurses comes on duty. In others, all bathing, weighing, and temperature taking of babies takes place in the nursery. Very frequently, nurses will urge overwhelmed new parents to turn their newborn over to the nursery staff by telling them that it's the "only way a tired new mother can get any rest." The best plan for avoiding these undesirable situations is to choose your birth setting carefully in the first place. Make sure that you are clear on your hospital's complete policy on rooming in *before* checking in to have your baby. If you find that you are continually being asked to hand your baby over to nursery staff despite your desire to have her with you, ask your pediatrician to put a note on the baby's chart stating that she has ordered *complete* rooming in. And of course, the best way to assure that you have privacy, relaxation, and contact with your new baby is to go home. Many women who have adequate help and support at home leave the hospital or birth center with their newborns within six to twelve hours of a healthy birth.

Gentle Care for Your Newborn

The days of obstetricians lifting terrified just born babies upside down and slapping them on the bum are (thankfully!) over. However, many routine hospital procedures still treat very new babies with disrespect for their personhood and for the monumental adjustment they are being asked to make in the hours and days directly after birth. Fierce advocacy for your child's rights is a fundamental part of attachment parenting and you may have to begin asserting yourself as a parent immediately after your baby's arrival. Insist that doctors, nurses and midwives who hold or examine your baby do so gently and respectfully. Unless it becomes necessary for medical reasons, your baby should stay in your arms or those of your partner during these early hours. You should take time before birth to educate yourself about routine newborn medical procedures that may be uncomfortable for your baby. As an example, most hospitals still insist on a painful injection of Vitamin K for all new babies immediately after birth in order to prevent an extremely rare situation in which babies' blood doesn't clot normally. However, new research suggests that for healthy newborns, this dose of Vitamin K is just as effective when given orally. Some parents choose to forego it altogether. You should discuss this with your HCP. As for a first bath by medical personnel, which can be quite upsetting and disorienting for your brand new baby, you may choose instead to gently sponge your baby yourself and then massage the white, creamy substance (called vernix) with which most newborns are coated, into your baby's skin over a period of several days in order to protect and moisturize his delicate skin.

> ▶ *"One of the reasons I liked the midwives at my birthing center so much is they they treated me like I was my baby's mother right from the first moment. They always asked whether they could hold him or bathe him or check something. They never acted like it was their right to take him out of my arms."*
>
> —*ALEX, MOTHER OF A NINE MONTH OLD*

Consider *Not* Circumcising Your Baby

Depending on your religious or cultural background, you may have very strong opinions concerning circumcision (removal of the sleeve of skin and tissue that normally covers the head of a healthy penis). Even if you don't have strongly held views on this controversial topic, you may have never met an adult male who was *not* circumcised, thus leaving you with the mistaken impression that this surgery is as inevitable for baby boys as cutting their umbilical cord. In fact, many attachment parents (and approximately half of *all* American parents today, as well as a much higher percentage of parents in Europe) are deciding against having their sons circumcised. Joining the major pediatric organizations in countries like Australia, Great Britain, and Canada in opposing routine circumcision, the American Academy of Pediatrics released a new policy on routine infant circumcision in 1999 which reads in part:

"After analysis of almost 40 years of available medical research on circumcision, the American Academy of Pediatrics (AAP) has issued new recommendations stating that the benefits are not significant enough for the AAP to recommend circumcision as a routine procedure . . . The new policy recommendations are based on analysis of all available medical literature on circumcision currently available, including new studies published in the last 10 years."

Why are so many parents and doctors now deciding against circumcision? Well, first, let's take a look at what happens in a routine medical circumcision. The newborn baby is strapped to a restraining board, with hands and feet secured. Approximately one-third of the nerve rich skin of the penis is then lifted, clamped and sliced off, generally without benefit of any pain relief at all. This is an inarguably traumatic and terribly painful procedure for a tiny new human to undergo. Some infants cry loudly afterwards, while others retreat into a deep sleep, which can indicate a type of mild shock. Many medical personnel have observed that newly circumcised babies have trouble sleeping and eating for hours and even days afterwards. The AAP's 1999 Policy Statement on Circumcision takes note of the pain involved in this procedure, stating that:

"For the first time in AAP circumcision policy history, the new recommendations also indicate that if parents decide to circumcise their infant, it is essential that pain relief be provided . . . Considerable new evidence shows that newborns circumcised without analgesia experience pain and stress measured by changes in heart rate, blood pressure, oxygen saturation and cortisol levels. Other studies suggest that

the circumcision experience may cause infants to respond more strongly to pain of future immunization than those who are uncircumcised. In response to this data, the AAP policy states that analgesia has been found to be safe and effective in reducing the pain associated with circumcision, and should be provided if the procedure is performed. Analgesic methods include EMLA cream (a topical mixture of local anesthetics), the dorsal penile nerve block and the subcutaneous ring block."

In addition to the issue of pain, what has been removed from the baby boy's body in a circumcision is *not* simply a useless piece of skin. The foreskin protects the penis from irritation and infection, and later in life, is an important part of a man's ability to experience sexual pleasure. It is for these reasons—the pain and trauma and the fact that they believe that the procedure is violative of a baby's body and rights—that increasing numbers of parents of all backgrounds are deciding against circumcision. Because you want your baby's entrance into the world to be as gentle and respectful as possible, you owe it to yourself and your baby to learn all you can about circumcision before making any decision.

If you choose not to circumcise, your son's intact penis will need no special care (unlike the cut penis, which will need to be treated as a painful and infection prone wound for several weeks after the procedure). Your baby's whole, healthy penis will also be less inclined to develop diaper rashes and irritation. One important thing to know about a baby's intact (uncircumcised) penis is that the foreskin should *never* be forcibly retracted. Sometime in the first one to five years of your son's life, his foreskin will loosen and begin to retract naturally on its own. If your pediatrician is not familiar with uncircumcised babies, she may try to convince you to force the foreskin back or even retract it herself. This can tear your baby's delicate tissues and cause scarring. Once your son's foreskin begins to retract on its own, you can teach him to gently wash himself, just as you would teach your daughter of the same age to clean the folds and crevices of her own external genitalia. If you do make the decision to circumcise your son, by all means make the effort to seek out an individual who will provide a local anesthetic to your baby during this procedure.

> ▶ *"My husband and I struggled for nine months of pregnancy over whether our son would be circumcised or not. He wanted Joel to look like him. I was adamant that this wasn't a good enough reason to subject our baby to the pain and insult of the procedure. I bombarded my husband with solid information on why circumcision just didn't mesh with our overall values as parents and he eventually decided against it. We are both very happy with our decision and I have no doubt that Joel will one day thank us for not removing part of his penis without asking him."*
>
> —LAURA, MOTHER OF TWO

The Very Best Resources for Learning More About Circumcision

BOOKS

Circumcision Exposed: Rethinking a Medical Cultural Tradition. rev. ed. Boyd, Billy Ray. Freedom, CA: Crossing Press, Inc., 1998.

The Joy of Uncircumcising! 2nd Ed. Bigelow, Jim. Aptos, CA: Marketscope Books, 1995.

WEB SITES

The Circumcision Information and Referral Pages
http://www.cirp.org

National Organization of Circumcision Information and Referral Centers
http://www.nocirc.org

Doctors Opposing Circumcision
http://weber.u.washington.edu/~gcd/DOC

Bonding After a Cesarean Birth

In the United States today, nearly one in four women gives birth via cesarean section. Although some of these surgeries are certainly necessary and lifesaving, many others are not. By taking a *natural* childbirth class, carefully choosing your birth attendant, and giving birth in a freestanding birth center or in a planned homebirth with a skilled attendant, you can dramatically reduce your risk of having to undergo this significant medical procedure. You should always inquire as to your midwife, doctor, or hospital's c-section rates when making your birth choices. If, however, you end up giving birth surgically rather than vaginally, rest assured that you too can begin attachment parenting your newborn from her first moments outside the womb. Again, you will want to include your preferences in your written birth plan in the event that you end up needing a c-section.

Have Your Partner Present for Your C-section

In recent years it has become the norm for a birthing woman's partner to accompany her into the operating room for a c-section. Except in the rare instance of extreme medical emergency, your partner should be able to hold your hand during your c-section, watch your baby being lifted from your womb, and hold him soon after birth. Because a c-section is major surgery and can leave a birthing mother more physically and emotionally shaky immediately after delivery, your partner can take over holding, talking to, and stroking your newborn until you feel strong enough to participate. As soon as you feel ready, your partner can gently position the baby in your arms while still providing extra physical support for the two of you.

Breastfeed Your Baby as Soon as Possible After Birth

Many women who give birth by c-section are able to begin breastfeeding their babies in the minutes or hour after birth, just as they would if they had had a vaginal birth. When a c-section goes smoothly, with no complications for mother or baby, a woman can nurse her baby (perhaps with her partner standing right there for extra support and safety) in the operating room as her doctor closes her surgical incision! Early breastfeeding is just as important for a baby who has been born via c-section; it may just take a few more pillows for positioning the baby at your breast, and a little more patience. If you find it difficult to get your baby positioned at the breast, a lactation consultant or La Leche League Leader can help you find the post surgery nursing position that is most comfortable for you.

Enlist Help with Rooming In

Many hospitals will not allow a mother who has just undergone a c-section to care for her own baby in her hospital room. This is because after major surgery, you will need help caring for *yourself*, much less a brand new baby. However, rooming in is just as important for you and your baby, even after a c-section. For this reason, you will need your partner, mother, doula or a friend to *also* room in with you in order to assure that you can be with your baby and still get the help you need.

Stay with Your Baby If She Can't Stay with You (When Your New Baby Needs Special Care)

It has been estimated that approximately one in ten hospital-birthed babies in the U.S. will need some type of specialized nursery care after birth. No one plans for their new baby to need special tests or a stay in the special care nursery, but occasionally these things become necessary and lifesaving. Some types of newborn health screenings can take place right in your hospital room and you should let your infant's doctor know that this is your strong preference. Many hospitals are used to shipping a newborn to the nursery for even the most routine tests when in fact, the same procedures could be performed without separating mother and baby. But even if your baby *does* need to go to the special care nursery, make it clear to your birth attendants and the baby's doctor that you, your partner, or another person of your choosing will be accompanying the baby. Just because your baby needs special care doesn't mean that he doesn't also need *you.* It is easy to feel intimidated by all the actvity and technology surrounding a premature or sick newborn, but you have to stay focused on the fact that your baby, like any baby, needs his parents to talk to him, touch him, snuggle him and breastfeed him as soon as he is able.

If your baby is whisked off to the nursery immediately after birth, you may not be up to hopping directly out of your birthing bed to go with him, but you will rest easier knowing that someone who loves your newborn and who can act as his advocate will be right by his side in your absence. As soon as you feel ready, ask that you be taken (by wheelchair if necessary) to the nursery so that you can be near your baby. It is likely that you will not be able to hold or even touch him immediately if he is experiencing serious complications. However, by just talking and singing to him, you will allow him to sense your presence and feel comforted and loved.

Most hospitals today do recognize the critical role that parents play in healing a premature or otherwise ill newborn. For this reason, up-to-date neonatal intensive care units (NICU) *encourage* parents to touch, hold and breastfeed their babies as soon as possible. This skin-to-skin contact with NICU babies is known as "kangaroo care" and studies have demonstrated its importance to the physical and mental health of parents and babies. Make it clear to your baby's HCPs that being able to touch, hold and breastfeed your baby is a priority for you. Sometimes you may have to be quite assertive and persistent about your wishes. If you feel that the nursery staff isn't listening, ask to speak with the hospital social worker. Until you are able to actually put your hospitalized baby to your breast to feed, you can pump your milk so that it can be given to your baby through his feeding tube. Most hospital nurseries will provide you with a good breastpump, a place near the nursery to pump in privacy, plus an on-site location to freeze and store your milk for your baby. Pumping is critical to keeping your milk supply up until that wonderful moment when you can first nurse him. You will want to avoid the use of bottles and artificial nipples in feeding your baby if possible. Many premature and sick newborns are able to transition directly from breastmilk given via nasal tube (or "cannula") to the breast, although NICU physicians and nurses are too often convinced that bottles are "the only way." As the parent of a hospitalized newborn, you will probably find it both helpful and comforting to work closely with a local La Leche League Leader or lactation consultant who is experienced with NICU situations in designing a plan for feeding your newborn.

▶ *"My third baby was critically ill at birth and was hospitalized in the NICU for two long weeks. For the first ten days we couldn't feed, hold or even touch him inside his oxygen tent. This was one of the most painful experiences of my life. I was by his side every possible moment and I pumped my milk at regular intervals so that he could have it through his nasal tube. Nurses urged me to allow him to have pacifiers and bottles, but they soon came to understand my commitment to having him go directly to breastfeeding. I think if I had been less sure of myself or less knowledgeable about the risks of artificial feeding, I might have given up. But on the twelfth day of his hospitalization, his neonatologist decided he was strong enough to nurse. Although he was still hooked to many wires and tubes, including a nasal cannula, I gently took his little mouth near my nipple, unsure what he would do. He eagerly latched on and began sucking away, and the rest is history! After I camped out in the NICU for twenty-four hours straight to 'prove' to the NICU staff that he could take all his nourishment from the breast, he was able to go home. Today, at eight months old, he is a healthy, chubby, fully breastfed baby!"*

—KATIE, MOTHER OF THREE

Tricia's Tried and True Tips for Attachment Parenting Your Hospitalized Preemie

Tricia and her husband Mike were taken by complete surprise when her uneventful pregnancy (she even planned to have a homebirth) suddenly took a frightening turn. For no discernible reason, Tricia's membranes ruptured prematurely and she was rushed to the hospital, where she gave birth to her daughter at twenty-six weeks' gestation. For several long months, Tricia and Mike parented their tiny baby from the NICU. Today, Tricia's daughter is a healthy, fully breastfed, ten month old.

Here are Tricia's thoughts on attachment parenting in the NICU and beyond:

1. Ask questions.

Make sure that you know what treatment your baby is receiving and why. Although you still may feel like things are beyond your control, you will feel better if you have a clear understanding of your baby's situation. Top quality medical personnel will respect you for your interest in your child's care. Insecure staff may be threatened by it, but that's their problem, not yours! There are several good books for parents of preemies. My personal favorites were *Kangaroo Care: The Best You Can Do to Help Your Pre-Term Infant* by Susan M. Luddington–Hoe and Susan K. Golant and *Premature Baby Book: A Parents Guide to Coping and Caring in the First Years.* Helen Harrison and Ann Kositsky (St. Martin's Press, 1983).

2. Be with your baby as often as you can manage.

On the other hand, don't be afraid to take a break from the NICU when you feel overwhelmed or exhausted. Your baby needs you to stay in good mental and physical health. Trade NICU shifts with your partner.

3. Create a home-like environment in your baby's NICU space.

Hang family photographs or drawings from siblings, and leave cassette tapes of you singing or talking to your baby for times when you can't be at the hospital. As soon as possible, begin dressing your baby in clothing (even if it's only booties and caps) that you have chosen. Assist in diapering and bathing your baby as soon as it's possible.

4. Learn all you can about infant massage and kangaroo care techniques.

If the medical staff resists your interest in these proven healing practices, try to figure out whether their objection is based on real medicine (ie, your baby is on a ventilator at the moment and shouldn't be handled to avoid jostling the tube) or merely on their own personal parenting philosophy (which might differ from yours). You may have to reinforce the fact that this is your baby and that the parenting choices should be your own. Research has demonstrated that maximizing the amount of skin to skin contact between parent and preemie is important and beneficial.

5. Pump, pump, pump . . . your breasts, that is!

I started pumping my milk a few hours after my daughter was born, and continued pumping five to eight times a day until she was strong enough to maintain the milk supply on her own (in my daughter's case, that was three months after her due date—six months after her birth). I pumped a vast quantity of milk, far more than she ever needed, and it was a good thing I did. My daughter's doctor had warned me that lots of moms of preemies can pump for only a few weeks before the milk supply dwindles to nothing, and that scared me so much that I pumped every drop that flowed. Apparently, some mothers pump only a little bit—just enough to feed their preemie —and my Lactation Consultant told me later that you need to pump as if you are nursing a full term baby. Otherwise, your milk supply may never become well established. If it turns out you don't need all that milk, a milk bank* will be happy to pay to have it shipped to them.

---

* Just as you can donate your blood to a blood bank, a growing number of breast-feeding mothers are donating their extra pumped breastmilk to milk banks. Milk banks carefully screen their donors for communicable diseases, and donors are given instructions in how to express their milk to meet the bank's safety criteria. Next, the milk is heat treated to kill any viruses or bacteria that may be present. The banked milk is then dispensed to mothers who are unable to produce enough or any breast-milk for their own babies. This often includes premature babies, for whom formula-feeding is extra risky. The milk may also be used for adopted babies, children and adults with immune deficiencies, and for research purposes. Donor milk can be obtained by physician prescription only. If you are interested in donating or obtaining banked breastmilk, you should talk to a breastfeeding-friendly physician. For more information or to find the milk bank nearest to you, see page 86.

6. Get competent breastfeeding help ASAP.

The hospital lactation consultants may not understand the unique challenges of breastfeeding a preemie (for example, a sleepy baby with a small mouth or weak facial muscles). If you do not feel that you are getting sufficient help from hospital staff, see if a local La Leche League Leader or private, International Board Certified Lactation Consultant (IBCLC) has experience with preemies. I don't think I would have persevered without the support of my excellent lactation consultant, who knew a lot about preemies. Although I already had one successful breastfeeding experience under my belt (with my son, four years earlier), this was a whole different ballgame.

7. Don't be afraid to try anything to help get breastfeeding started.

For example, conventional wisdom says that nipple shields** should be avoided. In our case, my daughter simply would not open her mouth wide enough to latch on well and I needed to use the shield to make my nipple stiff enough for her to latch on. Eventually, we weaned her off the shields.

8. Don't let your baby's medical equipment inhibit your bonding.

Once our daughter was finally home, we learned that her heart monitor did not suffer if an adult slept next to the baby and on top of

---

Human Milk Banking Association of North America, Inc.
c/o Mother's Milk Bank, PSLMC
1719 E. 19th Avenue
Denver, CO 80219
Phone: (303) 869-1888
Fax (303) 869–2490
E-mail: milkbank@capecod.net

**Nipple shields are devices placed over the mother's own nipple. They enable the baby to take hold of something very much resembling a bottle nipple when nursing. Unfortunately, they can cause nipple confusion and make it hard for the mother to receive enough breast stimulation to keep up a good milk supply. They do have some limited therapeutic uses, but should only be used with the advice and assistance of a Board Certified Lactation Consultant or La Leche League Leader.

the cable (we just had to pay attention when repositioning the baby, so that the wires didn't pull loose and set off a false alarm). And we got a daypack to put the monitor in, so that when the weather was nice and we felt she was strong enough, we went for walks with the baby in the sling and the monitor in the daypack. It was a twenty pound total load, but it meant *freedom!*

9. Don't stop pumping too early, or stop pumping suddenly.

I learned this the hard way. When my daughter was about four months old, I decided that I had had it with pumping and I quit altogether. My milk supply dropped suddenly, and as a result, my baby had a lot of difficulty getting anything from the breast. I then spent an anxious week of feeding and pumping frequently to build my milk supply up again.

10. Discontinue routine bottles as soon as possible (if you have used them at all).

Some preemies are fed expressed breastmilk via alternative methods (cup, spoon, syringe) and some go straight to the breast. Because our daughter had had so many bottles before she was able to nurse, we were fairly casual about using them after she was fully breastfeeding. We learned this lesson when she suddenly began refusing the breast in favor of bottles. She had developed nipple preference. This nursing strike*** scared me so much that we quit using bottles at all.

11. Consider sharing the nighttime feedings.

When we brought our daughter home, it took one and a half hours out of every three to feed her—she would nurse very slowly, then the

***A nursing strike is when your breastfed baby begins refusing the breast for any variety of reasons such as nipple preference, a sore mouth making it hard to eat, teething, a strange taste in the breastmilk due to mother's diet, etc. A nursing strike doesn't mean that your baby has "weaned himself." It means that there is a temporary issue in the breastfeeding relationship which can almost always be remedied with the right information or assistance.

weighing might show that she needed a supplemental bottle, and if she was too sleepy to drink it, we'd have to tube-feed her. Obviously, it became physically impossible for me to do every single feeding that way. My husband and I began alternating the late evening and night feedings. My LC assured me that as long as the baby was put to breast many times a day, she would learn.

And she did! What kept me going during the hard times was the dream that someday, we would be at the park together and she would need to eat, so I would just lift my shirt and nurse her. No muss, no fuss, no pump, and no bottles! In only a couple of months, my dream came true! Breastfeeding is worth it!

CHAPTER 4

Making the Breast vs. Bottle Choice

✦ **"Obstacles to the initiation and continuation of breastfeeding include physician apathy and misinformation, insufficient prenatal breastfeeding education, disruptive hospital policies, inappropriate interruption of breastfeeding, early hospital discharge in some populations, lack of timely routine follow-up care and postpartum home health visits, maternal employment (especially in the absence of workplace facilities and support for breastfeeding), lack of broad societal support, media portrayal of bottle-feeding as normative, and commercial promotion of infant formula through distribution of hospital discharge packs, coupons for free or discounted formula, and television and general magazine advertising."**

—*THE AMERICAN ACADEMY OF PEDIATRICS' POLICY STATEMENT ON BREASTFEEDING*

IT WILL CERTAINLY NOT COME AS A SHOCK THAT WE ARE GOING to tell you that you should breastfeed your baby: breastfeeding is a centerpiece of the attachment style of parenting. Of course, most parents today—whatever their parenting philosophy—are aware on some level that "breastfeeding is best." However, the fact that breastfeeding rates in the United States and other western nations remain relatively low reveals that many caring, responsible parents aren't truly informed as to the myriad reasons why breastfeeding is so critically important. In this chapter you will learn things about breastfeeding as a health, cultural, economic, and political issue that you may have never heard before. Additionally, you will discover that your choice as to how you feed your baby—while undoubtedly a personal one—isn't made in a vacuum; powerful corporate interests have a valuable stake in convincing you *not* to breastfeed. Lastly, your beliefs and biases may be challenged, and you will likely come away thinking of the breast vs. bottle choice in a whole new way.

Breastfeeding Isn't "Better"; It's Just Normal: A New Way of Thinking About Infant Feeding Choices

You have probably heard that breastfeeding is "better" for your baby and that it has many "advantages." Actually, breastfeeding isn't better; it's just normal. As the American Academy of Pediatrics (AAP) said in the exciting 1998 update of its position on infant feeding: *"The breastfed infant is the reference or normative model against which all alternative feeding methods must be measured with regard to growth, health, development, and all other short- and long-term outcomes."* In other words, breastfeeding doesn't have advantages; bottle-feeding has *disadvantages.* For example, childcare manuals often state that the diaper of a breastfed infant has a "mild, sweet, inoffensive odor." This is certainly true and is thus listed as one *"pro"* of breastfeeding. A more accurate way of looking at this, however, is to say that a definite *"con"* of bottle-feeding is that the diaper of a formula-fed infant has a foul, unpleasant, and very offensive odor, due to the indigestibility of the artificial product that the formula-fed baby has in his little tummy. In another example, breastfeeding mothers have often been made to worry needlessly over instances of "slow growth" and "low weight gain" in their babies. It has recently been revealed, however, that the growth charts used by a majority of pediatricians to calculate your breastfed baby's size were developed using only formula-fed infants who, as it turns out, are often abnormally fat! That's right: as a group, breastfed babies aren't *underweight*, artificially fed babies are often *overweight*. The World Health Organization is currently working to revise the weight charts for use with healthy infants in order to reflect this more accurate way of looking at babies' growth and development, using breastfed infants as the mean against which *all* babies will be measured. After all, humans are mammals and mammals are designed to nourish their young offspring with their own, species-specific milk. We should measure formula-feeding against the gold standard and biological norm: breastfeeding, rather than vice versa. It may take some mental adjustment to begin thinking of the issue in this way, but once you know the facts, we think you'll agree that this characterization makes sense.

The Breast-Bottle Decision and Your Baby's Health

Breastfeeding is among the most important things you can do to safeguard your baby's health, throughout infancy and beyond. Many parents today are under the mistaken impression that the health differences between breast and bottle-fed babies are minimal in modern, western societies like ours where commercial infant formulas and clean water are available. Unfortunately, this is not the case. It is true that, according to recent UNICEF statistics, more than one million infants in the developing world continue to lose their lives each year due to lack of breastfeeding, and the risk of death from diarrhea in less developed nations is twenty-five times greater for bottle-fed infants than for breastfed ones.[1] But bottle-feeding also carries significant health risks here in the United States. As Naomi Baumslag, M.D., M.Ph., and Dia Michels note in their book, *Milk, Money and Madness* (Greenwood, 1995): *"Even where bacterial contamination can be minimized, the risks of bottle-feeding are not inconsequential. Bottle-fed infants raised by educated women in clean environments, to this day, have significantly greater rates of illness and even death . . . In a study that analyzed hospitalization patterns for a homogeneous, middle class, white American population, bottle-fed infants were fourteen times more likely to be hospitalized than breastfed infants."* Further research has concluded that, for every 1000 bottle-fed infants, seventy-seven hospital admissions would result. The comparable figure for breastfed infants was determined to be five hospital admissions.[2]

The Texas Department of Health's Bureau of Nutrition Services says that bottle-fed infants in the United States are three to four times more likely to suffer from diarrheal diseases (the number one killer of infants worldwide) and are four times more likely to suffer from meningitis. Research also demonstrates that the risk for moderate to severe rotavirus gastroenteritis (a potentially deadly flu-like illness) in formula-fed babies increases by five-fold. Additionally, formula-feeding is consistently associated with immune system disorders, it accelerates the development of celiac disease, is a risk factor for Crohn's Disease and ulcerative colitis in adulthood, accounts for two to twenty-six percent of childhood-onset insulin dependent diabetes mellitus, and imposes a five- to eight-fold risk increase of certain cancers in children under fifteen (if they were formula-fed or breastfed for less than six months).[3] One of the most notable recent discoveries concerning breastfeeding is that it appears to offer protection to babies from Sudden Infant Death Syndrome (SIDS). The U.S. Centers for Disease Control reported in 1996 that lack of breastfeeding, along with exposure to tobacco smoke and a prone sleeping position, is now recognized as one of the only known modifiable risk factors for SIDS.[4] Even with the excellent medical care available to most American infants who do become ill with formula-related maladies, the infant mortality rate has repeatedly been shown to be higher for U.S. infants who are not breastfed. Research has determined that universal breastfeeding in the United States during approximately the first twelve weeks of life could lower the overall U.S. infant mortality rate by around five percent.[5] And predictably, it isn't just potentially fatal disorders to which bottle-fed babies are more prone; formula-feeding also raises your child's risk for everyday respiratory infections, urinary tract infections, ear infections, and allergies (see selected medical references at the end of the chapter).

> ✦ **"The only advantage that American women who formula-feed tend to have over third world women is better sanitation and medical care—and that's far from a culture-wide advantage. That in no way alters the long list of ailments to which their bottle-fed babies are prone."**
>
> —*Diane Weissinger, M.S., IBCLC*

Failure to breastfeed your baby may also impact his IQ. Several peer-reviewed medical studies have now revealed that lack of breastfeeding is clearly and consistently associated with learning deficiencies later in childhood. Researchers have demonstrated that, even after adjusting for socioeconomic and educational differences among parents, children who were not breastfed as infants experience markedly lower test scores on several measures of cognitive ability. In one study, test scores were directly correlated with duration of breastfeeding; the more months a child was breastfed, the higher he scored on the test (see selected supporting references at end of the chapter).

There's Just Something About Breastmilk. . . .

You may still be reeling from shock at discovering just how risky unnecessary formula-feeding can be, and wondering what exactly it is about breastmilk that confers such a clear protective effect on babies' health. The fascinating answer to your question would be that, to a large extent, we don't really know. Research *has* determined a great deal about the wonders of breastmilk. We know, for example, that human milk contains exactly the right proportions of fats, proteins, minerals and calories for human babies. We also know that breastmilk, unlike infant formula in a can, is actually a living substance—sort of like "super-blood"—teeming with infection fighting white blood cells and immunoglobulins (in fact, many experienced breastfeeding mothers use a few drops of breastmilk to prevent or cure infection when someone in the family gets a cut, scrape, or burn). Amazingly, both the nutritional and immunological elements of breastmilk actually *change* over time to best meet your baby's particular needs. For example, the milk that a mother's body produces for her premature baby has a different balance of nutrients than that of a mother breastfeeding her two year old. The preemie milk is higher in calories and special proteins, which is just what a preterm baby needs. Even more amazing is the fact that the living, anti-infective properties of mother's milk evolve constantly to reflect the immediate disease threats in your baby's particular environment. Your milk is full of specific antibodies to the germs that you and your baby face each day. You "immunize" your child against these germs every time you nurse him. It has even been discovered that vaccines work more effectively in the immune systems of breastfed babies. But even with all that we *do* know about breastmilk, there is still much that we haven't yet figured out about this amazing substance. Researchers are constantly discovering some critical new component or property of breastmilk, which is, of course, still absent from those cans of infant formula sitting on the grocery store shelf.

So What About Infant Formula?

> ✦ **". . . the best reason to breastfeed? 'Enzymatically hydrolyzed reduced minerals, whey protein concentrate, palm olein, soy, coconut, high oleic safflower oils, lactose, maltodextrin, potassium citrate, calcium phosphate, calcium chloride, salt, potassium chloride, magnesium chloride, ferrous sulfate, zinc sulfate, copper sulfate, manganese sulfate, potassium iodide, soy lecithin, mono and diglycerides, inositol, choline bitartrate, sodium ascorbate, alpha tocopheryl acetate, niacinimide, calcium pantothenate, vitamin A acetate, riboflavin, pyridoxine hydrochloride, thiamine mononitrate, folic acid, phylloquinone, biotin, vitamin D_3, vitamin B_{12}, taurine, L-carnitine.' That's what's in formula."**
>
> —*Janet Tamaro-Natt,*
> *author of* So That's What They're For!: Breastfeeding Basics

While formula is commonly perceived to be the medically recommended second choice infant food after breastfeeding, the World Health Organization (WHO) actually states: "The second choice is the mother's own milk expressed and given to the infant in some way. The third choice is the milk of another human mother. The fourth and last choice is artificial baby milk (formula)." The quality of infant formula is of paramount importance in the United States—where, despite the American Academy of Pediatrics' endorsement of breastfeeding for a *minimum* of twelve months and WHO's recommendations to breastfeed for at least two years—only approximately sixty percent of all mothers offer their newborns *any breastmilk at all.* Fewer than twenty-five percent of American babies are still breastfed at six months of age, and this figure drops to under ten percent by twelve months. Better educated and higher income mothers are far more likely to breastfeed their babies—and to breastfeed them for a longer duration—than other mothers. These statistics mean that the vast majority of American babies, and particularly those at socioeconomic risk, rely solely on synthetic breastmilk substitutes—infant formula—for their critical first year of life.

With so many American babies dependent on this single food source for their growth and nutritional well being, it is incumbent upon those concerned with infant-maternal health issues, as well as parents themselves, to examine breastmilk substitutes carefully and critically. Unfortunately, many health care professionals and public health officials avoid scrutinizing the production and marketing of commercial infant formula in the United States under the mistaken assumption that providing consumers with all the facts on formula will only cause bottle-feeding mothers to feel "guilty" for not breastfeeding. In fact, this unwillingness to explore the safety and nutritional competency of infant formulas only succeeds in retarding consumer pressure for better quality. As Marsha Walker, RN, IBCLC, has said, *"This paternalistic view seeks to protect women from making 'poor' choices for themselves and their infant, and robs parents of the right to informed decision making. Withholding information generates more anger than guilt in parents . . ."*[6]

Of course, formula manufacturers aggressively promote the idea that today's "highly scientific" breastmilk substitutes have been "specially formulated" to be "like breastmilk." One leading manufacturer's advertising campaign asserts that its product is a "miracle." Yet, the avalanche of formula advertising with which American parents are bombarded at every turn fails to reveal the rest of the story: researchers are quite convinced that despite advances, infant formulas cannot now and will not ever accurately imitate human breastmilk. According to the Food and Drug Administration (FDA), pediatric nutrition researchers at one of the largest formula manufacturers recently conceded that creating infant formula to parallel human milk is "impossible." These scientists, writing in a medical journal, stated that: *"[It is] increasingly apparent that infant formula can never duplicate human milk. Human milk contains living cells, hormones, active enzymes, immunoglobulins and compounds with unique structures that cannot be replicated in infant formula."*[7]

In the meantime, infant formulas are not only distant in composition from human milk, but various brands of synthetic baby milks aren't even comparable to one another! Contrary to what the name implies, there is no fixed "formula" for artificial baby milk. Content and quantities of nutrients vary widely between brands and types of formula (soy, cow's milk, and meat-based). According to formula manufacturers, a pediatrician should recommend an appropriate brand and type of formula for each bottle-fed baby—advice implying that every healthy baby's nutritional needs are unique and that physicians can recognize these special needs upon examination and select a formula accordingly. This is, of course, neither accurate nor possible.

Compositional variance between formulas persists because manufacturers are attempting to simulate a product for which there is no real recipe—a fact FDA officials recognize in their recent statement that ". . . the exact chemical makeup of breast milk is still unknown."[8]

✦ **"Hindsight shows the story of formula production to be a succession of errors. Each stumble is dealt with**

and heralded as yet another breakthrough, leading to further imbalances and then more modifications."

—Dr. Derrick Jelliffe

One of the least publicized risks surrounding the use of infant formula is inescapably inherent in the consumption of any commercially prepared and mass-marketed food product: between 1982 and 1994 alone, there were twenty-two significant recalls of infant formula in the United States due to health and safety problems. At least seven of these recalls were classified by the FDA as "Class I," meaning the problem was potentially life threatening. In several instances, random lots of lab-tested infant formula have been found to contain bacterial and elemental contaminants that, while clearly risks to infant health, did not rise to the level of threat considered appropriate for a widespread recall by the FDA. In February of 1995, FDA special agents uncovered a successful criminal scheme in California in which thousands of cans of substandard infant formula had been improperly labeled for resale. No one knows how many babies received this counterfeit product in their bottles.

Many bottle-feeding parents are under the mistaken impression that the FDA closely and carefully monitors infant formula, perhaps more scrupulously than other foods, since infant consumers are particularly vulnerable by virtue of their tender age and total dependence on this one product. In fact, the FDA sets forth only minimal standards regarding the production and sale of formula. The mandated nutrient requirements for formula are contained in the outdated Infant Formula Act of 1980, which was passed by the U.S. Congress in reaction to a formula manufacturing error that flooded the market with chloride deficient formula. Today, manufacturers are simply required to produce a relatively short list of ingredients and record them on the package.

Is there a role for the use of infant formula? Absolutely. As a medically indicated replacement for breastmilk, commercial infant formula is the appropriate feeding choice for babies without access to their mother's own milk or that of another mother. Until the day when breastmilk banks are able to provide donor milk to every family who needs it, infant formula will have to serve this purpose. Commercial infant formula should always be used for infants under twelve months in lieu of any type of homemade formula or whole cow, goat, or soy milk. The problem lies in the *routine* use of infant formula by mothers who are physically capable of nursing their babies. The vast majority of women who give birth *can* breastfeed their babies. Even women who work outside the home or who must be separated from their babies can use a breastpump to provide milk in their absence. Unfortunately, due to poor information and support, many women are still choosing to feed infant formula when they could be avoiding the risks associated with the unnecessary use of this product.

> ▶ *"When my sister and brother in law adopted my nephew from Korea, there was no question where he would get his milk: from me! I was breastfeeding my daughter at the time and I began pumping and freezing extra milk for him about eight weeks before they were due to pick him up. I continued pumping milk for him for eight months and was able to fill about three-fourths of his bottles with breastmilk. He got formula the rest of the time. My sister was very grateful that her baby was able to have breastmilk and I felt wonderful knowing that I was providing the best start possible for someone very dear to me."*
>
> —*SUSANNA, MOTHER OF TWO*

The Breast-Bottle Decision and *Your* Health

As with most aspects of attachment parenting, the benefits of breastfeeding aren't one-sided: nursing mothers are also protected from disease through breastfeeding. Although the fight against breast cancer has been receiving significant media attention in recent years, many women are still not aware of the strong evidence indicating the role that lactation plays in breast cancer prevention. Researchers have discovered that breastfeeding strongly correlates with a steeply reduced risk of premenopausal breast cancer. They have further concluded that the *longer* a woman breastfeeds, the more her risk of breast cancer goes down. Women who lactate for twenty-four months or more over the course of their lifetime have been found to have a whopping twenty-five percent reduction in rates of premenopusal breast cancer. Lacation, with its accompanying unique hormonal changes and suppression of menstruation, is a fundamental element of a woman's reproductive cycle. Not surprisingly, it appears that missing out on this piece of our body's natural life cycle can have negative consequences. Additionally, it has recently been determined that women who were not breastfed themselves as children also see an impact on their future breast cancer risk. In a study of more than one thousand American women, researchers found that women who were breastfed as children, even if it was for only a brief period of time, had a twenty-five percent lower risk of developing both premenopausal and postmenopausal breast cancer. Other research has revealed that women who breastfeed decrease their risk of ovarian cancer, osteoporosis, and hip fractures later in life. Is it any wonder that these diseases have been on the increase in the west during the past several generations, as a smaller percentage of chilbearing women than at any time in human history have experienced the critical lactational element of their reproductive lives? (For specific supporting research citations on breastfeeding's effect on women's health, see the selected medical references at the end of this chapter.)

"But I Wasn't Breastfed and I'm Just Fine!"

Today's mothers and fathers of young children were almost exclusively bottle-fed as babies because their own parents were, on the whole, completely unaware of the hows or whys of breastfeeding. Between the early part of the twentieth century and the present, the breastfeeding knowledge that had previously been passed from woman to woman for many generations was nearly destroyed in just a few decades of intense commercial pressure from infant formula manufacturers. Because of this, the odds are pretty good that you yourself were breastfed for less than a month, if at all. Your mother was probably told by her doctor that her milk was insufficient to meet your needs and that formula-feeding was the "modern," "scientific" way to feed you. "So," you may be asking, "if bottle-feeding was good enough for me, why isn't it good enough for my baby?" Well, it's likely that your parents also drove you around without a carseat and placed you to sleep on your tummy. Just because you are here to tell the tale doesn't mean that you would do these things with your own children. Your parents lacked all the information we now have to make a truly informed decision about car safety, SIDS risks, and yes, breastfeeding. They made the best decisions possible given the information they had. You, on the other hand, can't claim ignorance. You know just how risky artificial feeding can be. It is also worth considering how unhealthy many of today's bottle-fed adults actually are. Obesity, depression, cancer, asthma and a host of other chronic health problems are at an all time high.

Then again, you may have a friend whose breastfed baby has had lots of ear infections or a cousin whose bottle-fed baby has never been sick. "If breastfeeding is so great," you might be thinking, "why do some breastfed babies get sick anyway?" Well, even the most avid supporters of breastfeeding won't try to tell you that breastfeeding is an ironclad guarantee against all illness. The fact is that some breastfed babies do become ill, while many bottle-fed babies appear to remain healthy (although some formula-linked illnesses may not appear for many years). The evidence is clear, however, that, *as a group*, breastfed infants experience significantly lower rates of illness than bottle-fed babies. And when they do become ill, breastfed children get well faster and with fewer complications. Anecdotal observations can't compete with the huge, growing, and unanimous body of respected medical research demonstrating these facts (remember that the world looks flat out your own kitchen window!). After all, we have all known smokers who are healthy well into their nineties, or junk food junkies who never gain an ounce. Breastfeeding *lowers your baby's risk* of experiencing illnesses both minor and major, and we all want to do everything we can to keep our little ones healthy.

Wow! Why Don't Doctors Tell You This Stuff?!

That's a very good question. Why, with the huge and growing body of peer reviewed medical research demonstrating the many and serious potential health hazards of routine bottle-feeding, do so many otherwise competent doctors continue to take a neutral or even pro-formula stance with their patients? Even though all major medical organizations, including the American Academy of Pediatrics, have now taken a strong position in favor of breastfeeding, it is the rare individual obstetrician or pediatrician who will do more than offer a lukewarm "breast is best, but it's your choice . . ." statement to their patients, most of whom have no concrete understanding of why breastfeeding is so important to their babies' health. Many HCPs actually tell their patients that there is no real difference between breast and bottle feeding!

> ✦ **"This (infant feeding) seems to be the one area where you can practice medicine in the 1990s—with 1960s know-how—and not get sued."**
>
> —*Pediatrician Dr. Jay Gordon, quoted in* So That's What They're For!: Breastfeeding Basics, *by Janet Tamaro-Natt*

The failure of many medical professionals to fully inform their patients of the impact of infant feeding choices is due in large part to their own ignorance of the research. Very few medical or nursing school curriculae offer any significant or meaningful training in human lactation. Most obstetricians, pediatricians, and nurses graduate from their professional training having had little or no exposure to the most up-to-date literature or clinical practice in this area. In other cases, HCPs' views on breastfeeding are based on their own, highly personal experiences. A nurse who chose to formula-feed her own children, or a doctor whose wife weaned her baby at three weeks is unlikely to be an effective advocate for breastfeeding. Unfortunately, this glaring lack of knowledge doesn't prevent HCPs from authoritatively dispensing a lot of downright erroneous advice to new mothers on how to initiate and maintain a satisfying breastfeeding relationship. To make matters worse, many frustrated new mothers will tell you that they have been given *different* breastfeeding advice from every HCP with whom they have come in contact—from their OB to the maternity floor nurses to the baby's pediatrician! Any lactation consultant will tell you that a large part of her day is spent trying to salvage the nursing relationships of mothers and babies who are experiencing breastfeeding difficulties after following misguided advice given by physicians and nurses. Here are just a few actual instances in which breastfeeding women have been given poor counsel by their health care providers:

► *"My baby had severe tongue-tie* which was making it hard for her to latch on to my breast and get milk. As a result, she was losing weight and my doctor told me to put her on a bottle immediately. He never even looked at her mouth or tongue. He just told me that I didn't have enough milk and I believed him."*

—FRAN, *MOTHER OF A SIX MONTH OLD*

► *"My baby was very chubby at three months and my doctor told me that my milk was 'too rich.' She recommended that I wean him to a soy formula."*

—SANDRA, *MOTHER OF TWO*

► *"My nurse in the hospital told me I should mix breast and formula feedings every day right from the start or my baby would never get used to taking a bottle. By the second month, my milk supply was terrible and my baby wouldn't breastfeed at all."*

—JEANNINE, *MOTHER OF A TWO YEAR OLD*

► *"My doctor told me that I should never breastfeed more often than every two or three hours or my breasts wouldn't 'refill.'"*

—CATHY, *MOTHER OF TWO*

► *"My baby's pediatrician told me to stop night feedings completely by the third month so that my son would sleep*

---

*"Tongue-tie" is a fairly common physical anomaly in which a baby's frenulum—the piece of skin which attaches the tongue to the bottom of the mouth—is unusually short. This can cause real difficulties with breastfeeding in some babies, and for this reason, many informed HCPs are choosing to snip the piece of skin in tongue-tied babies as early as possible in order to facilitate nursing success. This is done in a minor procedure right in the doctor's office (often an ear, nose, and throat specialist) and the baby can usually nurse immediately.

through the night. We did as she suggested, but quit after one week as he was obviously starving and my milk supply was dropping."

—LORI, *MOTHER OF AN EIGHT MONTH OLD*

- *"My doctor told me that I could not breastfeed while taking antibiotics for mastitis."*

—KATIE, *MOTHER OF THREE*

- *"My baby went on a nursing strike at eight months and my pediatrician assured me that this was her signal to me that she wanted to wean."*

—SUE, *MOTHER OF TWO*

- *"My doctor suggested a hormone shot for birth control and never mentioned that it could essentially dry up my milk. I actually don't think she even knew this but it didn't stop her from prescribing it."*

—SARAH, *MOTHER OF AN ELEVEN MONTH OLD*

- *"At my baby's one year checkup, her nurse practitioner told me that I should wean her because there are no advantages and only disadvantages to breastfeeding a toddler."*

—ANN, *MOTHER OF FOUR*

The fact is, the HCP was simply dead wrong in each of the above instances. Perhaps in no other area of medicine is clearly misleading advice with potentially permanent consequences (the cessation of breastfeeding) tolerated so unquestioningly. There have been rumblings in recent years from within the lactation science community (and from mothers who feel angry and cheated that their opportunity to breastfeed their babies was destroyed through sub-optimal medical care) that HCPs should be held more accountable for the terrible advice that some of them give to so many breastfeeding women. In the meantime, however, a woman's best defense against the many misinformed HCPs out there is to arm *herself* with breastfeeding knowledge and support. Reading books about breastfeeding (including this one), talking with other nursing mothers at local La Leche League meetings, as well as surfing the Internet for the many Web pages, newsgroups and mailing lists geared to nursing mothers, can provide you with a wealth of practical information on starting and maintaining a successful breastfeeding relationship with your baby.

The Role of Infant Formula Manufacturers

> ✦ **"What makes a woman believe that she cannot breastfeed her baby is the constant undermining of her confidence by advertising."**
>
> —*Gill Wilcox, UNICEF UK*

If you live in the United States or another western nation and you are pregnant or the mother of an infant, you have undoubtedly been subjected to a barrage of advertising from the huge pharmaceutical companies that manufacture and sell commercial infant formula. This is true regardless of whether you plan to breastfeed or are currently a nursing mother. On your first visit to your OB or midwife, you were probably seated in a waiting room full of posters and popular parenting magazines loaded with colorful, appealing ads for particular brands of formula. When your HCP wrote down the name of your prenatal vitamin, she likely did so on a notepad with the name of a certain brand of infant formula emblazoned across the top. As you left the office, you were probably handed a folder or bag full of coupons, pamphlets and possibly even product samples, all courtesy of the formula companies. Soon after beginning your prenatal care, you almost certainly began receiving numerous direct mailings from infant formula manufacturers, including booklets on "your infant feeding choices," as well as "valuable coupons" for different brands of formula. You will probably continue to receive these mailings, carefully targeted to your stage of pregnancy or your baby's age, because your HCP, like most, provides the names, due dates and addresses of all of his patients to the infant formula manufacturers.

When you enter the hospital to give birth, your baby's bassinet will be marked with a small "It's a Boy!" or "It's a Girl!" card with name, weight, sex . . . and an advertisement for infant formula. When you are discharged from the hospital, you will probably receive a "free gift" from the hospital, including a diaper bag covered with the recognizable bunny logo of a major formula company, a breastfeeding "how-to" booklet produced by a formula company, bottles, nipples and at least one "free sample" of infant formula. "I know you plan to breastfeed," the nurse will tell you as she hands you the bag, "but you'll need this just in case things don't work out or your husband wants to feed the baby." In your first days home, you may answer the doorbell to discover that *an entire case* of infant formula has just been hand-delivered to your home, again compliments of one of the formula companies who are aware of the highly personal fact that you have just given birth.

> ▶ *"When I came home from the hospital after my stillbirth, there was a case of infant formula sitting on my front steps. Needless to say, this was very upsetting to me. My husband called the 800 number on the box, explained our situation and instructed the company to stop sending any further products or other advertising to our home, but it didn't do any good. For at least a year after my loss, we continued to receive numerous free samples, bottles, coupons, infant feeding booklets and surveys, all from about five different formula companies. It hurt every time."*
>
> —MARGIE, MOTHER OF THREE

Obviously, advertising and product giveaways on this scale cost infant formula companies millions and millions of dollars each year. But they aren't giving this stuff away just to be nice. It is because their own market research has clearly demonstrated that advertising, "educational literature," and especially product giveaways all make it statistically less likely that women will breastfeed without formula supplementation—or breastfeed at all.

Added to the cost of these companies' direct marketing is the amount they spend buying access to you and your baby through your doctor's office or hospital. Almost all American hospitals with maternity services have a contract with one or another of the infant formula manufacturers through which the facility receives free infant formula, "educational grants" (seminars and literature in which hospital staff receive lactation science training from, you guessed it, employees of the formula company), and even cash gifts in return for the formula company's exclusive right to market directly to that hospital's patients. Your doctor or midwife also likely receives monthly or quarterly office visits from a friendly formula sales representative. The rep brings free pens, calendars, T-shirts, tote bags, and sometimes even a delicious lunch for the office staff. Nurses or doctors who formula-feed their own children can depend on their sales rep to provide them with a year's supply of infant formula at absolutely no charge. Additionally, formula manufacturers routinely host lavish parties and receptions for pediatricians at AAP functions. Other medical groups such as the American College of Obstetricians and Gynecologists, the American Medical Association, the Association of Women's Health, Obstetric and Neonatal Nurses and the American Dietetic Association have received cash grants and advertisements for their publications totalling hundreds of thousands of dollars annually. Individual medical students and doctors receive loans, grants and "gifts" from the pharmaceutical companies which produce infant formula, and a 1991 study found that the U.S. pharmaceutical industry spends $6,000 to $8,000 per doctor each year on promotion. Sadly, vast and increasing amounts of medical research into infant health and nutrition is being underwritten by the infant formula industry.

Of course, the reasons behind all of this are crystal clear: the manufacture and sale of commercial infant formula is an unbelievably profitable enterprise. U.S. infant formula sales reached approximately $2.59 billion in 1993, representing a six percent increase over 1992. Since 1989, when formula companies lifted their previous voluntary ban on marketing directly to consumers, the market has grown by 54%. The average bottle-feeding family in the United States spends between $800 and $2,000 per year on infant formula. With such a lucrative product to promote, corporations have wisely enlisted the assistance of new parents' most trusted advisors—health care providers—in order to retain and increase their markets. Infant formula manufacturers attempt to hide behind the empty sounding "breast is best, but . . ." disclaimer that most of them include with their advertising. However, the simple fact is that breastfeeding itself is the formula companies' most dangerous and formidable competitor. Every time a woman chooses to breastfeed instead of bottle-feed her baby, the formula pushers lose *at least* one thousand dollars in sales. Because pharmaceutical companies which produce formula also develop and market medications and medical supplies, you can be sure that they are acutely aware that the better health enjoyed by breastfed infants and their mothers as a group also impacts their bottom line, possibly even more than the sale of the formula itself.

The Story of the "WHO Code"

During the 1970s and early 1980s, many Americans were shocked at television images of severely malnourished "bottle-babies" from various third-world nations, as consumer advocacy groups alerted citizens for the first time to the marketing practices being employed abroad by infant formula manufacturers. These advocacy groups described how physicians and other health care providers in the developing world were being bribed by formula manufacturers to steer patients away from breastfeeding and toward particular brands of artificial breastmilk substitutes. Age old cultural norms of exclusive and extended breastfeeding were disrupted, as subtly effective advertising campaigns convinced women that commercial infant formula was the "modern," "sterile," "western" way to feed their babies. New mothers were lured into giving birth in hospitals funded by infant formula manufacturers. Once there, these women were encouraged to offer their newborns bottles of formula. Mothers and babies were then sent home with a small "free" supply of the infant formula. By the time the supply ran out, the baby was refusing the breast, the mother's own milk supply was diminished, and the typical, impoverished family was unable to pay for any more infant formula. These practices, combined with an unsanitary water supply, lack of sterilization and refrigeration facilities, and poor access to medical care, have conspired to kill millions of third-world babies each year, according to the WHO and UNICEF.

In 1977, a worldwide boycott was launched against Nestlé Corporation, determined to be the most egregiously unethical actor in this sad drama. Consumers all over the world stopped purchasing Nestlé products, and WHO convened a meeting to discuss what could be done to influence corporations marketing infant formula to end their fatal practices. At the time, the acting World Health Director stated that, "In my opinion, the campaign against bottle-feed advertising is unbelievably more important than the fight against smoking advertisements."

WHO subsequently drafted the International Code on the

Marketing of Breastmilk Substitutes ("The WHO Code"). The Code's main points call for no advertising of infant formula or bottles directly to the public, and for the distribution by health care workers of factual, ethical information to parents. WHO intended for the Code to apply to all nations, including the United States. While the rest of the world signed onto the Code in the early 1980s, the United States withheld its support until 1994. Today, infant formula manufacturers openly flout the Code in the United States (check out the ads in any parenting magazine for clear evidence) and around the world. For this reason, the Nestlé Boycott was relaunched in 1988 and continues to this day.

Become a Lactivist!: The Very Best Resources for Learning More About Breastfeeding Advocacy

Once you understand the whole story behind the breast-bottle debate, it's likely that you will want to join many other attachment parents in working to promote breastfeeding.

BOOKS

Milk, Money and Madness: The Culture and Politics of Breastfeeding. Baumslag, Naomi and Dia L. Michels. Westport, CT: Greenwood, 1995.

This award-winning book provides the most comprehensive overview of the rise of the bottle-feeding culture and the threat it presents to infant-maternal health. The information is presented in an accessible, reader-friendly style.

The Politics of Breastfeeding. Palmer, Gabrielle. United Kingdom: Pandora Press, 1989.

The author carefully documents the role that big business plays in infant feeding choices around the world.

Beyond the Breast-Bottle Controversy. Van Esterik, Penny. Piscataway, NJ: Rutgers University Press, 1989.

A global, feminist perspective on the breast-bottle issue.

Breastfeeding: A Biocultural Perspective. Stuart-Macadam, Patricia, and Katherine Dettwyler. Hawthorn, NY: Aldine De Gruyter, 1995.

A fascinating compilation of essays from leading academic thinkers on a variety of topics related to breastfeeding.

BREASTFEEDING ADVOCACY ORGANIZATIONS

Promotion of Mother's Milk, Inc (ProMom)
P.O. Box 3912
New York, NY 10163
http://www.promom.org
E-mail: members@promom.org

National Alliance for Breastfeeding Advocacy (NABA)
254 Conant Road
Weston, MA 02193–175
Phone: (410) 995–3726
Fax: (617) 893–8608
http://members.aol.com/marshalact/Naba/home.html
E-mail: Marshalact@aol.com

Action for Corporate Accountability
910 17th Street, NW Suite 413
Washington, DC 20006
Phone: (202) 776–0595
Fax: (202) 776–0599

International Baby Food Action Network (IBFAN)
P.O. Box 781
10 Trinity Square
Toronto M5G IBI
Ontario

Canada
Phone: (416) 595–9819
http://www.gn.apc.org/ibfan/ibcoco.html
E-mail: infact@ftn.net

National Breastfeeding MediaWatch Campaign
Texas Department of Health
Bureau of Clinical and Nutrition Services
1100 West 49th Street
Austin, TX 78756
Phone: (512) 406–0744
Fax: (512) 406–0722
http://www.tdh.state.tx.us/lactate/media.htm

WEB SITES

The WHO Code
http://www.gn.apc.org/ibfan/thecode.html

The AAP Policy Statement on Breastfeeding
http://www.aap.org/policy/re9729.html

The Official Page of Breastfeeding Propaganda
http://members.aol.com/cgrapentin/brstfeed.html

McSpotlight on the Babymilk Industry
http://www.mcspotlight.org/beyond/nestle.html

Formula for Disaster
http://www.essential.org/monitor/hyper/mm0392.html#formula

INTERNET E-MAIL LISTS

The Lactivist List *is the list for discussion of breastfeeding promotion and advocacy. It has subscribers and participants from all over the world. For information on how to subscribe, go to:* http://www.promom.org

CHAPTER ENDNOTES

(1) Robbins, John. *May All Be Fed.* New York: Avon Books. 1992.

(2) Salisbury L., and Blackwell AG. *Petition to Alleviate Domestic Infant Formula Misuse and Provide An Informed Infant Feeding Choice.* San Francisco: Public Advocates, Inc., 1981, p. 45.

(3) Walker, Marsha. "A Fresh Look At The Risks of Artificial Infant Feeding," *J Hum Lact* 9(3) 1993.

(4) *Morbidity and Mortality Weekly Review* 45 (RR-10):1-6.

(5) Labbock, Miriam, MD, MPH. "Costs of Not Breastfeeding in the U.S." *Newsletter of the Academy of Breastfeeding Medicine,* (1995) 1(1):7.

(6) Walker, Marsha, "A Fresh Look At The Risks of Artificial Infant Feeding," *J Hum Lact* 9(3), 1993.

(7) Stehlin, Isadora. *FDA Consumer Magazine,* June, 1996.

(8) ibid.

SELECTED SUPPORTING MEDICAL REFERENCES ON THE RISKS OF ROUTINE ARTIFICIAL FEEDING

Compiled with Assistance From J. Rachael Hamlet, J.D. and ProMoM, Inc.

RESEARCH DEMONSTRATING THAT FORMULA-FED INFANTS ARE AT HIGHER RISK FOR A VARIETY OF INFECTIONS.

Borgnolo G, et al. "A case-control study of Salmonella gastrointestinal infection in Italian children." *Acta Paediatr* (1996) 85:804–8. *[Lack of breastfeeding was the single most important factor associated with a 5-fold increased risk of Salmonella infection.]*

Beaudry M, et al. "Relation between infant feeding and infections during the first six months of life." *J Pediatr* (1995) 126:191–7. *[Failure to breastfeed substantially increased risk of respiratory and gastrointestinal infections in first six months of life.]*

Aniansson, G, et al. "A prospective cohort study on breastfeeding and otitis media (ear infections) in Swedish Infants." *Pediatr Infect Dis. J.* 13 (1994):183–88 *[Acute otitis media frequency was significantly higher in the nonbreastfed children in each age group (2,6, and 10 months of age).*

The frequency of upper respiratory infections was also increased in those children, but reduced in the breastfed group.]

Lerman, Y, et al. "Epidemiology of acute diarrheal diseases in children in a high standard of living rural settlement in Israel. *Pediatr. Infect. Dis. J.* 13(2): (1994) 116–22 *[Children less than twelve months of age had a higher incidence of acute diarrheal diseases during the months they were being formula-fed than children who were breastfed during the same period.]*

Pisacane A; Graziano L; Zona G; Granata G; Dolezalova H; Cafiero M; Coppola A; Scarpellino B; Ummarino M; Mazzarella G; "Breast feeding and acute lower respiratory infection." *Acta Paediatr 83* (1994):714–18. *[Lack of breastfeeding is a strong risk factor for acute lower respiratory infection (i.e., pneumonia and bronchitis) in industrialized countries.]*

Pisacane A, Graziano L, Mazzarella G, et al. "Breast-feeding and urinary tract infection." *J Pediatr.* 120 (1992):87–89.

Harabuchi, Y, et al. "Human Milk secretory IgA antibody to nontypeable Haemophilus influenzae: possible protective effects against nasopharyngeal colonization." *J. Pediatr.* 124 (1994):193–98. *[Study demonstrating that infant formula lacks specific secretory IgA antibody present in breastmilk. The study suggests a mechanism to explain why formula-fed infants have higher incidence of infection.]*

Howie PW, et al. "Protective effect of breastfeeding against infection." *BMJ* 300 1990:11-16. *[As a risk factor, formula-feeding can account for 7% of all infants hospitalized for respiratory infections.]*

Duffy LC, et al. "The effects of infant feeding on rotavirus-induced gastroenteritis: a prospective study." *Am J Pub Health* 76 (1986):259–263. *[In industrialized nations, formula-fed infants have a 3–4 fold risk of diarrheal illness. Moderate to severe rotavirus gastroenteritis is five times more common in formula-fed infants.]*

Cochi SL, et al. "Primary invasive Haemophilus influenza b disease: a population based assessment of risk factors." *J. Pediatr.* 108 (1986):887-896. *[A 4–16 fold higher risk exists for H influenzae bacteremia and meningitis in North American formula-fed babies.]*

RESEARCH DEMONSTRATING THAT THERE IS A HIGHER INCIDENCE OF ALLERGIES AMONG FORMULA-FED CHILDREN.

Saarinen UM, Kajosaari M. "Breastfeeding as prophylaxis against atopic disease: prospective follow-up study until 17 years old." *Lancet* 346 (1995):1065–69. [From the study's author: "We conclude that breastfeeding is prophylactic against atopic disease, the effect extending into early adulthood. Breastfeeding for longer than 1 month without other milk supplements offers significant prophylaxis (prevention) against food allergy at 3 years of age, and also against respiratory allergy at 17 years of age. Six months of breastfeeding is required to prevent eczema during the first 3 years, and possibly also to prevent substantial atopy in adolescence." The article also states that the differences by infant feeding method were so pronounced that it "suggested an influence of early milk feeding that may exceed the heredity burden."]

van den Bogaard C; van den Hoogen HJ; Huygen FJ; van Weel C; "Is the breast best for children with a family history of atopy? The relation between way of feeding and early childhood morbidity." 25 *Fam Med* (1993) 471–45 [In families with a history of allergies, failure to breastfeed was related to higher levels of childhood illness both in the first and the first three years of life. In the first year of life the studied children had more episodes of gastroenteritis, lower respiratory tract infections, and digestive tract disorders. Over the next three years of life they had more respiratory tract infections and skin infections.]

Merrett TG, et al. "Infant feeding and allergy: twelve-month prospective study of 500 babies born in allergic families." *Ann Allergy* 61 1988:13-20. [Formula feeding is associated with higher incidence of wheezing, diarrhea, vomiting and prolonged colds.]

Host A., et al. "A prospective study of cow's milk allergy in exclusively breastfed infants." *Acta Paediatr Scand* 77 (1988):663–670. [Formula given to newborns in the hospital nursery contributed to the development of subsequent cow milk allergy among infants who were exclusively breastfed thereafter.]

Israel D, et al., "Protein induced allergic (PAC) colitis in infants." *Pediatr.*

Res. 25 1989:116A. [PAC is associated with formula-feeding and supplementation.]

RESEARCH LINKING FORMULA-FEEDING TO A HIGHER INCIDENCE OF CERTAIN CANCERS

Schwartzbaum, J. et al. "An exploratory study of environmental and medical factors potentially related to childhood cancer." *Med & Pediat Oncology* 19(2) (1991):115–21.

Davies, M. et al. "Infant feeding and childhood lymphomas [cancer]." *Lancet* 2 (1988):365–368. [There was as much as an eight-fold increase in risk of developing lymphomas among children artificially fed or breastfed less than six months.]

RESEARCH DEMONSTRATING THAT WOMEN WHO WERE FORMULA-FED AS INFANTS HAVE HIGHER RATES OF BREAST CANCER

Freudenheim, J. et al. "Exposure to breast milk in infancy and the risk of breast cancer." *Epidemiology* 5 (1994):324–331. [For both premenopausal and postmenopausal breast cancer, women who were breastfed as children, even if only for a short time, had a 25% lower risk of developing breast cancer than women who were bottle-fed as infants.]

RESEARCH DEMONSTRATING A LINK BETWEEN BREASTFEEDING AND BREAST CANCER PREVENTION IN MOTHERS

Newcomb, P.A. et al. "Lactation and a reduced risk of premenopausal breast cancer." *The New England Journal of Medicine* 330(2) (1994):81–87.

Romieu, I. et al. "Breast Cancer and Lactation history in Mexican women." *Am J Epidemiol* 143(6) (1996):543–52.

Michaels, KB et al. "Prospective assessment of breastfeeding and breast cancer incidence among 89887 women." *Lancet* 347 (1996):431–36.

Hirose, K. et al. "A large-scale, hospital-based case-control study of risk factors of breast cancer according to menopausal status." *Jpn J Cancer Res* 86 (1995):146–54.

Brinton, LA et al. "Breastfeeding and Breast Cancer risk." *Cancer Causes and Control* 6 (1995):199–208.

Yang, C. "History of Lactation and breast cancer risk." *Am J Epidemiol* 138(12) (1993):1050–56.

Chilvers C. "Breastfeeding and risk of breast cancer in young women, United Kingdom National Case-Control Study Group." *BMJ* 307 (1993):17–20.

Wolff, M, et al. "Blood levels of organochlorine residues and risk of breast cancer." *J Nat Cancer Inst* 85(8) (1993): 648–52.

Yoo, K, et al. "Independent protective effect of lactation against breast cancer: A case-control study in Japan." *Am J Epidemiol* 135(7) (1992): 726–33.

Reuter K, et al. "Risk factors for breast cancer in women undergoing mammography." *Am J Roentgenol* 158(2) (1992):273–78.

RESEARCH INDICATING THAT BREASTFEEDING LOWERS A WOMAN'S RISK FOR OVARIAN CANCER

Rosenblatt KA, Thomas DB, "WHO Collaborative Study of Neoplasia and Steroid Contraceptives." *Int J Epidemiol.* 22 (1993): 192–197.

RESEARCH INDICATING THAT BREASTFEEDING LOWERS A WOMAN'S RISK FOR OSTEOPOROSIS

Melton LJ, Bryant SC, Wahner HW, et al. "Influence of breastfeeding and other reproductive factors on bone mass later in life." *Osteoporos Int.* 3 (1993):76–83.

Cumming RG, Klineberg RJ. "Breastfeeding and other reproductive factors and the risk of hip fractures in elderly woman." *Int J Epidemiol* 22 (1993):684–691.

RESEARCH DEMONSTRATING THAT FORMULA-FEEDING IS A RISK FACTOR IN THE DEVELOPMENT OF JUVENILE DIABETES

Verge CF, et al. "Environmental factors in childhood IDDM. A population-based, case-control study." *Diabetes Care* 17 (1994): 1381–9 [*Study showed an increased risk of juvenile diabetes associated with early dietary exposure to cow's milk-based formula, short duration of exclusive breast-feeding, and high intake of cow's milk protein in the recent diet.*]

Virtanen SM, et al. "Early introduction of dairy products associated with increased risk of IDDM in Finnish children." *Diabetes* 42 (1993): 1786–90. *[Introduction of cow's milk-based formula is a significant risk factor for juvenile diabetes.]*

Mayer EJ, et al. "Reduced risk of insulin-dependent diabetes mellitus among breastfed children." *Diabetes* 37 (1988):1625–1632 [*Formula-feeding accounts for as much as 26% of insulin dependent diabetes mellitis in children.*]

Borch-Johnson, K., et al., "Relation between breastfeeding and incidence of insulin-dependent diabetes mellitus." *Lancet* (1984) 2:1083–86 [*It is postulated that insufficient breastfeeding of genetically susceptible newborn infants may lead to beta-cell infection and IDDM later in life.*]

RESEARCH DEMONSTRATING THAT FORMULA FEEDING IS A RISK FACTOR IN DEVELOPMENT OF CROHN'S DISEASE AND ULCERATIVE COLITIS

Rigas A, et al. "Breast-feeding and maternal smoking in the etiology of Crohn's disease and ulcerative colitis in childhood." *Ann Epidemiol* 3 (1993):387–92. [*Lack of breastfeeding was associated with higher rates of inflammatory bowel disease in children and adolescents.*]

Koletzko S., et al. "Role of infant feeding practices in development of Crohn's disease in childhood." *Br. Med. J.* 298 (1989):1617–18.

Bergstrand O; Hellers G. "Breast-feeding during infancy in patients who later develop Crohn's disease." *Scand J Gastroenterol* (1983) 18:903–6. [*Lack of breastfeeding appears to be a risk factor in development of Crohn's disease.*]

RESEARCH INDICATING THAT FORMULA-FEEDING APPEARS TO INCREASE THE RISK OF SUDDEN INFANT DEATH SYNDROME (SIDS)

Ford RPK, Taylor BJ, Mitchell EA, et al. "Breastfeeding and the risk of sudden infant death syndrome." *Int J. Epidemiol.* 22 (1993):885–890.

Mitchell EA, Taylor BJ, Ford RPK, et al. "Four modifiable and other major risk factors for cot death: the New Zealand Study."

J Paediatr Child Health. 28 (1992):S3–S8.

Scragg LK, Mitchell EA, Tonkin SL, et al. "Evaluation of the cot death prevention programme in South Auckland." *NZ Med J.* 106 (1993):8–10.

RESEARCH INDICATING THAT FORMULA-FEEDING IS ASSOCIATED WITH LOWER I.Q.

Horwood and Fergusson, "Breastfeeding and Later Cognitive and Academic Outcomes." Jan 1998 *Pediatrics* Vol. 101, No. 1 [*The latest study to support this statement was done in New Zealand. Here an 18 year longitudinal study of over 1,000 children found that those who were breastfed as infants had both better intelligence and greater academic achievement than children who were infant-formula fed.*]

Morrow-Tlucak M, Haude RH, Ernhart CB. "Breastfeeding and cognitive development in the first 2 years of life." *Soc Sci Med.* 26 (1988):635–639.

Lucas A., "Breast Milk and Subsequent Intelligence Quotient in Children Born Preterm." *Lancet* 339 (1992):261–62.

For a greatly expanded listing of peer-reviewed research exploring the risks of not breastfeeding, contact the American Academy of Pediatrics and ask for the exhaustive footnotes to the AAP's 1998 policy statement, *Breastfeeding and the Use of Human Milk (RE9729)*. The AAP can be reached at:

The American Academy of Pediatrics
141 Northwest Point Boulevard
Elk Grove Village, IL 60007–1098 USA
Phone: (847) 228–5005
Fax: (847) 228–5097
http://www.aap.org
E-mail: Kidsdocs@aap.org

CHAPTER 5

Breastfeeding: Much More Than Food

THROUGHOUT THE CENTURIES AND ACROSS CULTURES, THE IMage of a mother nursing her child has been seen as beautiful, tender, and emblematic of deep and abiding love. Many of the western world's most famous artists—from El Greco to Mary Cassat to Picasso—have immortalized the breastfeeding relationship in their work. Adults who are lucky enough to actually remember being nursed, as well as most women who have breastfed their own children recall the experience as uniquely meaningful and special. In other words, nursing your baby involves much more than food. The breastfeeding relationship plays an important role in the gentle, responsive, intuitive caregiving that is at the heart of attachment parenting.

► *"When I nurse my baby, a feeling of peace and love comes over me. I really can't describe it."*

—JOANNA, MOTHER OF A THREE MONTH OLD

▶ *"When I am rocking him and he's nursing so intensely, with those little cheeks working and sometimes with milk dribbling out the corner of his mouth, I can't believe I almost gave up on this during the first few weeks."*

—LARA, MOTHER OF AN EIGHT MONTH OLD

▶ *"I really thought that I would hate breastfeeding. I only tried it because I thought people would think badly of me if I didn't breastfeed. I figured I'd try it and then I could tell people it just didn't work out. Well, after about twenty-four hours, I was hooked. When we are alone together nursing and she looks up at me and thanks me with those big blue eyes, I am in heaven. I want to remember those moments long after she weans."*

—SARA, MOTHER OF A SIX MONTH OLD

▶ *"When I was hungry or thirsty, (my mother) would swing me 'round to where I could reach her full breasts; now when I shut my eyes I feel again with gratitude the sense of well-being that I had when I buried my head in their softness and drank the sweet milk that they gave."*

—KABONGO, A KIKUYU CHIEF OF EAST AFRICA,
AT AGE EIGHTY (QUOTED IN THE VITAL TOUCH)

▶ *"I love to nurse! My mama loves to nurse me!!"*

—JANE, AGE THREE

Breastfeeding and Attachment: Your Biological Connection with Your Nursling

✦ **"Besides the obvious nutritional and immunological factors in breast milk, recent research shows that**

there are other benefits of breast milk over artificial foods. Breast-feeding, with its hormonal storm of oxytocin and prolactin, has an opiate effect on mother and infant. In other animals, oxytocin is actually required for mothers to attach to their infants, but in humans, the exact role of oxytocin as a direct initiator of attachment is less clear. It does seem to play a role in making them both relax, concentrate on each other, and therefore must at some level be involved in fostering the bonding process."

—*Anthropologist Meredith F. Small, from* Our Babies, Ourselves

While it is certainly true that mothers can love and feel close to their babies no matter how they feed them, the attachment between a breastfeeding mother and her nursling is more than just a feeling. In fact, this connection is tangible and biological and is similar in many respects to the connection between a pregnant mother and the baby she is carrying. Anthropologists have determined that human infants—compared to other mammals—are exceptionally helpless and "unfinished" when they emerge from the womb. They still need the biological connection of breastfeeding for optimal development. Birth itself is not the end product of a new mother's reproductive cycle. For both mother and baby, there is one last step to human gestation: breastfeeding. While exclusively breastfeeding (no bottles, pacifiers, solids, juices, or supplementation for baby), most women will not ovulate or menstruate—just as if they were still pregnant. Scientists even have a name for this "fourth trimester"; it is called "exogestation" (imagine if breastfeeding women, instead of referring to their status as "nursing mothers," told people that they were "exogestating!"). Women who do not breastfeed lose this biological tie to their babies and with it, the many attachment promoting benefits it offers.

Breastfeeding and the Pleasure Principle

If you have never breastfed a baby before, you may have gotten the impression from popular culture, the media, or perhaps your own mother's description of an unsupported breastfeeding experience, that nursing a baby is unpleasant in some way. Maybe you have heard about sore nipples or painfully engorged breasts. While many women do require some adjustment to the new physical sensations that come with breastfeeding, and others—without adequate information in learning *how* to breastfeed—may experience real discomfort (which can almost always be overcome with appropriate lactation guidance), the fact is that—by design—nursing a baby is an experience meant to be enjoyed. The way in which your breasts produce milk for your baby helps to explain why nursing can be so pleasurable for you. During your pregnancy, the mammary glands located inside your breasts begin to grow. Whether your prepregnancy breasts were large, small, firm, or soft doesn't matter; women's breasts are designed to manufacture and eject milk. The hormones that promote the changes in your breasts during pregnancy are progesterone, estrogen, and lactogen, which come from the developing placenta, as well as prolactin, which you yourself produce. Prolactin is indicated in the production of endorphins, the brain chemicals that foster feelings of peace and human affection. By around the middle of pregnancy, your breasts are ready to begin making milk. The milk itself, which begins in the first days after birth as colostrum—a thicker, yellowish milk—is manufactured when the thousands of sacs called "alveoli" within your breasts' milk ducts absorb water, salts, sugar, and fats from your bloodstream and turn it into food for your baby. Your body is signaled to begin producing milk by the delivery of your placenta.

The key players in your milk production after birth are the prolactin and oxytocin, the same hormone that causes your uterus to contract during labor or an orgasm. Immediately after you give birth, your prolactin level drops, but it shoots back up again as soon as your baby first puts his mouth on your nipple. This process is repeated each time your baby nurses. Nerve endings within your areola send a message to the pituitary gland at the base of your skull, thus releasing the needed hormones. This is just the first of many examples of the concrete and continuing biological attachment between you and your breastfed baby even after you no longer carry him in your belly. Prolactin stimulates the production of your milk, while oxytocin is behind your "letdown," in which your breasts actually release milk for your baby to suckle. *Both* elements—milk production and milk ejection—must be doing their job in order for you to breastfeed effectively. Many women have a physical sensation of their milk letting down as it occurs. It can feel like a tingling, a sudden fullness or—when you are very relaxed and focused on your child—like a rush of indescribably pleasant sensations. Over time, as you become emotionally connected to your baby, you will likely find that the sound of his cry, the sight of his hungry little mouth opening wide, or even the very thought of him can cause your milk to suddenly begin to flow.

Many breastfeeding mothers describe a feeling of calm warmth washing over them as their milk lets down and their baby begins to nurse. Tension seems to melt away as these "mothering hormones" do their thing. Additionally, research shows that, within minutes after beginning a nursing session, a mother's cortisol levels subside and her blood pressure drops, fostering a further sense of peaceful relaxation. While nursing your baby, your body also reacts in ways much like a heightened sexual response: your temperature rises, your uterus contracts, and your nipples become erect. This is one more clue that breastfeeding is meant to be a natural part of the wide continuum of women's pleasurable physical experiences. Obviously, breastfeeding can be something that *you* enjoy and which promotes your attachment to your baby.

If you think about it, this makes perfect sense. Enthusiastically attentive mothers who keep their babies well fed are necessary to the continuation of the species. For modern mothers who often find themselves questioning every aspect of their own parenting, the relaxing and loving feelings that naturally accompany successful breastfeeding are welcome feedback that "this must be right."

How Does Your Baby Experience Breastfeeding?

> ✦ **"This entire intricate interaction involving the baby's sucking—which effects the mother's hormones, activates a milk let-down response, enhances warm maternal feelings, and deepens sensitivity and love—continues an age old human cycle. The fulfillment and gratification that occur for the infant during feeding may also be a beginning template for rewarding social and intimate relationships later in life."**
>
> — *From* Bonding: Building the Foundations of Secure Attachment and Independence *(Addison-Wesley, 1995) by bonding researchers Marshal H. Klaus, M.D., John H. Kennell, M.D., and Phyllis H. Klaus, C.S.W., M.F.C.C.*

When a baby is ready to nurse, which he may want to do out of hunger, thirst, or simply a need for comfort, he begins to root toward his mother's breast or exhibit some other individual cue to which a responsive parent is quite attuned. The willing breastfeeding mother can quickly and easily offer her baby just what he needs. The baby isn't asked to wait for anything to be opened, mixed, warmed or shaken before he can nurse. At the outset of the actual nursing session, the baby draws his mother's soft nipple far into his mouth, thus stimulating optimal oral-facial development. After sucking for a moment, the milk—warmed to precisely the right temperature—begins to flow. Thus, the baby learns that he can make good things happen for himself. As his digestive juices are stimulated by his suckling, the milk evolves into the heartier hindmilk, just as the baby is ready for it. Or perhaps the baby just wanted a nip, in which case the brief sucking soothed him and the foremilk satiated his thirst.

No one who has ever seen a nursing child at his mother's breast can doubt that, to a little person, breastfeeding is sheer delight. Skin to skin, with his mother's delicious smell enveloping his senses, a breastfed baby is frequently overcome with happiness as he nurses. Often he will pat or caress his mother's breast as he sucks, and older babies like to glance up at their mother's face and give a milky smile. These are the moments that breastfeeding mothers really treasure. Babies are strongly attracted to the scent of their own mother's milk and nipples and it isn't surprising; breastmilk is quite sweet. According to Dr. William Sears, human milk contains more lactose (sugar) than the milk of any other mammal, while infant formulas, on the other hand, are famous for their singularly unpleasant smell and taste.

Supply and Demand: You and Your Baby in Sync

So now your breasts are producing milk. You are lactating and feeding your baby. Obviously the mother of twins or triplets must produce more milk than the mother of a four pound preemie, but how does your body "know" how much milk your particular baby needs? The answer is another testament to the brilliant natural design of breastfeeding: the more your baby (or babies) stimulates your breasts with his nursing, the more milk you will make. The less he nurses, the less milk you will make. Sometimes in the first week or two of getting breastfeeding started, you will produce too much milk, causing your breasts to become swollen (called "engorgement"). But by allowing your baby free access to your breasts, the two of you will soon settle into your own unique rhythm as your milk supply harmonizes with his needs. During growth spurts, when your baby signals his need for greater numbers of calories by nursing more frequently, your body will produce extra milk to fuel his development. And as your baby grows into a toddler and beyond and very gradually replaces the breastmilk in his diet with things like bagels and yogurt and pizza, your breasts will slowly produce less and less milk (although some women say that they can express a little milk from their breasts long after their child has weaned). Theoretically, you could continue to lactate *forever*, as long as your breasts remained adequately stimulated by nursing.

Why Do So Many Women Believe That They "Don't Have Enough Milk" for Their Babies?

Talk to twenty average American women with young children and it's likely that at least one-third of them will tell you that they tried breastfeeding, but they weren't able to produce enough milk for their babies. But talk to twenty average mothers from Bangladesh, for example, and they will tell you that they have never heard of an otherwise healthy mother who couldn't producc enough milk to feed her baby. What's the difference? Why is it that the best nourished, healthiest women in the world seem to have the hardest time with their milk supply?

First, the *way* in which most western women are instructed to breastfeed their babies can actually *prevent* a mother from producing sufficient quantities of milk. Conventional wisdom in this culture has long held that breastfeeding mothers should feed their babies only every few hours (depending on the advice giver, women are told to nurse, or to expect their babies to *want* to nurse, only every two to four hours), and to control the amount of time the baby spends at the breast. Even with all of the emerging research on breastfeeding, his advice really hasn't changed much in the past several decades, as evidenced by these two excerpts from babycare manuals:

- **"Nurse your baby for four minutes on each side every four hours on the first day. Do not deviate from this schedule or your baby will become overfed and your breasts will produce too much milk."**

  —*INFORMATION FROM HOSPITAL BABYCARE BOOKLET GIVEN TO MOTHER WHEN SHE GAVE BIRTH IN 1967*

- **"Nurse for no more than two or three minutes per side at each feeding the first day, counting the time the baby mouths the breasts without sucking. Add two minutes each day until you reach ten minutes." And "Hourly nursing sessions are too much of a strain on you, both physically and emotionally, are likely to cause sore nipples, and may understandably result in your feeling resentment toward your baby for taking up so much of your day and night with his greedy habit. As for your baby,** overnursing **(authors' emphasis on this made-up word) isn't only unnecessary, it's unhealthy."**

  —*INFORMATION FROM THE 1989 EDITION OF* WHAT TO EXPECT THE FIRST YEAR *(EISENBERG, MURKOFF AND HATHAWAY, WORKMAN PUBLISHING) GIVEN TO 1960S MOTHER'S DAUGHTER AT HER OWN BABY SHOWER IN THE '90S.*

Despite what many childcare manuals will tell you, the fact is that sometimes, thriving, perfectly healthy breastfed infants will want to nurse very frequently—sometimes more than once an hour. This is particularly true during the early months. In societies where babies are routinely allowed free access to their mother's breasts, "insufficient milk syndrome" is virtually unheard of. This is because *it is the frequency, not the duration of nursing sessions that determines how much milk you produce!* Limiting your baby's feedings according to some arbitrary, predetermined schedule can lead to diminished milk production.

In addition to the fact that increased breastfeeding frequency generally equals better milk production, another indication that human babies should be nursed more often than most women have been led to believe, is the composition of our milk. Human breastmilk is low in fat and protein and very high in water. This is consistent with the milk content of other "continuous contact" species. As anthropologist Meredith Small explains, "In species where mothers are expected to feed only occasionally and leave babies in the nest for long periods, the milk is high in fat and protein so that infants can be both nutritionally compensated (by protein) and satisfied (with fat) for long periods alone. When milk is low in fat and protein, as it is in humans, it is an indication that breastfeeding is designated or intended to be more continuous." However, since many new mothers today are under the mistaken impression that a "normal" breastfed baby will always naturally fall into a "two to four hour schedule," they may become alarmed if their (completely normal) baby signals that he wants to eat (or simply nurse for comfort) every forty-five minutes or so, believing that his frequent nursing is a sure signal that he "isn't getting enough." As long as a baby is healthy and gaining well, very frequent breastfeeding isn't anything to worry about. In this case, it is the mother's expectations, not her milk supply or her baby that need adjustment.

Limiting how *long* a baby spends at the breast during each feeding (as per the "expert" advice: "Nurse for no more than two or three minutes per side at each feeding the first day, counting the time the baby mouths the breasts without sucking . . .") can also lead to milk supply problems. When your baby begins a nursing session, the first milk that your breasts produce is called the "foremilk." This milk is thin and dilute (though still loaded with important immunological and nutritional value). As your baby continues nursing, more of the hormone oxytocin is released into your breasts, thus contracting the milk glands further and spurring the release of a thicker, creamier second wave of milk, known as the "hindmilk." Hindmilk has greater amounts of fat and calories than the foremilk. Predictably, it's also more filling and satisfying to the nursing baby. Babies who are only permitted to nurse for a short period on each breast may get *only* the foremilk, thus leaving them hungry and fussy. Continued for any length of time, these limited feeds may even lead to a baby who is gaining weight too slowly or not at all. A frequently fussy baby or one who is not thriving can lead a mother to believe that she isn't producing enough milk for her baby when in fact, the problem may be that she isn't allowing her baby to nurse *long enough* to get the milk he needs. Different babies may require different periods of time on the breast in order to get enough of both kinds of milk. Some may be slow, leisurely nursers while others get right down to business and take all they need within a very short time. That's why any type of one-size-fits-all baby feeding schedule can lead to real or perceived milk supply issues. And contrary to what you may have heard, allowing your baby to nurse at the breast for long periods will not, under normal circumstances, lead to sore nipples. A ravenously hungry baby who isn't getting enough at each feeding is actually much more likely to mouth your nipple in such a way that you become sore.

Another common cause of low milk supply is offering *unnecessary* (meaning, not medically indicated by a well-informed health care provider) supplementary bottles of formula. Every time your baby takes a bottle of formula is one less time he has stimulated your breasts. The more bottles he takes, the less milk you will make. The same is true of sucking on a pacifier. And there are other reasons why a woman might have or believe that she has milk supply problems. Many mothers become disheartened when they see how little milk they are able to extract with a breastpump. They may believe that this is indicative of their overall milk supply. But this isn't always the case. Successful pumping requires practice, patience, and usually, a high quality breastpump. In the absence of any one of these factors, it's possible that you might not be able to express very much milk. With a good latch-on and suck, however, your baby herself is the world's most efficient breastpump! Many women who are unable to express their own milk have a perfectly abundant milk supply when it's their own baby extracting it from their breast. Don't assume that the amount of milk you are able to pump is necessarily representative of the amount your baby is getting. In other instances, women become convinced that they aren't producing enough milk because their mother/sister/best friend says that *she* couldn't. Questions such as, "Are you sure that baby's getting enough milk?" or other negative feedback can play a role in how a woman feels about her milk supply.

How Can I Be Sure My Breastfed Baby Is Getting Enough Milk?

In order to determine whether your baby is getting enough milk, consider the following factors, remembering that your baby herself is the best indicator of your milk supply. As lactation consultants often tell mothers, output equals input!

- Your baby should have *at least* six to eight very wet diapers per day (remember that disposable diapers make it much harder to determine how much your baby is wetting. You may want to consider using cloth diapers).
- Your baby should also have *at least* three bowel movements per twenty-four hour period (although some breastfed babies have one after every feed) during the early months. After about six to

eight weeks, his dirty diaper count may drop off sharply—often to only a couple per week.

- Your baby should be nursing *at least* eight times per twenty-four hour period.
- Your baby should, when appropriate, produce tears, saliva and perspiration.
- Your baby should seem alert, vigorous, and well.
- You should be able to hear your baby swallowing milk as he nurses.
- Your baby should be gaining weight.

If at any time you have questions regarding your baby's well being—whether he is breast or bottle-fed—you should never hesitate to have him examined immediately by a qualified health care provider. In addition, routine well baby checkups, especially in the first days and weeks after birth, can assure you that your baby is thriving.

Cloth Diapering

Many attachment parents enjoy covering their babies' delicate bums in soft cotton diapers, considering cloth diapering to be a part of the "art of parenting." Chemical-laced disposables are relatively new to baby care and no one really knows what threat they may pose to children's health. Today's ultra-absorbent single use diapers contain chemicals called polyacrylates. This is the "gel" found in the center of disposable diapers. The bleached paper used in disposables is also loaded with dioxin, a potent cancer causing agent. Considering that infants and toddlers wear these items—wet, and leaching potentially harmful elements onto their bodies—for 24 hours a day, it is wise to be concerned about these chemical agents. Too often, however, today's parents are intimidated by the thought of using anything but "wearable garbage" to diaper their children because their only exposure to cloth diapering has been old-fashioned squares of leaky cotton, combined with sharp pins and rubber pants. Disposables just seem so much easier!

In fact, however, cloth diapering has become just as convenient as disposable diapering, with many easy-to-use diapering supplies on the market. The biggest innovation in cloth diapering has been the use of Velcro and snaps on diapers and covers. Cloth diapers now come preshaped just like disposables, with Velcro fasteners or snaps where the disposables would have tapes. Parents can then cover the diapers with the traditional rubber pants or the newer Velcro diaper covers in a variety of waterproof fabrics. Diapers come in many different types of cotton, with most parents finding that flannel and terry are easily as absorbent as the disposables. There are even all-in-one diapers now, with both the diaper and the waterproof outer layer combined into one package. Just fasten the Velcro or snaps and go!

If parents have a washer and dryer at home, laundering is not as much trouble as clipping coupons and shopping for the costly disposables. Parents can employ one of the reusable Gore-Tex® diaper pail liners in the diaper pail and discard the used diapers in the pail. When the pail becomes full, parents simply lift the liner full of dirty diapers out of the pail and empty it into the washer, throwing the liner in with the diapers. Presoaking with a good detergent, followed by a long cycle on hot with borax gets the diapers clean and sanitary. Drying on high heat or on a line in the sunshine makes sure that the diapers are fresh, soft and healthy for baby. Since most good cloth diapers are now preshaped like disposables, no time-consuming folding is needed.

The initial costs of purchasing high quality cloth diaper supplies can seem daunting. However, over the long run, a parent will spend approximately half what she would have spent on disposables. Cloth diapers are an even better value when the supplies are handed down to other babies.

The Very Best Resources for Cloth-Diapering Parents

BOOKS

Diaper Changes: The Complete Diapering Book and Resource Guide. 2nd Ed. Rodriguez Farrisi, Theresa. Richland, PA: Homekeepers Publishing, 1998.

Available from the publisher at:
P.O. Box 439
Dept WWW
Richland, PA 17087
Phone: (800) 572–1826

This concise guide explains everything you need to know about diapering. It includes a complete discussion of the differences between disposables and cloth, including cost, convenience, and ecological considerations, as well as an extensive Resource Section offering over fifty pages of mail-order sources for diapering products and other parenting supplies.

WEB SITES

Diapering Choices
http://webhome.idirect.com/~born2luv/CHOICES.HTML

The Diaper Information Page
http://www.geocities.com/~sharra2/cloth.html

INTERNET E-MAIL LISTS

N-DIAP *is an e-mail list for cloth-diapering parents. To subscribe, you send a message to* n-diap-request@kjsl.com with "subscribe" in the body (no quotes).

Learning How to Breastfeed

Zoo-kept primates who haven't been raised around other breast-feeding mothers of their own species often have trouble breastfeeding their babies. The same is true for human mothers who lack breastfeeding support. Breastfeeding *is* natural, meaning that as mammals, our healthy bodies are designed to do it. However it is also cultural, meaning that women best learn *how* to breastfeed from other women. Knowing how to comfortably position your baby at the breast, guiding enough of your areola into his little mouth, and feeling confident that he is getting what he needs sometimes require support and guidance, particularly in the early weeks. In many cultures around the world, new mothers receive generous amounts of assistance in learning how to breastfeed from other experienced women in their family or community. If a new mother is having difficulty getting her baby to latch-on well or if her nipples are becoming sore, these breastfeeding helpers can offer her the information and hands-on guidance she needs to overcome any problems.

In our bottle-feeding culture, however, you may have never known anyone who breastfed a baby. Even if you have encountered breastfeeding mothers, they may have hidden themselves away with blankets, shawls, or even gone into the bathroom when they fed their babies. Thus, your direct experience with breastfeeding may be quite limited when you embark upon your own breastfeeding relationship with your new baby. *The best way to enjoy nursing your baby and prevent problems is to educate yourself.* Read a good breastfeeding book or two while you are pregnant, attend La Leche League meetings during pregnancy and afterwards, and talk with other experienced breastfeeding mothers in your community or on the Internet. As with most things in life, an ounce of prevention equals a pound of cure when it comes to initiating breastfeeding. However, the most important key to success in breastfeeding your baby is to relax, feel confident that this is what you and your baby are designed to do, and *savor* this lovely time of your life. As mothers of older children will tell you, it passes all too quickly.

The Very Best Resources for Learning *How* to Breastfeed

BOOKS

So That's What They're For: Breastfeeding Basics. Tamaro-Natt, Janet. Holsbrook, MA: Adams Media, 1998.

A witty and comprehensive overview of the most common breastfeeding questions and concerns. Especially useful for the woman starting out with little to no exposure to breastfeeding information.

The Nursing Mother's Companion. Huggins, Kathleen. Boston: Harvard Common Press, 1995.

A nationally known lactation consultant's complete and reassuring guide to every aspect of breastfeeding. Always completely up-to-date.

Breastfeeding Your Baby. rev. ed. Kitzinger, Sheila. New York: Knopf, 1998.

Gorgeous photographs of mothers and nursing babies are the hallmark of this comprehensive breastfeeding book from Sheila Kitzinger, one of the world's best-known childbirth educators.

The Baby Book: Everything You Need to Know About Your Baby—From Birth to Age Two. Sears, William, and Martha Sears, New York: Little, Brown & Co., 1993.

This is the modern "bible" of baby care. Breastfeeding information is presented within the context of all the information you will need to care for your new baby.

The Womanly Art of Breastfeeding. La Leche League International Staff. New York: Plume, 1997.

This book is like a gentle, warm embrace for new mothers who want to learn more about mothering through breastfeeding. Lots of practical information as well.

Breastfeeding Answer Book. 2nd expanded rev. ed. Mohrbacher, Nancy, and Julie Stock. Schaumburg, IL La Leche League Intl, 1997.

This is the same book that many lactation consultants, La Leche League Leaders and informed HCPs use to find answers to every possible question about breastfeeding. If the information isn't here, you probably won't find it anywhere!

Bestfeeding: Getting Breastfeeding Right for You: An Illustrated Guide. Renfrew, Mary, Chloe Fisher, and Suzanne Arms Berkeley, CA: Celestial Arts Publishing Co., 1995.

If you aren't sure what breastfeeding should look like, this is the book for you. Clear (and beautiful!), easy to follow photographs lead you step by step through many breastfeeding concerns.

Medications and Mother's Milk. Hale, Thomas W., R.Ph., PhD. Pharmasoft Medical Publishing, 1998.

Although this book is directed primarily at medical professionals, mothers who have questions about drugs and breastfeeding will also find it a useful reference. If your own physician says that it isn't (or is) safe to take a particular prescription while nursing, you can double check her advice with Dr. Hale's book.

BREASTFEEDING SUPPORT IN YOUR COMMUNITY

La Leche League International
Phone: (800) LALECHE (US) or (847) 519–7730
http://www.lalecheleague.org

International Certified Lactation Consultant
International Lactation Consultants Association (ILCA)
Phone: (919) 787–5181
Fax: (919) 787–4916
E-mail: ilca@erols.com

Nursing Mother's Counsel Chapter
Phone: (415) 599–3669
http://www.nursingmothers.org/index.html

WEB SITES

The LACTNET archives

http://peach.ease.lsoft.com/archives/lactnet.html

Nursing mothers can search and read the LACTNET database for authoritative answers to all their breastfeeding questions. The LACTNET mailing list is for medical professionals involved with breastfeeding. Many of the world's foremost experts in human lactation have information archived here.

The Official La Leche League International Website

http://www.lalecheleague.org

Dr. Jack Newman's Breastfeeding Articles

http://www.erols.com/cindyrn/drjack0.htm

Jane's Breastfeeding and Childbirth Resources

http://www.breastfeeding.co.uk/janelnk6.html

Breastfeeding After C-Section

http://www.greatstar. com/lois/bfcsec.htm

NursingMother.Com

http://www.nursingmother.com

Why You Should Breastfeed

http://www.erols.com/cindyrn

Questions About Breastfeeding

http://www.ecr.net/betz/bamenu.htm

Promotion of Mother's Milk, Inc (ProMoM)

http://www.promom.org

Answers to Common Breastfeeding Concerns

http://www.parentsplace.com/readroom/medela/problems.html

Breastfeeding at Suite 101
http://www.suite101.com/page.cfm/5046/bfeeding

The Christian Parent's Guide to Breastfeeding
http://www.christianparent.com

INTERNET E-MAIL LISTS

Parent–L *is a forum for discussing issues related to breastfeeding and parenting the nursing baby or child. The topics for discussion vary widely, and include subjects related to life with a nursing toddler or baby, nursing during pregnancy, tandem nursing, societal attitudes towards breastfeeding, weaning, and any other related topics. To subscribe to parent–l, send the following command in the body of an e-mail message to:* parent–l–request@uts.edu.au: "subscribe parent–l"

BFAR *is the list for mothers who are breastfeeding after breast reduction or other breast surgeries. For information, send an email to* bfar@storefront.com. *If you are interested in subscribing, send your request, along with a brief description of your history and current situation to* bfar@storefront.com.

The Nursing Mothers' Sewing List *is designed to provide support for breastfeeding women who want to sew their own nursing clothing or adapt "regular" clothing with nursing access. To subscribe send an email to:* nmsl-request@kjsl.com with "subscribe" (no quotes) in the body of the message.

INTERNET NEWSGROUPS

misc.kids.breastfeeding
alt.support.breastfeeding

What Is La Leche League?

La Leche League was founded in 1957 by a handful of Illinois mothers who wanted to support the (at that time) minuscule percentage of women who were choosing to breastfeed their babies. In the 1950s, the word "breastfeeding" wasn't considered appropriate for polite company, so LLL's founding mothers had to come up with a name that would allow them to discreetly discuss their activities, as well as list their meetings in the local newspaper. La Leche is Spanish for "the milk," and is pronounced *"la LAY-chay."* The idea for the fledgling organization's name came from a statue in St. Augustine, Florida (USA) honoring *"Nuestra Señora de la Leche y Buen Parto,"* which translated, means: "Our Lady of Happy Delivery and Plentiful Milk."

Today this nonprofit group has grown into the world's foremost authority on breastfeeding. La Leche League representatives are welcomesd as experts at national and international conferences on infant-maternal health. La Leche League Leaders—volunteer women specially trained to assist other women in their communities with breastfeeding—lead more than 3,000 La Leche League groups in community centers, places of worship, and homes around the world. It is very likely that you will be able to locate one or more regular La Leche League meetings in your area. Additionally, anyone can telephone a local Leader for free, friendly, and accurate answers to all your breastfeeding questions. La Leche League considers this mother-to-mother breastfeeding support an important complement to a nursing family's medical care.

La Leche League sums up its philosophy in the following ten statements:

- Mothering through breastfeeding is the most natural and effective way of understanding and satisfying the needs of the baby.
- Mother and baby need to be together early and often to establish a satisfying relationship and an adequate milk supply.

- In the early years the baby has an intense need to be with his mother which is as basic as his need for food.
- Breast milk is the superior infant food.
- For the healthy, full term baby, breast milk is the only food necessary until the baby shows signs of needing solids, about the middle of the first year after birth.
- Ideally the breastfeeding relationship will continue until the baby outgrows the need.
- Alert and active participation by the mother in childbirth is a help in getting breastfeeding off to a good start.
- Breastfeeding is enhanced and the nursing couple sustained by the loving support, help, and companionship of the baby's father. A father's unique relationship with his baby is an important element in the child's development from early infancy.
- Good nutrition means eating a well balanced and varied diet of foods in as close to their natural state as possible.
- From infancy on, children need loving guidance which reflects acceptance of their capabilities and sensitivity to their feelings.

Obviously, many attachment parents find information, support and friendship through membership in La Leche League. In the past, some women found La Leche League's traditional views on the family rather off-putting. However, in recent years the organization has made great strides in its support for and inclusion of working mothers and nontraditional families. If you have never breastfed before, you will definitely benefit from attending a couple of La Leche League meetings while still pregnant. However, La Leche League welcomes women and their young children to their meetings at any time. Although regular LLL meetings are for mothers only, fathers are welcome to attend special family meetings, as well as conferences. Locate a meeting or Leader near you by calling (800) LaLeche. If the first meeting you try doesn't appeal to you, you might want to attend another. Each regular meeting tends to have a unique personality and flavor.

When Breastfeeding Is a Challenge

▶ *"My own hang-ups about allowing other people to get close to me made it difficult for me to feel good about being so physically intimate with this little person who seemed to need me so much. This was something I had to overcome in order to breastfeed."*

—KATE, *MOTHER OF A SIX MONTH OLD*

▶ *"I had one inverted nipple, so I had to work closely with a lactation consultant to get my baby to nurse on that side. Our learning curve was hard, but well worth it."*

—BARBARA, *MOTHER OF TWO*

▶ *"Because of an earlier cosmetic breast surgery, I was very worried about whether I would be able to breastfeed. My fears made it hard for me to even try."*

—DONNA, *MOTHER OF A TWO YEAR OLD*

▶ *"I take medication for depression. I really need my medicine, so my doctor and I worked with a lactation consultant to find the best antidepressant for me to take while breastfeeding. Incidentally, I have found that my depression has greatly improved since I had the baby."*

—GWYNN, *MOTHER OF A ONE YEAR OLD*

▶ *"I developed a yeast infection called thrush on my nipples within weeks after starting breastfeeding. It made nursing really unpleasant and I seriously considered quitting. Thankfully a friend encouraged me to call a La Leche League Leader right away. She told me what medications I would need, I told my doctor, she prescribed them, and I was enjoying nursing within a day or two."*

—KAREN, *MOTHER OF A NINE MONTH OLD*

For some women, particularly women living in our own bottle-feeding culture, breastfeeding can be a challenge even when they are well-informed. Physical, emotional, or other issues may occasionally make nursing your baby more difficult. In virtually every instance, however, these problems can be addressed and overcome with help from a La Leche League Leader or Board certified lactation consultant. Sometimes—especially if your own partner, family, or friends are lukewarm in their support for your nursing relationship with your baby—you may need an emotional boost from a kind and knowledgeable breastfeeding helper. Other times, you may need more specialized or even medical breastfeeding support. Your local La Leche League Leader or Board certified lactation consultant can talk with you on the phone or come to your home to help you with proper positioning, milk supply issues, physical discomfort, or any other breastfeeding concerns. If you are experiencing difficulties in breastfeeding your baby, it is very important that you seek assistance immediately. Don't wait. Additionally, be sure that you get the right kind of help. Anyone can hang out a shingle and call herself a "lactation consultant." Be certain that you find someone with the "IBCLC" (International Board Certified Lactation Consultant) credential, or an accredited La Leche League Leader. Unfortunately, even some hospitals advertise the availability of "lactation consultants" (usually staff nurses who actually have little or no formal training in lactation science). And if you do find yourself facing unexpected breastfeeding challenges—in the beginning or later in your breastfeeding relationship—don't give up too quickly! With the right information and support, it is very likely that you can solve your problems and happily breastfeed your baby.

Very infrequently, a woman *is* actually physically incapable of breastfeeding, even with the right kind of support and information. Although this situation is quite unusual, that fact alone doesn't make it any less upsetting for those women to whom it occurs. As we explained previously, a small percentage of women may have an insurmountable problem with milk *production*, milk *ejection,* or both. In a very few other cases, babies themselves are physically unable to effectively suckle at the breast. No one knows exactly what percentage of mothers lack the physical capability to breastfeed, but all agree that the numbers are *significantly* lower than popular culture and the media have led parents to believe. Remember: *it is a virtual certainty that you will be able to successfully breastfeed your baby for as long as you want to do it.* However, if a well-informed lactation specialist ultimately determines that you are, in fact, among the small number of women who really cannot breastfeed, skip ahead to the section on bottle-feeding for information that may be helpful to you. And remember that sometimes, even when breastfeeding doesn't work out with one baby, it will with the next.

Breastfeeding and Guilt

> ✦ **"In my experience, the guilt comes later," says Dr. Jay Gordon, a nationally recognized pediatrician and breastfeeding expert, who often finds the mother of a sick child weeping in his office when she finds out that breastmilk might have prevented or minimized the illness. "Women say, 'Why didn't someone tell me?,' or 'I wish I had gotten a second opinion because my doctor never told me how important it was.' "**
>
> —*Quoted in* So That's What They're For: Breastfeeding Basics, *by Janet Tamaro-Natt*

The topic of breastfeeding—who does and who doesn't and why—has become an emotionally charged one. There is a widespread misperception that breastfeeding supporters purposefully set out to make "all the women who can't breastfeed" feel guilty. In fact, as we have discussed, very few women actually *cannot* breastfeed. Given that a relatively low percentage of American women nurse their babies for more than a few weeks, that leaves an awful lot of women who are—for a wide variety of reasons—simply *not choosing* to breastfeed. Of course, there is no reason to feel negative or defensive about a choice that is made confidently and in consideration of all the relevant information. However, many women quit breastfeeding in the first few months—with little information or support, and before giving nursing a real chance—and then proceed to tell people that they "couldn't breastfeed." There is a very real difference between freely choosing to discontinue breastfeeding, and being literally *incapable* of breastfeeding, as any woman who has experienced the pain of being truly unable to nurse her baby will tell you. If for any reason you decide that you don't want to breastfeed your baby—as opposed to actually being *unable* to do so—be honest with yourself and others. That is certainly your decision to make, and no one but you yourself can know your own circumstances well enough to make that call. And again, if you make your choice confidently and armed with all the facts, the most strident breastfeeding supporter in the world cannot make you feel guilty.

But a lot of bottle-feeding women *do* seem to struggle with feelings of defensiveness and guilt regarding their feeding choice. Too often, this guilt manifests itself as an illogical lashing out at breastfeeding mothers, advocates, and researchers. Many bottle-feeding parents react to their own inner conflicts by vociferously asserting that the mountain of peer reviewed scientific research demonstrating the risks of routine artificial feeding is flawed in some way. "People can make research say anything they want," is an oft-heard refrain. "I was bottle-fed and I'm just fine!" is another. Bottle-feeding mothers who are experiencing guilt should spend some time exploring the foundation for their feelings. Clearly, for one reason or another, they do not feel good about the choice they have made. Perhaps (even likely) they didn't have enough information or support to make a well-thought-out decision, and maybe they have regrets. Some women, after digging deeply into what's making them feel so conflicted about their bottle-feeding choice even find that they have real grief feelings about the loss of their opportunity to nurse their baby. Any discussion of the topic—no matter how benign, can feel like salt in their wounds.

Women need to support one another in our mothering journeys. Judgment and criticism are pointless and painful. Infant formula manufacturers are laughing all the way to the bank as parents turn on one another in their frustration over how difficult breastfeeding is made for women in this society. Bottle-feeding mothers can direct their energy toward changing the elements of our culture which robbed them and their children of their nursing relationships. Breastfeeding advocates, on the other hand, must continue to make it possible for women to get *all* the facts before making their infant feeding choices, as well as offer support for new mothers in learning *how* to breastfeed.

▶ *"I quit breastfeeding my first baby after only a few weeks because—at that time—I just didn't want to do it. For several years I told people (and even thought to myself) that I wasn't able to produce enough milk. After I became pregnant with my second baby, I began learning more about breastfeeding. I soon knew that I really wanted to breastfeed my new baby, which I have done and am still doing. I am now much more comfortable saying that I made the decision to bottle-feed my first child. I no longer tell people that I 'wasn't able to breastfeed.' And I no longer feel defensive about it. I used to direct a lot of the guilt I felt about not breastfeeding toward other women who were breastfeeding. I called them 'zealots' and 'militant.' Now I realize that this was just misguided anger toward the doctor who gave me bad breastfeeding advice and the formula companies who sent me home from the hospital with the free samples that started us on the path toward bottle-feeding."*

—JENNIFER, MOTHER OF TWO

► *"My first failure as a parent came swiftly when I was unable to overcome nipple confusion and illness, both my own and my son's. Back then, I didn't know what nipple confusion was—or that there were lactation consultants and La Leche League Leaders I could turn to. I only knew that I was shell-shocked and bereft when I returned from the hospital to realize I was a bottle-feeding mother, something I had never thought I would be. The experience plunged me into a depression I battled for three years. I remember, when Zack was an infant, watching my sister-in-law nurse my nephew so easily. I had to sneak away, crying in huge heaving sobs that I thought would break me in half. I was tempted to justify it all to myself by saying that my formula-fed son was healthier or that it wasn't so important anyway. But I'm not a person who can lie to myself, especially when it comes to my children. This experience has brought a lot of anger at the people and institutions who deliberately sabotaged my efforts to breastfeed. Still, I carry guilt and regret; I own this failure. Guilt and regret, though, are appropriate responses to a loss so profound, and they have made me work harder to parent Zack lovingly. The experience has made me determined to tell the truth about formula and all the people who are so tied up in promoting it that they don't care how many mothers and children suffer by losing the breastfeeding relationship. I did scads of research on breastfeeding and was well prepared when Gina was born. She is now two years old and still nurses frequently, and I am happy that I gave my son, through his sister, the opportunity to learn about mothering through breastfeeding. He is a staunch advocate of breastfeeding and gentle parenting."*

—JANICE, MOTHER OF TWO

Slaying the Most Common Breastfeeding Myths

Jack Newman, M.D., F.R.C.P.C.

- **Many women do not produce enough milk.** Not true! The vast majority of women produce more than enough milk. Indeed, an overabundance of milk is common. Most babies who gain too slowly, or who lose weight, do so not because the mother does not have enough milk, but because the baby does not get the milk that the mother has. The usual reason that the baby does not get the milk that is available is that he is poorly latched on to the breast. This is why it is so important that the mother be shown on the first day after birth how to latch a baby on properly by someone who knows what she is doing.
- **It is normal for breastfeeding to hurt.** Not true! Though some tenderness during the first week or so is relatively common, this should be a temporary situation and should never be so bad that the mother dreads nursing. Any real and lasting pain is abnormal and is almost always due to the baby latching on poorly. Any nipple pain that is not getting better by day three or four or lasts beyond five or six days should not be ignored. A new onset of pain when things have been going well for a while may be due to a yeast infection of the nipples. Limiting feeding time does not prevent soreness.
- **A breastfeeding baby needs extra water in hot weather.** Not true! Breastmilk contains all the water a baby needs.
- **Breastfeeding babies need extra vitamin D.** Not true!

except in extraordinary circumstances (for example, if the mother herself was vitamin D deficient during the pregnancy). The baby stores vitamin D during the pregnancy, and a little outside exposure, on a regular basis gives the baby all the vitamin D he needs.

- **A mother should wash her nipples each time before feeding the baby.** Not true! Formula feeding requires careful attention to cleanliness because formula does not protect the baby against infection and can also be a good breeding ground for bacteria and contamination. On the other hand, breastmilk protects the baby against infection. Washing nipples before each feeding makes breastfeeding unnecessarily complicated and washes away protective oils from the nipple.
- **Pumping is a good way of knowing how much milk the mother has.** Not true! How much milk can be pumped depends on many factors, including the mother's stress level. The baby who nurses well can get much more milk than his mother can pump. Pumping only tells you how much you can pump.
- **Breastmilk does not contain enough iron for the baby's needs.** Not true! Breastmilk contains just enough iron for the baby's needs. If the baby is full term he will get enough iron from breastmilk to last him at least the first six months. Formulas contain too much iron, but this quantity may be necessary to ensure the baby absorbs enough to prevent iron deficiency. The iron in formula is poorly absorbed, and most of it, the baby poops out. Generally, there is no need to add other foods to breastmilk before about six months of age.
- **It is easier to bottle-feed than to breastfeed.** Not true! Or rather, this should not be true. Unfortunately, breastfeeding is too often made difficult because women often do not receive the help they should to get started properly. A poor start can indeed make breastfeeding difficult. But a poor start can also be overcome.
- **Breastfeeding ties the mother down.** A baby can be nursed anywhere, anytime, and thus, breastfeeding is liberating for

the mother. No need to drag around bottles or formula. No need to worry about where to warm up the milk. No need to worry about sterility. No need to worry about how your baby is, because he is with you.

- **Modern formulas are almost the same as breastmilk.** Not true! The same claim was made in 1900 and before. Modern formulas are only superficially similar to breastmilk. Every correction of a deficiency in formulas is advertised as an advance. Fundamentally, they are inexact copies based on outdated and incomplete knowledge of what breastmilk is. Formulas contain no antibodies, no living cells, no enzymes, no hormones. They contain much more aluminum, manganese, cadmium and iron than breastmilk. They contain significantly more protein than breastmilk. The proteins and fats are fundamentally different from those in breastmilk. Formulas do not vary from the beginning of the feed to the end of the feed, or from day one to day seven to day thirty, or from woman to woman, or from baby to baby . . . Your breastmilk is made as required to suit your baby. Formulas are made to suit every baby, and thus no baby.
- **If the mother has an infection she should stop breastfeeding.** Not true! With very, very few exceptions, the baby will be protected by the mother's continuing to breastfeed. By the time the mother has fever (or cough, vomiting, diarrhea, rash, etc) she has already given the baby the infection, since she has been infectious for several days before she even knew she was sick. The baby's best protection against becoming ill is for the mother to continue breastfeeding. If the baby does get sick, he will be less sick if the mother continues breastfeeding. Besides, maybe it was the baby who gave the infection to the mother, but the baby did not show signs of illness because he was breastfeeding. Also, breast infections, though painful, are not reasons to stop breastfeeding. Indeed, the infection is likely to resolve itself more quickly if the mother continues breastfeeding on the affected side.
- **If the baby has diarrhea or vomiting, the mother**

should stop breastfeeding. Not true! The best medicine for a baby's gut infection is breastfeeding. Stop other foods for a short time if necessary, but continue breastfeeding. Breastmilk is the only fluid your baby requires when he has diarrhea and/or vomiting, except under exceptional circumstances. The push to use "oral rehydrating solutions" is mainly a push by the formula (and oral rehydrating solutions) manufacturers to make even more money. Additionally, the baby is comforted by breastfeeding.

- **If the mother is taking medicine she should not breastfeed.** Not true! There are very, very few medicines that a mother cannot take safely while breastfeeding. A small amount of most medicines appears in the milk, but usually in such minute quantities that there is no concern. If a medicine is truly not appropriate for a breastfeeding mother, there are usually equally effective, alternative medicines available. The loss of benefit of breastfeeding for both the mother and the baby must be taken into account when weighing whether breastfeeding should be continued.
- **A breastfeeding mother has to be obsessive about what she eats.** Not true! A breastfeeding mother should try to eat a balanced diet, but she doesn't need to eat any special foods or avoid certain foods. A breastfeeding mother does not need to drink milk in order to make milk. A breastfeeding mother does not need to automatically avoid spicy foods, garlic, caffeine, cabbage or alcohol. A breastfeeding mother should eat a normal healthful diet. Although there are situations when something the mother eats may affect the baby, this is unusual.
- **A breastfeeding mother has to eat more in order to make enough milk.** Not true! Women on even very low calorie diets usually make enough milk, at least until the mother's calorie intake becomes critically low for a prolonged period of time. Some women worry that if they eat poorly for a few days this also will affect their milk. There is no need for concern. Such variations will not affect milk supply or quality. It is commonly said that women need to eat 500 extra calories a day in order to

breastfeed. This is not true. Some women do eat more when they breastfeed, but others do not, and some even eat less, without any harm done to the mother or baby or the milk supply. The mother should eat a balanced diet dictated by her appetite. Rules about eating just make breastfeeding unnecessarily complicated.

- **A breastfeeding mother has to drink extra fluids.** Not true! The mother should drink according to her thirst. Some breastfeeding mothers feel they are thirsty all the time, but many others do not drink more than usual. The mother's body knows if she needs more fluids, and tells her by making her feel thirsty. Do not believe that you have to drink at least a certain number of glasses a day. Rules about drinking just make breastfeeding unnecessarily complicated.
- **Premature babies need to learn to take bottles before they can start breastfeeding.** Not true! Premature babies are less stressed by breastfeeding than by bottle feeding. A baby as small as 1200 grams and even smaller can start at the breast as soon as he is stable, though he may not latch on for several weeks. Still, he is learning and he is being held, which is important for his well-being and his mother's. Actually, weight or gestational age do not matter as much as the baby's readiness to suck, as determined by his making sucking movements. There is no more reason to give bottles to premature babies than to full term babies. When supplementation is truly required there are ways to supplement without using artificial nipples.
- **Babies with cleft lip and/or palate can never breastfeed.** Not true! Some do very well. Babies with only a cleft lip usually manage fine. But many babies do indeed find it impossible to latch on. There is no doubt, however, that if breastfeeding is not tried, it will not work. The baby's ability to breastfeed does not always seem to depend on the severity of the cleft. If bottles are given, they will undermine the baby's ability to breastfeed. If the baby needs to be fed, but is not latching on, a cup can and should be used in preference to a bottle. Finger feeding occasionally is successful in babies with cleft lip/palate, but not usually.

- **A woman who has had breast augmentation surgery can never breastfeed.** Not true! Most do very well. There is no evidence that breastfeeding with silicone implants is harmful to the baby. Occasionally this operation is performed with an incision through the areola. These women do have problems with milk supply, as does any woman who has an incision around the areolar line.
- **Breastfeeding does not provide any protection against becoming pregnant.** Not true! It is not a foolproof method, but no birth control method is. In fact breastfeeding is not a bad method of child spacing, and gives reliable protection during the first six months after birth. But it is reliable only when breastfeeding is exclusive, when feedings are fairly frequent (at least six to eight times in twenty-four hours), there are no long periods during which the baby does not feed, and the mother has not yet had a normal menstrual period after giving birth. After the first six months, the protection is less reliable, but still present. On average, women breastfeeding into their child's second year of life will only have a baby every two to three years without using any artificial method of contraception.
- **A woman who becomes pregnant must stop breastfeeding.** Not true! If the mother and child desire, breastfeeding can continue. There are many women who continue nursing their older child even after delivery of the new baby. Some mothers do decide to stop nursing when they become pregnant because their nipples are sore or for other reasons, but there is no rush or medical necessity to do so. In fact, there are often good reasons to continue. The milk supply may decrease during pregnancy, but if the baby is taking other foods, this is not a problem.
- **Babies need to know how to take a bottle.** Therefore a bottle should always be introduced before the baby refuses to take one. Not true! Though many mothers decide to introduce a bottle for various reasons, there is no reason a baby *must* learn how to use one. Indeed, there is no great advantage in a baby's taking a bottle. At about six months of age, the baby can start

learning how to drink from a cup. If the mother is going to introduce a bottle, it is better if she waits until the baby has been nursing well for four to six weeks, and then give it only occasionally. Giving a bottle when breastfeeding is going badly is not a good idea and usually makes the breastfeeding even more difficult.

- **If a mother has surgery, she has to wait a day before restarting nursing.** Not true! The mother can breastfeed immediately after surgery, as soon as she is up to it. Neither the medications used during anaesthesia, nor pain medications, nor antibiotics used after surgery require the mother to avoid breastfeeding, except under exceptional circumstances. Enlightened hospitals will accommodate breastfeeding mothers and babies when either the mother or the baby needs to be admitted to the hospital, so that breastfeeding can continue. Many rules that restrict breastfeeding are more for the convenience of staff than for the benefit of mothers and babies.
- **Breastfeeding twins is too difficult to manage.** Not true! Breastfeeding twins can be easier than bottle feeding twins, if breastfeeding is going well. This is why it is so important that a special effort should be made to get breastfeeding started right when the mother has had multiples. Many women have breastfed triplets exclusively. This obviously takes a lot of work and time, but twins and triplets take a lot of work and time no matter how the babies are fed.
- **Women whose breasts do not enlarge or enlarge only a little during pregnancy, will never produce enough milk.** Not true! There are a very few women who cannot produce enough milk. Some of these women say that their breasts did not enlarge during pregnancy. However, the vast majority of women whose breasts do not seem to enlarge during pregnancy will still produce more than enough milk.
- **A mother whose breasts do not seem full has little milk in the breast.** Not true! Breasts do not have to feel full to produce plenty of milk. It is normal for a breastfeeding

woman's breasts to feel less full as her body adjusts to her baby's milk intake. This can happen suddenly and may occur as early as two weeks after birth or even earlier. The lactating breast is never "empty" and actually continues to produce milk *while* the baby nurses.

- **If the baby is off the breast for a few days or even weeks, the mother should not restart breastfeeding because the milk sours.** Not true! The milk is as good as it ever was. Breastmilk in the breast is not animal milk or formula in a bottle.
- **A mother should not breastfeed after she exercises.** Not true! There is absolutely no reason why a mother would not be able to breastfeed after exercising. The study that purported to show that babies were fussy after mothers exercise contradicts the everyday experience of millions of mothers around the world.
- **A breastfeeding mother cannot get a permanent or dye her hair.** Not true!
- **Breastfeeding is blamed for everything.** *True!* Family, health professionals, neighbors, friends and taxi drivers will blame breastfeeding if the mother is tired, nervous, weepy, sick, has pain in her knees, has difficulty sleeping, is always sleepy, feels dizzy, is anemic, has a relapse of her arthritis (migraines, or any chronic problem), complains of hair loss, change of vision, ringing in the ears or itchy skin. Breastfeeding will be blamed as the cause of marriage problems and the other children acting up. Breastfeeding is to blame when the mortgage rates go up and the economy is faltering. Whenever something goes wrong, women are often advised to discontinue breastfeeding.

JACK NEWMAN, M.D., F.R.C.P.C. is a pediatrician, a graduate of the University of Toronto medical school. He started the first hospital based breastfeeding clinic in Canada in 1984. He has been a consultant with UNICEF for the Baby-Friendly Hospital Initiative in Africa. Dr. Newman has practiced as a physician in Canada, New Zealand, and South Africa.

Breastfeeding Multiples: One Mother's Experience

▶ *"When we discovered halfway through my third pregnancy that we were expecting twins, it came as quite a shock. My husband and I had mentally prepared ourselves to become a family with three children, not four! Soon after getting the news, I began spending time connecting with other moms who had successfully nursed their multiples so that I could learn from women who had 'been there, done that.' Because I had breastfed my two older children (and actually continued to nurse my then-two-year-old daughter throughout my pregnancy and until she self-weaned when the twins were about four months old), I understood the 'basics' of breastfeeding, but I wanted to find out all I could about the special challenges that might come with nursing twins. I never considered formula-feeding or the possibility of failure. After all, nursing has been such an important part of my mothering experience and I didn't want my new babies to be deprived of its many benefits. My preparation paid off and I am still happily breastfeeding my nine-month old son and daughter. When the babies were eight weeks old, I returned to my part-time consulting position. I was away from home one full day a week and my husband would bring the babies to the office for me to nurse at noon time. I also left pumped milk for them to drink in the afternoon, but Helen and Max never cared much for bottles, so my husband perfected cup feeding rather quickly!*

Here are some of my most useful tips for mothers who will be breastfeeding multiples:

1. If at all possible, have the babies room in with you at the hospital so that you can easily breastfeed on cue and avoid unnecessary bottle use.

Although most hospitals claim to be breastfeeding-friendly, actual support for breastfeeding is dependent upon which staff members happen to be on duty at the moment. I arrived at the hospital with preprepared signs for my babies' bassinets stating that no pacifiers or bottles (water or formula) were to be given without written permission from me or my husband. I caught up on sleep in the late afternoon and was sure to keep the babies with me all night at the hospital in order to respond to their wakings promptly.

2. Purchase a nursing pillow specially designed for nursing twins, and take it to the hospital with you.

I love mine. It's called the 'EZ–2–Nurse.' It is made by a company called Double Blessings at (800) 584–TWIN. The pillow allowed me to nurse both babies at the same time, a crucial survival technique in those early weeks. I am still using the pillow, but of course, now they don't always nurse at the same time, since they have too much fun poking each other in the eye, pulling hair, vaulting over the pillow, etc.

3. When the babies are young, nurse them together as much as possible.

We have a family bed and when one baby would wake at night, I would simply wake the other one as well and then change both, feed both at the same time, and then we would all fall back asleep together. The few nights that I tried only responding only to the single baby who had awakened, I would lose track of who had eaten last. By feeding the babies together, I was able to avoid the hassle of having to keep a chart of which baby had eaten when. I only had to remember to keep an eye on their wet and dirty diaper counts and general health to ensure that all was well.

4. Switch breasts by day, not by feeding.

For example, I would nurse my son, Maxwell, on the left side on odd numbered days and then on even days he would switch places with baby Helen. This allowed both babies to get the mental and visual stimulation of nursing on opposite sides, but avoided the confusion of wondering which baby had nursed on which side on a feeding-by-feeding basis. It also helps to even out any suck problems. Max had a less vigorous suck than Helen, so by alternating days Helen was able to really boost my milk supply, with each breast getting the stimulation of a full day of strong, effective nursing.

5. Line up your nursing support system (La Leche League Leader or IBCLC), *before* your babies are born.

Attend La Leche League meetings, learn as much as you can about breastfeeding, and don't hesitate to ask for help. The more quickly any breastfeeding challenges are addressed, the more satisfying your nursing relationship will be. I had latch on problems with Maxwell, and he was also a sleepy baby. My La Leche League Leader spent about two hours with me one afternoon, teaching me latch on tricks and helping to get started. It was very helpful.

6. Line up household support for yourself.

Educate your partner or family about breastfeeding multiples as you educate yourself. My husband was already incredibly supportive of breastfeeding, but we both had some things to learn about nursing twins. As for help, I was fortunate to have my stepmother, with whom I get along with very well, and my dad came to visit for the first month. They came specifically to help with the house and older children, allowing me to focus on nursing the new babies. I could not have done it without their help. You will need help too!

7. Here is my personal mental health tip for breastfeeding mothers of multiples: try to get out of the house frequently with the babies.

Yes, taking twins out (and breastfeeding them in public) can sometimes make you feel like a sideshow act at first, but you will be amazed at the supportive and admiring comments you will receive. This can do wonders to lift your spirits when you feel overwhelmed or tired.

8. Use a sling with the babies.

Don't be tied into the double stroller trap. Try combining a sling and stroller. This allows additional closeness for mom and baby. And of course be sure to alternate which twin gets to ride in the sling and who goes in the stroller.

And last but not least, try not to become so overwhelmed by the physical aspects of caring for multiples that you forget to relish and treasure the tremendous gift you have been given. Becoming a mother changed my life forever; having twins has just increased the joy and wonderment two-fold."

—*Susan, mother of four, ages seven, three and nine months*

Cue-feeding: Breastfeeding Success, Attachment, and Convenience . . . All Rolled into One

✦ **"If a baby is allowed to nurse whenever he feels inclined, and for as long as he likes, he will ensure exactly the right amount of milk for himself today, when he weighs eight pounds, and in six months' time when he weighs seventeen pounds. Mothers not only do not need to exercise control over their babies' suckling, they ruin the process if they do."**

—*Penelope Leach in* Children First

Earlier in the book, we mentioned that, unlike many other child-care books, we aren't going to tell you precisely when or how much you should feed your baby. After all, we can't tell you what your baby's eating habits might be without knowing him any more than we can ascertain your favorite flavor of ice cream. But there *is* someone who can tell you when you should offer your breast . . . and that someone is your child himself. A healthy infant can be counted on to let you know when he needs to nurse, *as long as you remain in close and attentive contact with him*. There is no need to worry about nursing your healthy infant "too much." You can and should feed him whenever he lets you know that he wants to nurse. Allowing your baby to set the pace for your breastfeeding relationship in this way is sometimes called "feeding on demand." However, the negative connotations of the word "demand" aren't really descriptive of this gentle, responsive, attachment style of feeding. When you think of a "demanding" child (or anyone else, for that matter), you are likely to envision someone who is selfishly and unreasonably asking more of you than you can give. But there is nothing selfish or unreasonable about your baby's need to nurse. Instead, when he becomes hungry, thirsty, tired, frightened, or overstimulated, his desire to seek out the comfort and security of the breastfeeding relationship that you share with him is his natural and involuntary response. In light of this, a better way to describe breastfeeding "by the baby" instead of "by the clock" is "natural feeding," "free-feeding" or, most accuratly, "cue-feeding."

✦ **"Newborns should be nursed whenever they show signs of hunger, such as increased alertness or activity, mouthing, or rooting. Crying is a late indicator of hunger."**

—*The American Academy of Pediatrics*

As long as your baby is nursing a minimum of eight times every twenty-four hours and is growing and thriving, you can safely allow *her* to decide when and how much she nurses (babies who nurse too infrequently or who aren't thriving may need you to encourage them to eat more often and for longer stretches). At times, your baby may want to nurse every hour. Other days she may go three or more hours at a stretch. Sometimes she may need to suck for only a moment after bumping her head while learning to crawl, and other times she may want a thirty-minute feast. By remaining physically close to your baby and open to her individual cues, you are able to actually "intuit" her varied and changing nursing needs. Instead of worrying about when you "should" feed your baby, you will be able to truly *know* when to take her to your breast. As long as you are sure (using the guidelines on page 133) that your baby is getting enough milk, you do not need to worry about nursing her "too often" or "too much." Because our culture is obsessed with exerting maximum control over every aspect of babies' lives, you may worry (or be told by others) that, by offering the breast whenever the baby asks, you can "overfeed" or even "spoil" her. You can't. A baby's desire to nurse is healthy and fundamental: *it is a need, not a habit.* Every mother-nursling pair develops their own individual nursing language through which they communicate and negotiate with one another. Some common "I want to nurse" signals that your infant might send you include:

- "Rooting," in which your baby turns her head from side to side, looking for your breast (she may do this even when other people hold her)
- Sucking on fingers and hands
- Rubbing or twirling hair
- Blinking or looking around
- Increased alertness
- Fussing and whimpering
- Crying (usually after her other cues weren't "heard")

Each baby's nursing cues are slightly different and it won't take long before you can tell that your baby wants to nurse well before anyone else notices her signals. The close and sensitive physical attachment that you share with her and the biological bond of breastfeeding itself allow you to sense her needs, usually before she makes a peep. In one interesting phenomenon, many nursing mothers report that they actually wake up seconds *before* their nursling begins to stir for a night feeding.

> ► *"One day during the first week home from the hospital with my son, he was fussing and my mother—who has never breastfed a baby—was trying everything to soothe him: rocking him, patting him, singing to him, and offering*

him a pacifier that he kept spitting back out at her. All the while, he was madly rooting around and sucking his little hands. And my breasts were literally spraying milk! I kept saying to her, 'I think he wants to nurse.' and she kept saying, 'He can't be hungry, he just ate an hour ago!' I believed her because I thought that she must know more about this motherhood business than I! Soon I realized that I could trust my baby, body, and instincts to tell me when to nurse him. Even now my mother shakes her head at how often he nurses, but she loves to tell people proudly that he's still nursing at twenty months and that he has never been sick."

—*CAROLINE, MOTHER OF A ONE YEAR OLD*

► *"Before I had Caleb I kept reading and hearing that he would have many different cries—one for hunger, one for being tired and so on. It wasn't long before I figured out that ninety-nine percent of the time, he just wanted to nurse. He nurses when he's hungry, thirsty, tired or just upset. When I offer my breast, he's happy. It's great. I love knowing that I have just what he wants and needs. All my friends who are breastfeeding say the same thing. It's clear that this is what babies are supposed to do much of the time in the first year or two."*

—*JACLYN, MOTHER OF AN EIGHTEEN MONTH OLD*

The many benefits of cue-feeding your baby include:

• **Breastfeeding success.** As you already know, frequent and effective nursing sessions are the most important element of successful lactation. If you follow your baby's lead and nurse him whenever he signals his need, you can count on your baby to work with you to ensure an abundant milk supply.

• **Healthier babies.** Cue-fed babies eat frequently and for exactly the amount of time they need. This highly individualized feeding "schedule" is just right for your baby. It ensures the proper calories and nutrients for his optimal growth and development. When your baby feels ill, he will nurse more frequently for comfort, thus exposing himself to the customized infection fighting properties of your milk and allowing him to get well more quickly. Your baby knows what his little body needs to grow and thrive.

• **Confident mothers.** Discovering that you are able to understand and anticipate your baby's feeding needs better than anyone else (including some stranger who has devised an "infant management system" and written a book about it) is a real confidence booster for new moms. With cue-feeding, mothers only have to look at their thriving baby each time he nurses to know that they are doing a great job. Denying babies what they really want and forcing them to wait until the next "scheduled" feeding often leads to unhappy (or even depressed) babies and a mother who can't figure out why her baby is so lethargic, fussy, frantic, or "colicky."

• **Delayed return of your menstrual period.** Women who cue-feed their babies have been shown to remain period-free for a greater number of months after birth. This is because increased breastfeeding frequency delays the return of fertility. In one study, the average length of time during which cue-feeding mothers went without menstruation was thirteen months as compared to eight months for women who were breastfeeding on a schedule. Some attachment parenting mothers find that they go as long as two years or even longer without menstruating as a result of their nursing style.

• **Convenience.** Cue-feeding frees parents from the cumbersome burden of trying to follow a schedule made up by someone who isn't familiar with you, your baby, or your lifestyle. Wherever you are and whatever you're doing, you can nurse your baby and keep her content and well-fed. There is no need to schedule appointments, outings, or even a date with your partner around a set feeding time. Your family's comings and goings don't become enslaved to the baby's feedings.

• **Ability to take your baby anywhere, anytime.** Because you know you can soothe your baby with the breast, you can take him just about anyplace. Young babies can go to movies and nurse quietly through the show; toddlers can go out to dinner and you can nurse them to sleep in your lap—even if you stay out late. An impromptu stopover at the park is no problem when you know your baby's favorite snack is readily at hand.

• **Sets the stage for your child's healthy relationship with his own body.** A child who is cue-fed learns that he can trust his hunger signals. He isn't left hungry because it isn't "time to eat" yet or alternately, offered food and pushed to eat when he doesn't feel the need. Cue-feeding encourages him to feel confident in his ability to know what nourishment his body needs at any given time.

• **Builds your child's self-esteem.** Your responsive attention to your child's signals that he wants to nurse teaches him that he has the power to make good things happen for himself.

• **Teaches your child that he can trust you.** A baby who learns that his mother can be counted on to give him what he needs when he needs it is better able to develop a foundation of trust and attachment with others in his life.

The Problem with Parent-Directed Schedule-Feeding

> ✦**". . . the best feeding schedules for babies are the ones babies design themselves . . . Scheduled feedings designed by parents may put babies at risk for poor weight gain and dehydration."**
>
> —The American Academy of Pediatrics in a 1998 Media Alert regarding Parent Directed Schedule Feeding

> ✦**"The evidence is very strong that arbitrary (defined as set by external influences, such as averages)**

scheduling of breastfed infant feedings is inadvisable for any mother who desires to breastfeed successfully, most especially for the recommended longer periods of up to a year or more . . . Empirical and theoretical evidence combined continue to support current recommendations of the American Academy of Pediatrics that babies, most especially breastfed babies, need to be fed on cue and should be allowed to set their own routine, rather than placed into a predetermined schedule. It is our further conclusion that practices which interfere with respecting babies' cuings have been responsible for low weight gains, failure to thrive, milk supply failure, involuntary early weaning, and possibly even some cases of colic, not to mention infant regression and depression due to lack of parental responsiveness to baby's frantic cues."

—*FROM*, EXAMINING THE EVIDENCE FOR CUE-FEEDING OF BREASTFED INFANTS *BY LISA MARASCO, BA, IBCLC* AND *JAN BARGER, MA, R.N., IBCLC*

Our mothers and grandmothers who, for the most part, bottle-fed us, considered a baby who ate only every four hours a "good" baby. Even today, many parents believe that there is something inherently desirable about a feeding schedule with ever-lengthening intervals between feedings, especially at night. Certainly a rigid schedule like this can be convenient for adults practicing a detached parenting style. It requires a bare minimum of touching and little attention to a baby's cues. After all, there's no need to tune in to your baby's signals when you have already decided when he will and will not be permitted to eat. Today's parents aren't usually advised to wait as long as four hours between feedings. Instead they are generally instructed to expect and even *require* their babies to go "two to four hours" (two or three hours in the newborn period and four hours after a few months).

It's true that artificially fed babies usually won't want to eat as frequently as their breastfed counterparts, because infant formulas are much less digestible than breastmilk and tend to sit in the stomach for longer periods. But, as we have already discussed, normal human infants have a physiological need to eat frequently. Breastfed babies who are allowed to direct their own feedings will rarely go more than a couple of hours during the day without nursing (actually, few adults routinely go several hours at a stretch without a drink or a snack), although every baby is different. A particular baby may change his nursing habits from day to day, eating every hour during growth spurts or teething spells, and going much longer as he becomes engrossed in a new-found motor skill. Parent-directed schedule-feeding—in which a baby is fed only at set intervals—doesn't allow for this healthy variation in an infant's day-to-day needs and development.

Schedule-fed infants who become hungry between feedings will generally adopt one of two dispositions. Some will become very fussy and cranky out of hunger and the frustration that no one seems to be listening to their cues. They can't understand why no one will feed them even though they feel hungry or need to comfort-nurse. These are the babies whose mothers—in an attempt to make them happy without offering the breast or bottle—will jiggle them, rock them, walk them, sing to them and sometimes, become annoyed with them. A mother who believes that her baby shouldn't eat—or shouldn't *want* to eat—more often than every few hours may feel at a loss when he cries and fusses between scheduled feeding times. She may dejectedly decide that *she* is doing something "wrong" or that he has gas or "colic." Often she believes that she has no alternative other than to simply let him cry. In fact, some babycare advisors even tell parents that crying between scheduled feedings is simply a normal part of baby behavior, instead of a possible (and likely) nursing cue. It can be terribly difficult on a parent who can't figure out what is causing her baby's distress because she is under the mistaken impression that she shouldn't offer to nurse him. On the other hand, many schedule-fed babies simply give up and do eventually adapt to long stretches between feedings. Because they have learned that no one listens to them when they announce—in the only ways they know how—that they need to nurse, they stop saying anything at all. These babies are said to be "good" and are often held up as proof of the benefits of scheduling.

But what about a "flexible schedule" for feeding a baby? Certainly a healthy cue-fed baby will eventually fall into his own routine. Many factors—including the pace of a particular family's days, a mother's need to be separated from her child for work or school, and a baby's personal activity level—all play a role in determining a baby's routine. Attached parents and attuned substitute caregivers will soon become comfortable in their familiarity with their baby's nursing routine. However, with the rapid physical and cognitive development that occurs in the first few years of life, a child's nursing needs can vary tremendously from day to day and month to month. For this reason, trying to force a baby to adapt perhaps the most important activity in his early life—nursing—to a predetermined schedule, is a real lose-lose proposition for baby and parents.

The Difference Between Breastfeeding and *Nursing* Your Child

✦"I don't think breastfeeding is 'just' about feeding the baby, any more than sex is 'just' about creating babies. As long as breastfeeding is seen as simply a way to feed the baby, then bottle-feeding will be seen as equivalent or 'good enough.' We need to really try to get away from this idea that if the sucking is 'non nutritive' then it is optional, or can be replaced by a pacifier. Unfortunately, this is the way many people feel—that baby shouldn't want to nurse again. How

could it possibly be hungry already? Well, maybe this time it wants to nurse because it is cold or lonely or agitated or sleepy or cranky. All of these are equally legitimate needs. We really need to start teaching people that breastfeeding is a multi-factorial, complex interaction between two people that has ramifications for the child's nutritional status, to be sure, but also its ability to deal with disease, its physiology and its emotional and cognitive development."

—Katherine Dettwyler, Ph.D.,
Associate Professor of Anthropology and Nutrition at Texas A&M University

✦**"It is a natural, appropriate and desirable part of development for a baby to be dependent. A baby needs to have needs. A baby who is forced into independence (to become a self-soother) before his time misses the needs stage. A baby first needs to bond to people before things. If a baby can't have needs, who can? If the parents can't fill those needs, who will? Later in life you may be very distressed to see who or what will be used to fill needs that went unmet during infancy."**

—Dr. William and Martha Sears

"Breastfeeding" directly refers to the transfer of nutrition and calories from you to your baby. *Nursing*, on the other hand, describes a style of parenting through breastfeeding. It encompasses the wide variety of ways that breastfeeding satisfies your baby and solidifies your relationship with him. Children nurse for many reasons besides hunger, all of which are perfectly legitimate and deserving of respect. You can enjoy and appreciate the fact that—in addition to feeding your baby with your breasts—you are able to calm, soothe, relax, and demonstrate your love for him as well.

Warm, delicious breastmilk is nature's perfect soporific. You will likely find that for many, many months after birth, you are able to easily mother your baby to sleep by simply nursing him in your arms, baby sling, or bed. Nothing could be easier! Enjoy this while you can because the day will come all too quickly when your active toddler or preschooler will probably require more complicated parenting in order to settle in for the night.

Sometimes mothers are told that they shouldn't let their babies "use them as a pacifier" by nursing for reasons other than immediate physical hunger. This is a very misguided piece of advice. Infants and young children have a physical and psychological *need* to suck for comfort. That being the case, to whom would you rather have your baby develop his first attachment and turn for comfort: you or a piece of latex and plastic? Don't be afraid to nurse your baby when he needs you, whatever the reason.

Breastfeeding in Public

> ► *"With my first baby, my discomfort with breastfeeding in public caused me to wean him to the bottle. I was determined not to allow this to happen with my second baby, so I invested in some nursing clothes and spent a lot of time around other nursing mothers. Now that my daughter is a nineteen month old nursling I feel quite comfortable feeding her anywhere. In fact, I never even give it a second thought!"*
>
> —SARAH, MOTHER OF TWO

In many cultures all over the world, women and their breastfeeding babies are a common sight. You might see them in the park, on the bus, in worship services, or at the grocery store. This includes societies in which women are kept "covered up" in general.

In the United States and many other western nations, however, breastfeeding mothers are quite an *uncommon* sight. Many of today's new parents have literally never seen a woman nursing her baby—especially not up close—before the momentous day when they first find themselves outside the house with their own hungry breastfed baby. Surveys have revealed that far too many women are uncomfortable at the thought of nursing their baby in public and that this discomfort is a common cause for disruption of the breastfeeding relationship. We would like to strongly encourage you to relax and feel comfortable feeding your baby wherever you happen to be. Breastfeeding mothers shouldn't feel that they must retire to a separate room, their car, or the bathroom to feed their babies. *It is your right to nurse your baby in any setting where a bottle-feeding mother would feel welcome and comfortable meeting her child's needs.* Many people are under the impression that breastfeeding in public is considered "indecent exposure" under the law. But according to Florida attorney Elizabeth Baldwin, the nation's foremost authority on breastfeeding and the law, this is not the case:

"In the United States, breastfeeding legislation has been enacted in over one-third of the states over the past four years, and many more states have pending bills. The legislation typically clarifies the fact that breastfeeding is not indecent exposure, and thus not criminal behavior. Many states have clearly set forth that a woman has a right to breastfeed any place she has the right to be. Some of the laws provide mothers with legal recourse if they are prevented from breastfeeding. For instance, New York's law protects the right to breastfeed in public as a mother's civil right! Why is breastfeeding legislation necessary? Legislation is not being enacted because it is currently illegal to breastfeed in public, but because it is the public perception that breastfeeding is indecent exposure. The laws generally clarify that it is not illegal, and emphasize the importance of encouraging this preferred method of infant feeding. Mothers have the right to breastfeed in public, with or without legislation."

Here are some points to remember about feeding your baby when you are away from home:

• **The right clothes will make it easy to breastfeed.** As we discussed previously, attachment parenting mamas will want to be able to easily meet their child's need to nurse wherever they might be. For this reason, when you go out you'll want to wear clothes that allow comfortable, discreet access to your breasts. Many a new and inexperienced breastfeeding mother has found herself out with her new baby for the first time in clothes that require her to literally undress to nurse! You should choose clothes (and the options are numerous) that will facilitate breastfeeding when you and your child go out.

• **Most people find the sight of a mother and her nursling very beautiful.** Although you may worry that people will be made uncomfortable when you feed your child in their presence, the opposite is often true. You will be surprised by the many friendly smiles and approving nods you will get from those you encounter when you sit down to feed your baby at the mall, a restaurant, or in the park.

• **Breastfeeding "in public" is a misnomer.** When your baby is properly latched on and you are wearing clothes with good nursing access, less of your chest will show than if you were in a tank top or a bathing suit. Way less. There really isn't anything "public" about nursing away from home. It's a quiet, private interaction between you and your child.

• **Your confidence in feeding your baby encourages other mothers.** Every time you nurse your baby outside your home, you have made a positive impression for breastfeeding. Young girls will learn about their breasts' biological function, and other women will see that they too can feed their babies wherever they happen to be. If you hide in the bathroom or behind a shawl or "nursing cape," the message you are sending is that there is something "secret" or even "unclean" about what you are doing.

• **A baby sling makes it easy to feed your nursling anywhere.** Once you get the hang of it, carrying your breastfed baby in a sling-style baby carrier while wearing a top with nursing access will allow you to walk, sit, eat, and converse while your baby is happily latched on—all without anyone having a clue that you are nursing. Slings provide hands-free and totally discreet nursing away from home.

To be sure, there may be times when you simply *choose* to nurse your baby in a quiet, out of the way spot—not because you are hiding what you are doing, but because you or your baby want a little peace and few distractions. Of course you should nurse wherever you are most comfortable. Just remember that you don't *have* to hide yourself from view in order to mother your baby at the breast.

The Breastfeeding Father

Breastfeeding involves an intimate interaction between a mother and her baby, but this doesn't mean that fathers must be left out. Unfortunately, a great many men have been encouraged to believe that the *only* way they can participate fully in the care of their baby is to give him a bottle. Not surprisingly, one of the biggest promoters of this fallacy is the infant formula industry. In fact, if you take a look at informational booklets and advertisements put out by the formula companies, you will notice many pictures of men bottle-feeding babies, accompanied by commentary strongly suggesting that exclusively breastfeeding mothers will *completely* miss out on the enthusiastic help and participation of their partners.

In deciding whether your breastfed baby will receive "relief bottles" from his father, it is important to undertake a risk-benefit analysis. If you have read this far, you are now well aware of the significant health risks that your baby faces from *unnecessary* formula use. Obviously, there will be some babies and some situations for which the benefit of formula-feeding outweighs the risk. But if breastfeeding is going well for you and your baby, and you aren't required to be separated from him at feeding times, or can provide pumped milk when you are, why expose him unnecessarily to the potential hazards of artificial feeding simply so that your partner can offer a bottle? And even if what your partner will be offering is in fact your own pumped milk, excessive or ill-timed bottle use can cause nipple confusion in a breastfed baby, not to mention supply problems in a nursing mother. Unless your husband (or anyone else, such as a grandparent or sibling) has a true *need* to replace your breast with a bottle (due, for example, to your work schedule), it is best to avoid bottle use in your breastfed baby. There are scores of ways that the father in a breastfeeding family can do his share, support his baby's mother as she gives their child the very best in nutrition and good health, and bond and interact with his little one as well.

- *"I kept my wife well-fed and the house cleaner in the first year so that she could concentrate on the job she did best: feeding the baby."*

—TIM, FATHER OF TWO

- *"I handle all diaper changes, solid food feedings and baths. All of them. In fact, I get sort of huffy if she tries to invade my turf!"*

—MICHAEL, FATHER OF A TEN MONTH OLD

- *"When I see another father giving a bottle, it looks totally strange to me. I just no longer think of that as the way babies get their food."*

—DEAN, FATHER OF A TWO YEAR OLD

- *"My daughter so obviously loves to nurse. She smiles and pats and massages Linda's breast. Why would I want to interfere with that relationship just so I can stick a piece of plastic and rubber in her little mouth?"*

—BLAKE, *FATHER OF A SIX MONTH OLD*

► *"I get so sick of bottle-feeding parents assuming that I am not as involved in my baby's care simply because I don't give a bottle. First of all, we made the decision that James would be breastfed based on reading all the literature together. Only my wife can actually breastfeed him, but we made the decision together. I was as big a part of the feeding choice as she was and frankly, after learning about the differences between breastfeeding and formula-feeding, I can't imagine anyone making another choice. Secondly, I am as hands-on with James as she is. We all sleep together, with him between us. I change him, bathe him, feed him his baby food, play with him, read to him, rock him, and take him walking in the backpack. It's true that only she can nurse him but I never forget that only I can be a father to him."*

—DANNY, *FATHER OF A THIRTEEN MONTH OLD*

Nursing Your Bottle-Fed Baby

✦**"It can be argued that bottle-fed babies should be exempt from the need for cue-feeding, but even though the composition and availability of their milk is relatively stable and without the immunity factors of human milk, they, too, may benefit from being allowed to eat when hungry, rather than being forced to take in possibly larger amounts on less frequent intervals in order to meet their daily caloric needs, stretching their stomachs unnecessarily in the process."**

—*FROM* EXAMINING THE EVIDENCE FOR CUE-FEEDING OF BREASTFED INFANTS, *BY* LISA MARASCO, *BA, IBCLC* AND JAN BARGER, *MA, R.N., IBCLC*

Although we intend to have made a powerful and convincing case in favor of breastfeeding over bottle-feeding, we now want to turn our attention to those readers who are—for one reason or another—already bottle-feeding their babies. Perhaps you have picked up this book after having already weaned your baby to a bottle. Or maybe you are an adoptive parent* or you are among the small percentage of women who are truly unable to breastfeed. Whatever your personal circumstances, we want to offer you some supportive and concrete information on minimizing the artificiality of bottle-feeding and developing the most positive, attachment promoting feeding relationship with your baby possible:

- **Bottle-feed like a breastfeeding mother.** When feeding your baby from the bottle, you should attempt to replicate the breastfeeding relationship as closely as possible. Although it may be tempting to routinely hand bottle-feeding duties off to Dad, Grandma or siblings, you should remember that nature designed *mothers* to feed their babies, not a rotating band of friendly helpers. Human infants need the one-to-one interaction of a feeding *relationship* with a primary caregiver. Decide early on who the

---

*Many adoptive attachment parents are able to nurture their babies at the breast. There is a rapidly growing amount of good information available for adoptive mothers who wish to induce lactation (which occurs when a women who has not recently been pregnant works to successfully produce breastmilk for her baby) so that they can provide some or all of their baby's nutritional needs, but perhaps more importantly, also experience the nursing relationship and its important attachment-promoting benefits with their child. Here are some of the best resources on this topic:

BOOKS

Breastfeeding the Adopted Baby. Peterson, Debra.
San Antonio, TX: Corona Publishing 1995.

WEB SITES

The Adoptive Breastfeeding Resource Web site
http://www. fourfriends.com/abrw/

The Adoption and Breastfeeding Message Board at ParentsPlace
http://rainforest.parentsplace.com/dialog/get/adoptionandnursing/5.html

primary bottle-feeder for your baby will be and, as much as possible, have that person consistently share feeding times with your baby.

• **"Nurse" your bottle-fed baby.** Remember when we described the difference between breastfeeding and nursing? Well, there is also a difference between bottle-feeding your baby and nursing your bottle-fed baby. Do not think of feeding times as simply a transfer of calories and nutrition from the bottle to your baby. Instead, think of each feeding time as an opportunity to actively parent and show your love for your baby.

• **Continue to feed your baby even after she can hold her own bottle.** Many bottle-fed babies are able to feed themselves after only five or six months. This is much too early for a baby to stop receiving generous daily doses of nursing time from a parent. Although it may seem like an admirable developmental milestone when your baby is able to hold her own bottle, remember that a six month old can also stuff sand in her mouth at the beach, but that doesn't mean it's a good idea! Continue to hold your baby in a nursing position and offer the bottle yourself for at least the first year. (Needless to say, you should *never* "prop" a baby's bottle. Not only is this a very detached parenting practice, it can allow your infant to gag and choke.)

• **Try some skin-to-skin bottle-nursing.** Breastfed babies and their mamas can't help but get large doses of skin-to-skin contact while nursing. This tactile interaction is important to both parent and child as a conduit to attachment. The sensual pleasure of this loving touch is something that bottle-feeding pairs shouldn't miss out on. Whenever you can, hold your baby against your bare chest while offering the bottle.

• **Switch sides.** Offer your baby her bottle from both sides of your body, just as if you were breastfeeding.

• **Warm the bottle.** Breastfed babies get warm milk; so should bottle-fed babies.

• **Don't schedule your bottle-fed baby too rigidly.** It *is* possible to overfeed an artificially fed infant. Because a formula-fed baby can't consume more and more of his food source whenever he feels like sucking (as a breastfed baby can), you will probably only offer a bottle of formula every two to four hours, as per your baby's doctor's instructions. But try to be open to your baby's individual cues in determining how long to go between formula feedings, and allow him to set the pace as much as possible.

• **Respect your bottle-fed baby's need to suck.** Your baby doesn't label himself "bottle-fed" or "breastfed"; he just knows that he's a human baby with a normal need to suck for comfort. Since you cannot offer a bottle full of formula every time your baby is fussy, tired, tense, or over stimulated, you need to offer him something else to fill his very intense and healthy need to comfort-nurse. This is where a pacifier can be a very useful and beneficial helper to a bottle-feeding attachment parent. There is no reason not to give thriving bottle-fed babies a pacifier whenever they want it. You might also try a freshly washed parental pinky to fill this sucking need, or encourage your baby to find his own hands and fingers.

• **Allow your bottle-fed baby to have a say in weaning.** There is no set age after which a child should no longer be allowed to have a bottle or pacifier. Every child's sucking needs are different and deserving of respect. Many two and three year old children—or even older—still enjoy and are comforted by sucking their bottle or pacifier. Be wary of giving too much juice or milk in bottles, as this can rot baby teeth. Instead you might eventually make the transition to bottles of water after your child is off formula, eating solids, and drinking from a cup. Don't let others attempt to shame you or your child regarding bottle or pacifier use past the first year. Your child will outgrow his need to suck when he is ready.

• **Consider using a Supplemental Nutrition System**

(SNS) for some or all feedings. An SNS is a type of "feeding necklace" in which very tiny tubes connected to a hanging pouch of formula or breastmilk are taped to your breasts. The baby suckles at your breast—just like the baby of a lactating mother—in order to get the food from the tubes. Used by women attempting to build their milk supply (the suckling stimulates their milk production) or induce lactation from scratch, the SNS can offer a bottle-feeding mother the opportunity to nurse her baby for some or all feedings. You can get an SNS and instructions for how to use it from a certified lactation consultant or La Leche League Leader.

CHAPTER 6

Attachment Parenting All Through the Night

✦ **". . . nighttime parent-infant co-sleeping during at least the first year of life is the universal, species wide normative context for infant sleep, to which both parents and infants are biologically and psychosocially adapted . . . Solitary infant sleep is an exceedingly recent, novel, and alien experience for the human infant."**

—*Dr. James McKenna, Professor of Anthropology and the Director of the Center for Behavioral Studies of Mother-Infant Sleep, Notre Dame University*

▶ *"My only experience with babies had been what I saw on TV. You know, where the mother puts the still-awake baby down in her crib and tiptoes out of the room to allow the baby to fall asleep on her own? Well, this is what I expected my own child to do and I was completely frustrated when she wouldn't stay in her crib. When Sasha became old enough to crawl, I was forced to buy a special net to put over the top of the crib so that my anxious baby wouldn't climb out and hurt herself. One night, after I had gotten up about four times to put Sasha back in her crib, I was crying, she was crying, and it suddenly occurred to me that I had been trying to get my baby to sleep in a cage! It even looked like a cage with the net on top and the bars. I took her out and brought her into bed with us. The very next night, after she fell asleep nursing in our bed, she slept seven hours straight! I couldn't believe it!"*

—*MARSHA, MOTHER OF A THREE YEAR OLD*

Desperately Seeking Sleep . . . and Finding It Right in Your Own Bed

Today's new parents are tired. In fact, if you talk to mothers and fathers—at the playground or pediatrician's office—that may be the first thing they tell you. Parents are so tired that an entire cottage industry has sprung up around the issue. New books are released each year promising to teach parents how to get their babies and young children to sleep. Expensive mechanical devices that hum, thump, vibrate, and rock are sold by the thousands to parents seeking a sleepy baby. Television programs and movies wrap entire plots around the sleeplessness of new parenthood. Convinced that everyone else's baby is sleeping soundly all night long, desperate parents resort to harsh "cry it out" sleep training techniques to solve what some book has advised them is a true "sleep disorder" in their eight month old. In fact, most parents are willing to try just about anything to get a good night's sleep—anything, that is, except the attachment parenting solution that is staring them right in the face: bringing their babies and young children into their own bed.

For decades, the foremost rule of family sleep, as promulgated by mainstream American parenting experts, has been that infants and children should *never* be allowed to sleep with their parents. This, we've been told, will lead to poor sleep habits, unhealthy dependencies, ruined marriages, and even infant suffocation. Anxious new mothers inching through grocery store checkout aisles are accosted by glossy magazines touting articles such as "Teach Your Baby to Love Her Crib" and "The Hidden Dangers of Sleeping with Your Child." The message is clear: a conscientious parent shouldn't allow her baby or young child into her bed.

▶ *"On the first night after my daughter's birth, I rested soundly with her nestled beside me in my narrow hospital bunk. Until I was awakened by the nurse on the overnight shift; she waved a clipboard in my face and insisted I sign a release stating that, if I persisted in bringing my baby into bed with me, I understood I was putting my daughter's life at risk. I groggily signed the form and went back to sleep."*

—Katie, mother of three

In spite of such (ridiculous) warnings and widespread approbation of the "family bed," as sleep sharing is often called, a growing number of parents are challenging conventional wisdom each and every night—with support from a new wave of experts. Emerging research, anthropological studies, and anecdotal evidence have demonstrated the many benefits of parents sleeping with or very near their little ones. As you will learn, family sleep sharing can actually provide a safer, sounder sleep for everyone in the household. While some parents inadvertently fall into the practice after allowing their kids into their bed and discovering better sleep as the result, others make an informed decision to create a family bed after careful consideration of this warm, attachment promoting, safe, and *restful* nighttime arrangement.

How Humans Sleep

> ✦ **"Co-sleeping has always had survival value, both physical and psychological. In the past, if a mother and infant shared a bed . . . the baby was better protected from predators, and both stayed warm . . . After millennia of co-sleeping, how do we tell our nervous system and our baby's just to 'relax' when sleeping alone? We can't."**
>
> —*SHARON HELLER, PH.D.*

American society's deviance from the still widespread human practice of sleeping with one's young is a relatively recent development. For millennia, family co-sleeping was the way *all* human beings spent their nights. Only 150 years or so ago in the United States, it was still generally assumed that young children would sleep with their parents or other relatives. Most families could not afford separate sleep quarters for everyone in the household. Additionally, sharing sleep was a reliable way to make sure that the youngest family members stayed safe and warm. Today's emphasis on materialism, however, leads many to equate bed sharing with poverty. A prosperous, modern family, so the theory goes, shouldn't need to engage in this "third-world parenting practice"(an actual term taken from one of today's best-selling childcare guides!).

It is true that in many, if not most developing nations around the globe, family sleep sharing remains the norm. However, this isn't all a matter of economics. To mothers and fathers in many other cultures, the idea of leaving a vulnerable baby or young child all alone during the night seems downright neglectful, if not cruel—sort of like if we left our napping baby to go out to the mall for a few hours. When anthropologists explain to Central American Indian mothers, for example, that in the United States, babies are left to sleep alone in a bed with bars—usually in another room—these women are appalled. They can't imagine how a conscientious mother could do such a thing! But family sleep sharing certainly isn't limited to the developing world. In one sample of 136 different societies all over the earth, parents shared a bed with their babies in two-thirds of them. In the remaining one-third, babies slept very near their parents in the same room. In Japan, one of the world's most bustling, modern, productive societies, children often sleep with their parents until late childhood.

As a rule, human beings do not like to sleep alone. Baby, child or adult—most of us are strongly attracted to the idea of spending our nights cuddled up next to someone we love. Across cultures and centuries, this has always been the case. Yet today's American parents have somehow been led to believe that our own babies and young children are different from all other human beings. We have mistakenly bought into the bizarre idea that the smallest, weakest, neediest members of our families "should learn to sleep by themselves." As we struggle to force our babies into a solitary sleeping arrangement that runs counter to their very human nature, is it any wonder that American parents describe themselves as sleep deprived and exhausted, and that "sleep problems" are rampant among American children?

The Many Benefits of Family Sleep Sharing

► *"With my first baby, I had him in a crib down the hall and because I wasn't willing to let him cry, I remember being up every few hours during the night to feed him and settle him. Clearly he just wanted human contact, but I was trying to follow the rules and be a 'good mother,' so I never considered bringing him to bed with us. By the time my second baby was born, I had read some stuff about sleeping with your baby, but I still had hang-ups left over from thirty-three years of hearing how terrible sleeping with a baby was, so I would only bring her into our bed as a last resort. It always worked to provide everyone with more and better sleep. With baby number three, we invested in a king sized bed with bedrails and we all get plenty of sleep. I can't believe the difference in my mental state. I have had absolutely none of that wrung out, exhausted, new parent feeling that I had when my first child was a baby. I feel like I've discovered the best kept secret of motherhood and I preach it to every pregnant woman I meet. Sleep with your baby! You'll get more sleep!"*

—*Terri, mother of three*

✦ **"For our species, the natural nighttime arrangement is for kids to sleep alongside their mothers for the first few years. At least, that's the norm in hunter-gatherer societies, the closest things we have to a model of the social environment in which humans evolved. Mothers nurse their children to sleep and then nurse on demand through the night. Sounds taxing, but it's not. When the baby cries, the mother starts nursing reflexively, often without really waking up. If she does reach consciousness, she soon fades back to sleep with the child. And the father, as I can personally attest, never leaves Z-town."**

—*Robert Wright, author of* The Moral Animal: Why We Are the Way We Are: The New Science of Evolutionary Psychology

So, now you know the real story: it's normal and natural for parents and their children to share sleep. But this isn't the only reason why attachment parents are hooked on this nurturing style of nighttime parenting. Here are just a few of the many benefits of the family bed:

• **Babies and children usually sleep better.** Parents who have raised a first child in a nursery with a crib and then another in a family bed report that their family-bedded babies—particularly those who spend their nights beside their parents from the very beginning—just plain sleep better. A primary reason for night wakings is the desire to be close to parents. Many parents who sleep separately from their young children find themselves engaged in a nightly struggle of trying to keep their little ones from migrating into their bed. With a family bed, your child feels your physical warmth as he sleeps next to you. There is no need for him to fully wake out of fear, loneliness, cold, or a sense of "disorganization." Your smell, touch, and body heat, as well as the sound of your breathing, all help to keep him relaxed and quiet. If he does rouse during the night (and everyone—even adults—wakes occasionally during the night for a snack, drink, trip to the bathroom, or from a dream), he will usually quickly resettle. There are some babies who seem to prefer to sleep alone, but they are few and far between.

• **Parents sleep better.** When your baby is in a separate sleep space, you are unlikely to sleep well. In addition to having to actually get out of bed to tend to your baby's needs, an attached parent—particularly a breastfeeding mother—often feels "incomplete" when her baby is sleeping elsewhere. You may worry whether the baby is too cold or too hot, whether you remembered to lock the window, how you would get to him in the event of a fire or storm, whether you have missed hearing his cry, or even whether he is still breathing! Many an anxious new parent has trudged down the hall to the nursery in the middle of the night just to reassure herself that her baby is well. When your baby is nestled nearby in the same room, you are acutely aware of his physical well-being, enabling you to relax and get a good night's sleep.

• **Night feedings are *much* easier.** Breastfeeding while

lying down makes night feedings easy and convenient. With your baby beside you, you simply roll to your side and offer the breast, then drift back to sleep. There is no need to get up, sit up, or even completely wake up! Once you have been doing it a while, it's unlikely you will even be aware of how often or whether you feed your baby during the night.

• **Provides fathers with built-in "snuggle time."** Fathers who work outside the home are frequently away from their babies and young children for most of their waking hours. With a family bed, fathers are able to get plenty of time to drink in the smell, feel, and sounds of their children, all in the most warm, relaxing environment imaginable. This recharges the father-child relationship each and every night.

> ▶ *"I am a full-time working father. If my two young children didn't sleep with us, I would come home around 6:00 or 6:30 pm, eat with my family, and then an hour later the kids would be off to bed and I would spend little if any time with them. In the family bed, I can actively nurture and be with my kids at times other than the weekends. My younger son is still nursing at night. With my wife's attention focused on him, my older son has found a growing amount of security in having my attention, not only for falling asleep, but for night time wakings or other incidences. I am often his primary nighttime parent."*
>
> —EVAN, FATHER OF TWO

> ▶ *"I actually had a demonstrably easier time bonding with our second baby—who slept in our room or in our bed from birth—than I did with our first baby who always slept in his own nursery."*
>
> —JEFF, FATHER OF TWO

• **Teaches babies that nighttime is for sleeping.** If your goal is to raise a child with healthy sleep habits, the best way for him to learn is by observing how other people sleep. You can't model sleep for your baby when he is in a crib in another room. In fact, you can't really expect a young child who has never observed our cultural norms for nighttime routines to know what is expected of him.

• **It's a cozy and pleasant part of family life.** Families who enjoy sharing sleep with their young children can't imagine doing without the attachment promoting benefits of staying close all through the night. The feeling of waking up with the people you love most in the world is a truly special one.

• **Can make up for a hard day.** Every family with babies and young children sometimes has a challenging day. A cranky child and an impatient parent can really benefit from some relaxing physical downtime with each other during the nighttime hours.

The Family Bed: A How-To Manual

Now say you have decided that you would like to adopt a family bed, but you're not sure how to pull it off. The practical solutions for sharing sleep are accessible and numerous:

• **Buy a bigger bed.** Many sleep sharing parents invest in the largest bed available for maximum comfort. Attachment parenting families usually find that upgrading to a king-sized bed with bedrails is a better bargain than a bunch of expensive nursery furniture. If you try family bedding in a too small bed, it's likely that you won't enjoy it.

• **Build a "sidecar."** Securely attach a crib to one side of the parents' bed, next to the mother (for easier breastfeeding). Three sides of the baby's crib are then left intact, but the side next to the parents' bed is lowered or removed, allowing mother and baby to have easy access to one another. Basically, the parents' bed serves as the fourth "side" to the crib. The sidecar set up is a great solution for parents (or the occasional baby) who sleep better with a little more kicking space.

Authors' Note: A new product, the "Arm's Reach Co-Sleeper" (available at http://www.littlekoala.com, among other places) provides a ready-made sidecar to attach to any bed.

• **Take to the floor.** Some larger families or households with older children place futons or mattresses all over the bedroom floor so that everyone has plenty of room to stretch out, creating a "family sleeping room."

> ✦ **"Co-sleeping is often discussed as if it were a discrete, all-or-nothing proposition (i.e., should baby sleep with parents?). Many parents fail to realize that infants sleeping in proximity alongside their bed, or with a caregiver in a rocking chair, . . . in a different room other than a bedroom, or in their caregiver's arms all constitute forms of infant co-sleeping."**
>
> —DR. JAMES MCKENNA

• **Create a "modified" family bed.** When parents feel unsure about a full scale family bed but wish to have their children nearby at night, they have other options. For example, family members can sleep in separate beds in the same bedroom, or an infant's bassinet or crib can remain within arm's length of resting adults. Alternatively, toddlers or older children can sleep on a futon on the floor beside their parents' bed. Another version of the "modified" family bed provides a child with her own bedroom along with free access to the parents' bed at any time. For every household in which the children spend the entire night in the family bed, there is another in which children start their overnight hours in a separate sleep space but are welcomed into the parents' bed after a night waking. The key is to be open to *your* child's individual needs for nighttime nurturing, and to encourage an arrangement that provides the most sleep for the entire family.

• **Make sleep your decorating theme.** For a family bedding arrangement of any kind to work, *sleep* has to be the priority. Don't worry if the way you have your bedroom set up (with several futons on the floor, for example, or with a sidecar attached to your bed) doesn't exactly look like something out of a Martha Stewart decorating book. You have plenty of years ahead of you to worry about matching bedskirts and night tables. For now, let sleep—for your whole family—be the driving force behind your decorating scheme. If one adult has to get up and get dressed for work every morning, you might want to consider relocating his clothes and toiletry items into another room so that he can head out the door without disturbing those who are still asleep.

Safety and the Family Bed

Some pediatricians and others advise new mothers to avoid sleeping with their babies as a protective measure against infant suffocation. However, parents who enjoy a family bed and doctors who advocate its use point out that the same internal signals that prevent you from rolling out of bed and injuring yourself will also prevent an aware parent from rolling on top of her infant. The sad fact is that many cases of nighttime infant suffocation have actually been cases of intentional infanticide. Remember that tonight, families all over the world will sleep safely and soundly with their babies and young children nestled beside them. You can do it too. Here are the important safety tips to remember when creating your own family bed:

• **When using a standard, off-the-floor bed, be absolutely sure that your baby cannot roll or fall off the sides.** This can be accomplished with the use of bed rails, available at any baby store. Bed rails easily attach to your bed's frame and many models even flip down for storage during the day. The safest models are designed from plastic and soft mesh. If you plan to use the wall as one "bed rail" by pushing your bed against it, be absolutely *certain* that the bed is flush against the wall, allowing no space into which a tiny baby could fall. Alternatively, some families pack their bed frame away for a few years and place their box springs and mattress or futon directly on the floor, thus relieving any concern about a baby falling out of a high bed.

• **Young infants should sleep between their mother and the bed rail, not between both parents or beside an older sibling.** Fathers and siblings are usually not as attuned to the movements and breathing of tiny infants. Attached mothers—particularly those who are breastfeeding—are acutely aware of their baby's presence. As your child gets older, you can allow him to sleep between both parents or next to a sibling if he chooses.

• **Make sure that your mattress or futon provides a firm sleeping surface.** Never, ever allow an infant to sleep on a waterbed, featherbed, beanbag, deep pillowtop mattress or other inappropriately soft surface. Of course, this advice holds true for *all* babies, whether you use a family bed or not.

• **Never sleep with your baby if you are under the influence of drugs, alcohol or prescription medication that makes you unusually groggy or sleepy.**

• **Exceptionally obese parents should use a sidecar arrangement rather than having a young infant in the bed with them.**

• **Do not overload your bed with excessive pillows, blankets or stuffed animals.** Again, this advice is important for *any* bed in which your baby sleeps, including a cradle, bassinet, or crib.

• **Never fall asleep on a couch, sofa, or overstuffed chair with your baby.** She could become wedged between the cushions and suffocate.

• **Do not stuff too many bodies into a bed with a small baby.** If you share sleep with more than one child, adequate space is necessary for both comfort *and* safety.

- **Make sure that your baby isn't overdressed.** Remember, the body heat in a family bed makes most bedtime bundling unecessary.
- **Dress your baby in safe sleepwear.** Flame retardant with no strings or ties, just as you would if she were sleeping alone.

Sleeping with Your Baby May Prevent SIDS

✦ **"Judging from the infant's biology and evolutionary history, proximity to parental sounds, smells, gases, heat, and movement during the night is precisely what the human infant's developing system 'expects,' since these stimuli were reliably present throughout the evolution of the infant's sleep physiology. The human infant is born with only twenty-five percent of its adult brain volume, is the least neurologically mature primate at birth, develops the most slowly, and while at birth is prepared to adapt, is not yet adapted. In our enthusiasm to push for infant independence (a recent cultural value), I sometimes think we forget that the infant's biology cannot change quite so quickly as can cultural child care patterns. Infants sleeping for long periods in social isolation from parents constitutes an extremely recent cultural experiment, the biological and psychological consequences of which have never been evaluated."**

—*DR. JAMES MCKENNA*

▶ *"It feels natural and much safer to me to have my baby in our room. I like knowing where he is and what's going on with him."*

—*DANIEL, FATHER OF AN EIGHT MONTH OLD*

In addition to the understanding that a family bed can be perfectly safe for your baby, a growing number of pediatricians, scientists, and lactation specialists are beginning to conclude that sleeping with your baby is actually *safer* than leaving him all alone in a crib at night. In research funded by the National Institutes of Health, Dr. James McKenna, Professor of Anthropology and the Director of the Center for Behavioral Studies of Mother-Infant Sleep at Notre Dame University, has theorized that infants who sleep alone are at an increased risk for Sudden Infant Death Syndrome (SIDS). According to the National SIDS Alliance, one in every 500 American infants, or 7,000 to 8,000 babies a year, die of this still mysterious phenomenon. This number represents a larger proportion of the U.S. infant mortality rate than cancer, heart disease, pneumonia, child abuse, AIDS, cystic fibrosis and muscular dystrophy combined.

McKenna and coresearcher Dr. Sarah Mosko, a psychobiologist and sleep specialist at the University of California Sleep Disorders Laboratory, performed two pilot projects on the physiological influences that sleep sharing mothers and babies exert on one another. McKenna monitored the breathing patterns, heart rates, brain waves, and chin and eye movements of mothers and their infants in various sleeping arrangements, and with infrared cameras, videotaped mothers' and infants' sleeping behavior. Results from these tests showed that mothers and babies who sleep together are extremely attuned to one another even while asleep. Neither partner disturbed the other's rest. Mothers and babies seemed to move simultaneously through the various sleep stages, and yet co-sleeping infants spent less time overall in the deepest state of sleep—the period most dangerous to SIDS-vulnerable infants. In one of the observed pairs, the infant spent eighty-seven percent of her time within twelve inches of her mother's face. This behavior allows co-sleeping babies to inhale some of the parent's expelled breath. According to McKenna, when a parent's expelled carbon dioxide is mixed with oxygen, it induces her infant's stable breathing.

McKenna's studies strongly suggest that American parents heighten the risk of SIDS by expecting their babies to sleep alone and for long stretches at too tender an age. Vulnerable infants, he posits, need to "learn" safe sleeping habits, such as moving through varying sleep states and breathing patterns, or they risk falling into a period of heavy, uninterrupted slumber from which they might not awaken. McKenna's research suggests it may be through sleeping alongside an adult that an infant develops these skills and receives the continuous contact and vestibular stimulation that can protect against SIDS. Additionally, a mother who sleeps with her infant has been shown to be keenly aware of her child's breathing and temperature throughout the night, and is thus able to quickly respond to any significant changes. Two factors that have been conclusively *proven* to lower a baby's risk for SIDS—breastfeeding and the back or side sleeping position—are more common in mother-infant pairs who co-sleep. Breastfed babies who sleep with their mothers are far less likely to end up in the risky face down sleeping position.

Data collected from other countries also supports McKenna's theory. In Hong Kong, Japan, and China, where mothers almost always sleep with their infants, SIDS rates are a fraction of what they are in the United States, which has the highest SIDS rate in the world. SIDS rates also remain low among communities of Asians who immigrate to the United States. However, the number of SIDS deaths rises in direct relation to the amount of time an Asian parent lives in the United States, quite possibly due to the adoption of American style customs, such as bottle-feeding and separate sleeping quarters for mothers and babies.

Questions About the Family Bed

Maybe you are ready to try sleeping with your baby or young child, but you still have a few nagging questions. Or perhaps you're convinced about the benefits of the family bed but your partner isn't so sure. Or possibly you want to respond to the questions that others (like grandparents) may have. Here are some answers to commonly asked questions concerning family sleep sharing:

- **What about our sex life? Isn't the parents' bed supposed to provide private time for parents?** The idea that the parental bed should be the locus of all sexual activity or even emblematic of the sexual relationship between mother and father is a cultural construct. Your baby's need for nighttime nurturing, on the other hand, is a biological necessity. Parents who enjoy a family bed don't stop having sex. Instead, they have sex in other areas of the house. Many couples claim that the act of seeking alternative locations for intimacy adds creativity and spontaneity to their lovemaking. You might also have your child start the night in her own bed or crib and then bring her back into your bed if she awakens later in the night. Lots of sleep sharing families have second, third, or even more children, so clearly the family bed isn't wrecking their sex lives!

> ✦ **"Psychiatrists should not take their children to bed with them. . . . but it is quite alright for everyone else!"**
>
> —*SARCASTIC COMMENT BY WELL-KNOWN PEDIATRICIAN AND AUTHOR, THE LATE ROBERT MENDELSSOHN, WHEN CONFRONTED BY MENTAL HEALTH SPECIALISTS WHO FEARED "SEXUALIZATION" OF THE FAMILY BED*

- **If we allow our baby into our bed, I've heard that she will never want to leave. Is this true?** Nope, it's not true. Although no substantive studies have looked at this issue, long term family bedders find this concern to be totally without merit, and it appears to spring from the same obsession American society has with rushing children through other developmental milestones such as weaning from the breast. Children who sleep with their parents leave the family bed when they are ready: earlier for some children and later for others, just as with many other stages of maturity. As a baby moves out of infancy, some attachment parents decide to promote a gentle transition away from complete co-sleeping by installing a small futon on the floor next to their bed, so that their child can still feel safe and protected at night. Other families ease into the change by having a parent begin the night in her child's bed and then leave for her own bed after he has fallen asleep. Children who remain most comfortable sleeping with another person can share a bed with siblings as they grow. However, it's important not to push children out of the parental "nest" before they are ready. As an attached, attuned parent, you will be able to make the nighttime choices that are right for your family as the years pass and options present themselves.

> ✦ **"(Some critics of the family bed) state that children who sleep in bed with parents will not make the decision to start sleeping in their own bed. Where do these self-described "experts" think all the children who were allowed to sleep in their parents' bed and are now adults are sleeping today? Should babies never be put in a stroller for fear that they may not learn how to walk? Children do, of course, progressively develop the desire to move on and have their own space, including their own sleeping space. Maybe not always on the same schedule as every other child, but on their own schedule, just like they learn to speak, to walk and to control their bodily functions."**
>
> —*Psychiatrist and Neuroscientist*
> *David Servan-Schreiber, M.D., Ph.D.*

• **I am a single parent. Can I still have a family bed with my kids?** Absolutely! There is no reason why single parents and their little ones should miss out on the comfort and security of the family bed. In fact, in many families, coupled parents take turns singly sleeping with their baby or other children in order to best meet everyone's needs. When parents break up, continuing to offer your child the nighttime security of co-sleeping can ease a difficult transition. A word of caution: *do* use good judgment and extreme discretion in deciding how long any new adult partner should be a member of your family's life before allowing him/her to share sleep with your children. Co-sleeping is an intimate part of *family* life and any adult partner should be a true family member in every sense of the word before sharing sleep with your children. This is not something to rush into.

• **What if I just don't enjoy sleeping with my baby?** Before deciding that family bedding definitely isn't working for you, be sure to give it a real chance. Is your bed big enough? A cramped sleep space is one of the primary reasons why some parents aren't able to enjoy sleeping with their little ones. You might also try the sidecar arrangment for maximum space combined with lots of great nighttime closeness. Is your partner pressuring you to get the baby out of the bed? If so, try having a respectful, heart-to-heart talk with him or her, explaining the many benefits of family bedding and reiterating what a short period early childhood is in a parent's life. Compare the amount of sleep you get with the baby snuggled up beside you with the amount you would get having to rouse yourself from the bed to tend to your baby's needs. Do you find that your own hang-ups about sleeping with another person are making it hard for you to relax with your baby in your bed? Try to recognize the root causes for your feelings of discomfort and work through them. Remember that your baby shouldn't be denied having his needs met as a result of your own past experiences. If after careful consideration and a real opportunity to try it out, you decide that sharing sleep with your baby isn't for you, then you can still strive toward maintaining an attached nighttime parenting style without a family bed.

Infant Sleep: What's "Normal"?

In our culture, an inordinate amount of value is placed on getting a child to "sleep through the night" (usually defined as sleeping the exact same amount of time that his particular parents desire to sleep each night) as early as possible. Because mothers and fathers so often sleep apart from their babies and feed them artificial milk from a bottle, the headaches associated with feeding babies at night can indeed be tremendous.

With the attachment style of nighttime parenting, however, the desire to see a baby "sleep through the night" becomes less urgent because: (a) parents have realistic sleep expectations of their babies, (b) parents understand the concept that babies "need to have needs," and don't feel the necessity to rush very young children through developmental stages, and (c) with a family bed and the convenience of breastfeeding, nighttime wakings are generally not a big hassle. This may be hard to believe if you haven't tried it, but it's true! It has been demonstrated that breastfed babies in close physical contact with their mothers at night *do* naturally tend to nurse more frequently than babies sleeping alone (a fact that gives further weight to the evidence that babies are *designed* to eat at night). However, babies who understand that they have only to stir slightly to garner their mother's (almost reflexive) attention during the night won't usually become fully awake, cry, or otherwise seriously disturb anyone's sleep. If your child *does* become overly fretful or fussy during the night, you will know immediately that something—possibly teething or a fever—is bothering him. Dr. William Sears has referred to this sleep communication between attachment parents and their babies as "nighttime harmony." Everyone is comfortable and having their needs met in a way that is respectful of both the parents' desire for sleep and the baby's normal, healthy sleep physiology.

Because every baby is different, it is impossible to predict when yours may begin sleeping on a schedule much like an older child or adult. The rare baby does indeed begin sleeping eight hours at a stretch—without any coercion from parents—before the six month mark (these will be the amazing babies you will be told about *constantly* as you adjust to the demands of early parenthood!), while many others wake one or more times a night well into toddlerhood. *Both* of these variations are normal (although the latter is more common) and anyone who tells you otherwise is preying on your insecurities as a new parent.

It's important to remember that an infant's need for nourishment during the nighttime hours *is not a sleep disorder*. It's an adaptive behavior arising from the fact that babies must grow both their bodies and their brains at a *monumental* rate during the first year or so of life. They don't stop growing—or needing to fuel that growth—between sundown and sun-up. And, of course, babies and toddlers also wake at night for many other equally legitimate reasons: thirst, cold, fear, a wet diaper, dreams, or teething. None of these necessarily constitutes a sleep disorder in need of "corrective measures." Additionally, sleep researchers have determined that infants and young toddlers naturally have shorter sleep cycles than adults do. As your baby moves from REM to nonREM sleep during each of these approximately sixty minute cycles (as compared to ninety minute cycles in an adult), he is vulnerable to waking.

It is important to approach your young child's sleep patterns with realistic expectations. Human infants and very young children simply don't sleep in the same way that adults do; in fact, human beings tend to have different sleep patterns at each life stage (just ask your seventy-five year old grandfather who now finds himself quite wakeful during the overnight hours). It's easy to become frustrated when you mistakenly believe that *your* nine month old is the only one in the city awake for a feeding at three A.M. Don't believe it when people tell you that "all" babies sleep through the night by two months or four months or when they double their birth weight or when they start solids. Remember: *your baby is unique!* What experienced attachment parents will tell you is that you will enjoy your little one much more and find yourself much better rested during the day if you adapt your own nighttime routine to your baby's (for example, by adopting a family bed so that any awakenings are barely noticed) rather than expecting your baby to sleep just like a little adult. Your baby *will* eventually sleep for eight hour stretches. In fact, on those mornings down the road when you practically have to use a bullhorn to jump start your seven year old out of bed each morning, you may actually recall your baby's current wakefulness with fondness!

Sleeping Through the Night: Don't Rush It (Yes, you read that correctly!)

> ✦ **"I strongly feel that an infant's sleep pattern is 'infantile' so that the infant can more easily communicate his survival needs."**
>
> —DR. WILLIAM SEARS

Because getting a baby to sleep on an adult-like schedule as early as possible is so frequently encouraged in new parents and promoted as desirable, too few parents are aware of the pluses of "natural nighttime parenting," which usually includes night feedings at least through the first year. In addition to lowering your baby's risk for SIDS, as we have previously explained, the positives include:

• **Breastfeeding success.** Particularly during the first six months, mother-baby pairs who cut out all night feedings risk compromising their milk supply. Many breastfeeding mothers have been baffled to find their milk drying up "for no good reason" after they listened to misinformed advice and refused to feed their infants during the night.

• **Healthier babies.** Babies have a tremendous amount of growing to do during their first year. Left to their own devices, virtually all healthy cue-breastfed babies will seek at least one feeding during the nighttime hours. During growth spurts—when they need extra calories—or during illness, when babies instinctively seek out their mother's protective antibodies—they may nurse more often than once a night. Clearly, their little bodies *need* this nighttime nurturing to continue to develop brain capacity, gain weight, and thrive. One of the best known remedies for a baby who isn't gaining weight adequately is to tell the mother to take the baby to bed with her and nurse, nurse, nurse!

• **Night nursing significantly delays the return of menstruation and fertility.** Breastfeeding during the night plays an important role in suppressing ovulation in nursing mothers. When breastfeeding is more concentrated during the daytime hours, as opposed to being spread out over a full twenty-four hours, women are much more likely to see the speedy return of their menstrual periods, an aspect of breastfeeding which most women find appealing.

• **Night nursing reduces a new mother's risk of developing engorgement or mastitis.** Particularly during the first six months of a breastfed baby's life, attempting to abruptly cut out night nursings can lead to painful engorgement and even mastitis—a painful breast infection which may require antibiotic treatment. Your lactating breasts need to be drained regularly in order to stay healthy. Any changes in nursing frequency should take place very gradually for maximum maternal comfort. Not coincidentally, your baby will *gradually* begin sleeping longer and longer stretches without any special efforts on your part, following her natural sleep pattern as a growing human.

• **Night feedings are a special time.** Late at night, as you tenderly rock your nursling in your arms or cradle him beside you in your bed, you will experience some truly memorable moments. With a hushed household around you and moonlight streaming in the window, it can feel that the two of you are the only people awake on earth. Most mothers have very warm memories of this quiet nighttime nurturing.

• **Nighttime feedings can help working mothers with breastfeeding.** Mothers who are separated from their nurslings during the daytime hours often find nighttime feedings to be an important element of breastfeeding success. Although pumping while on the job or at school is essential to keeping supply up, nighttime feedings give your baby a chance for skin-to-skin nursing, thus stimulating the hormonal support for breastfeeding and keeping your baby "in practice" so that he is less likely to begin to prefer a bottle to you.

Nighttime Parenting

> ✦ **"People have the unreasonable expectation that they should be able to essentially turn their children off at seven or eight p.m. and not have to deal with them until the next morning."**
>
> —*Anthropologist Katherine Dettwyler*

> ✦ **"When the researcher explained to the Mayan mothers how babies were put to bed in the United States, the Mayan mothers were shocked and highly disapproving, and expressed pity for the American babies who had to sleep alone. They saw their own**

> **sleep arrangments as part of a larger commitment to their children . . . closeness at night between mother and baby was seen as part of what all parents do for their children."**
>
> —ANTHROPOLOGIST MEREDITH F. SMALL

Sometimes—even if you have a family bed and use cue-breastfeeding, and *definitely* if you don't—parenting your child at night can be . . . well . . . tiring. In the first few months after your baby is born, when you are physically recovering from childbirth and your baby is probably sleeping in shorter stretches (and frequently only in your arms) than he ever will again—as is normal for a newborn—you may find yourself to be *very* tired. Later on, toddlers and preschoolers might suffer from occasional bad dreams, a wet bed, a night of coughing or vomiting from a virus, or some other temporary factor that makes them more wakeful than usual. And *much further* down the road, you may find yourself sitting up late at night, anxiously awaiting your child's return from a date.

We mention these things because it's important to recognize that *parenting your child is indeed a twenty-four hour job*. Children cannot and should not be expected to confine all of their nurturing needs to the hours most convenient to adults. Nighttime parenting is just as important as the parenting you do during the day. It's part of the job description, so you shouldn't expect to always put your child down for the night and not see her again until your alarm goes off the next morning.

Many infants, young children, and even some perfectly normal school-aged children require active parenting on your part in order to comfortably fall asleep. You should never hesitate to rock, nurse, or snuggle your little ones to sleep, or to read and lie down with your older children until they are able to drift off. Yes, this can be time consuming, but the most important things in life usually *do* take time, and parenting your child is one area where you surely do not want to cut corners. As your child grows in age and in the secure knowledge that you will always be there for her if she needs you, she will become increasingly able to fall asleep on her own. All children arrive at this point on their own timetable. Don't worry that your child is becoming too dependent on you to fall asleep or stay asleep. Attachment to and dependency on parents—including at night—is a normal, healthy aspect of childhood and not something that needs to be discouraged. After all, you want to raise a child who turns to *people* for love and comfort, rather than *things.*

"Q: I've heard that if a baby is used to going to sleep at my breast or in Dad's arms, when he wakes up he will expect the same thing and won't be able to get himself back to sleep without us. Is this true?

A: True, true—and so what? This is a valid criticism of nighttime attachment parenting. But your baby is a baby a very short time and this is a stage where you are building foundations of trust. Consider what may happen if a baby wakes up alone and is forced, before his time, to become a self-soother. The style of parenting called self-soothing, which is creeping into the "let's have babies conveniently" mindset emphasizes techniques of teaching babies how to comfort themselves—by leaving them alone or setting them up to devise their own methods—rather than relying on mother or father. On the surface, this sounds so convenient and liberating, but watch out for shortcuts, especially in nighttime parenting. This school of thought ignores a basic principle of infant development: A need that is filled in infancy goes away; a need that is not filled never completely goes away but recurs later on in 'diseases of detachment'—aggression, anger, distancing or withdrawal, and discipline problems. We have a practical rule of thumb for you to consider: During the first year, an infant's wants and needs are usually one and the same."

—DR. WILLIAM AND MARTHA SEARS FROM THE BABY BOOK

Gentle Weaning from the Family Bed: One Family's Story

► *"When my son Trevor was five years old, I became engaged to be married. For the previous fifteen years, I had been a single mom. As a strong advocate of attachment parenting, I had happily shared a family bed with my son for his entire life. As we discussed our plans for our new family, Dave, my husband-to-be, asked if I would consider moving Trevor to his own bed. After much thoughtful deliberation, I decided that Trevor was probably old enough to start moving towards his own bed. I agreed to try it but insisted that the process be slow, gentle, and respectful of Trevor's needs. The process of gentle weaning from the family bed started well before Dave came to live with us and continued for several months after we were married. Before any changes were made, I talked to Trevor and let him know what our ultimate goal was: for him to feel comfortable sleeping in his own special bed. I also assured him that I wouldn't ever leave him alone or frightened. I let him know that he could come into our bedroom any time he needed me. After a period of gradual transition lasting several months, one night when I laid down with him in his room, Trevor said, 'You can go sleep in your room, Mommy. Just leave your light on until I go to sleep; then turn it off.' I see what happened in our household as a wonderful example of attachment parenting. My nighttime parenting has evolved with Trevor's growth and our changing family. Things worked out in such a way that the needs and wants of all three people in the house were considered. I wanted Trevor to move to his bed at a pace that was comfortable for him. I didn't want him to feel that he was being pushed out of our bed. I think the pace and process were comfortable for Trevor and respectful of his needs. He truly seems to enjoy sleeping in his own bed now. I wanted him to feel comfortable and welcome to come to our room any time he wanted or needed to, and he does. I have time alone with my husband, but we never close the door to our room unless we have guests sleeping in our house. I believe with all my being that babies and toddlers (or beyond) who are still nursing belong in bed with Mama, but, when the time comes for an older child to be in his or her own bed, there are respectful and gentle ways to accomplish that goal."*

—CECILIA, MOTHER OF TWO

Sleep Problems

> ► *"If your baby is able to sleep when she is in her parents' bed then she doesn't have a sleep problem."*
>
> —LAURIE, MOTHER OF TWO

As we have already pointed out, most of what parents believe to be "sleep problems" in their babies and young children are actually a problem of parental misunderstanding or unrealistic expectations. However, attached parents who *are* meeting their child's nighttime needs in a hands-on, nurturing way *do* sometimes encounter sleep behaviors in their little ones that they sincerely believe to be a problem. When are you as a parent facing a real sleep problem in your child? When, despite your acceptance of your child's natural nighttime needs, your own lack of sleep begins to exceed your ability to cope. *All* parents trudge through the occasional day or two in a fog after a child was particularly wakeful the night before due to illness, teething, or some other temporary factor. However, if you are *consistently* finding yourself physically or mentally exhausted and overwhelmed from lack of nighttime sleep, you may need some help. Here are some ideas:

- In the short term, you should make catching up on sleep for *yourself* a real priority. No one can parent effectively—or do much of anything else for that matter—without adequate sleep.
- Go to bed much earlier than usual so you can have a few hours of uninterrupted sleep before any night wakings begin.
- Try using a grandparent or sitter in the afternoons for at least a week so that you can snooze for a few hours.
- If you can, take a sick day from work and sleep all day.
- Some parents with wakeful toddlers *diligently* childproof their bedroom so that if their child wakes during the night and wants to play, parents can continue to sleep while their child tod-

dles around the room. Eventually even the most wide awake little person will probably decide to crawl back in bed next to your resting body and go to sleep.

• Now may be the time to begin asking your partner to do more of the nighttime parenting. A breastfed toddler may initially resist having Dad take over some of the overnight rocking, patting and soothing, but with a gradual, respectful transition, he can and will adjust.

• You might want to give some thought to what your nursling has been ingesting via breastmilk. Have you had changes in your diet recently? Have you perhaps begun eating or drinking more caffeine, sugar, alcohol, or dairy? Are you (or your child) taking a new medication? Have you begun offering new solid foods to your child that could be upsetting his stomach or causing an allergic reaction?

• Is your child on the verge of a major developmental milestone? Children who are just about to walk or talk frequently wake more often at night until they master the new skill.

• Have you recently begun leaving your child to go to work or school? If your child is learning to adjust to your absence during the day, he may feel the need to nurse more often or attract your attention during the nighttime hours as he adjusts to the transition.

• It is also important to rule out medical problems that may be causing your child discomfort at night. These are especially likely if the waking began suddenly. If your child cries inconsolably at night, physical pain—from teeth, a headache, nausea or an ear infection—might be the problem. A child who is crying a lot at night should definitely have a medical evaluation.

It's crucial that you get some sleep yourself before you begin making decisions about how to best handle the larger issue of your child's sleep patterns. Sleep-deprived parents aren't in any position to make good decisions. If you are psychologically exhausted and physically run down, you may make choices regarding how to deal with your child at night that you will later come to regret (like deciding to abruptly wean her or allowing her to cry herself to sleep). Once you *have* gotten some sleep under your belt, the first thing you should do is brainstorm with the people who know your child best and see if you can figure out what the underlying cause for chronic wakefulness at night might be. Frequently, children begin sleeping less soundly after the occurrence of major changes in the household, such as a new sibling, parent-led weaning, or parents' marital discord. Situations such as these may require *more* active, nurturing parenting—including at night—in order to ease your child through them.

The Very Best Resources for Solving Your Child's Sleep Problems

BOOKS

The Baby Book: Everything You Need to Know About Your Baby—From Birth to Age Two. Sears, William M., and Martha Sears. New York: Little, Brown & Co., 1993.

This comprehensive baby/toddler care guide includes an extensive and reassuring section on trouble-shooting and solving a wide variety of sleep problems. Written by a pediatrician and a nurse who are themselves the parents of eight very different children, it is likely that any question you have regarding your child's nighttime behavior will be covered here.

Nighttime Parenting: How to Get Your Baby and Child to Sleep. Sears, William M. Sears. Schaumberg, IL: La Leche League Intl., 1985.

This is Dr. Sears' bestselling guide for parents who want to learn how to develop healthy sleep habits in their children. It also contains lots of great information on identifying and solving specific sleep problems.

Crying Baby; Sleepless Nights: Why Your Baby Is Crying and What You Can Do About It. Jones, Sandy. Edited by Linda Ziedrich. Boston: Harvard Common Press, 1992.

Written with empathy for the parent and child alike, this reassuring, comprehensive guide to the many causes of infant crying and wakefulness will enable parents both to make their babies happier and to cope better with their own emotions. Includes an up-to-date listing of resources for parents.

The Family Bed: An Age Old Concept in Child Rearing. Thevenin, Tine. Garden City, NY: Avery Publishing Co., 1987.

The author explains how sleeping with your children can solve a variety of sleep issues. She also delves into the history and future of the concept of family sleep sharing.

SIDS: A Parent's Guide to Understanding and Preventing Sudden Infant Death Syndrome. Sears, William, MD. New York: Little, Brown & Co., 1996.

Although the primary subject of this fascinating book is the latest research into SIDS, parents will learn a great deal from it about what to expect from their healthy infant in terms of sleep patterns and habits.

Please, Please, *Please* Don't "Ferberize" Your Baby

► *"I think there are very few legitimate sleep problems—narcolepsy, chronic fatigue syndrome maybe?—that sort of thing. I can't imagine a situation of any kind with my child—sleep disorder or not—for which abandonment would be appropriate."*

—AMY, *MOTHER OF TWO*

✦ **"I don't generally complain about oppressive patriarchal social structures, but Ferberism is a good**

example of one. As 'family bed' boosters have noted, male physicians, who have no idea what motherhood is like, have cowed women for decades into doing unnatural and destructive things. For a while doctors said mothers shouldn't feed more than once every four hours. Now they admit they were wrong. For a while they pushed bottle feeding. Now they admit this was wrong. For a while they told pregnant women to keep weight gains minimal (and some women did so by smoking more cigarettes!). Wrong again. Now they're telling mothers to deny food to infants all night long once the kids are a few months old."

—*Psychologist and Author, Robert Wright*

If you are the parent of a baby or young child, it's more than likely you've heard about this. It goes by different names: "Ferberizing" (named after Dr. Richard Ferber, physician-author and the best-known advocate of its use), the "*Babywise*" program (named after a highly controversial childcare guide), or simply the "cry it out" technique. What is it? Well, it's a popular method for "training" babies to fall asleep alone and then stay asleep all night by leaving them to cry (or in the case of many sensitive children, scream in terror, bang their heads, throw their bodies against crib bars, or even vomit) in their cribs with no adult company. Different proponents of this training regimen offer slightly varying versions of the method. Some advocate waiting until a baby is six months old to try it while others suggest starting earlier. Dr. Ferber asks that parents periodically go in to check on their baby and "reassure" him before once again leaving the room. The *Babywise* books even urge parents to allow babies to cry before and after daytime naps if they haven't slept for what the author believes to be the "correct" number of minutes for *all* babies to nap each day.

After reading or hearing about this method, you may have found yourself wondering if it would be right for you and your baby. "Hmmm," you may think hesitantly to yourself. "I *am* sort of tired. Even though we really enjoy having the baby in bed with us and it seems like she really needs to nurse at night, all my friends expect their babies to be sleeping all night in their nursery by now. Maybe we should try it."

If you take only one message from this entire book, let it be this: No you shouldn't! The cry it out method for prematurely forcing a baby to fall asleep by himself and sleep for unnaturally long stretches is dead wrong. Why? The reasons are compelling and numerous:

- **It's simply unkind.** Babies are *people,* extremely helpless, vulnerable, and dependent people. Your baby counts on you to lovingly care for her. When she cries, she is signalling—*in the only way she knows how*—that she needs you to be with her. To draw an analogy, elderly people—who are often vulnerable and dependent—also wake a lot at night and sometimes have trouble falling asleep. However, there would be a terrible uproar if anyone suggested that nursing home staff should lock the doors to their patients' rooms and let them cry or scream themselves to sleep. What if we told these older people that—no matter how hard they yelled or how much they begged—they simply would not be permitted to get out of bed for a snack, a drink of water, clean bedclothes, or even a comforting hug until the following morning?
- **It's dangerous.** Babies who are pressured into sleeping through the night too early may not get enough to eat or drink. They also may be at higher risk for SIDS if they are left alone to sleep for long stretches at night before their own circadian rhythms signal that it's "time" for their sleep pattern to lengthen on its own. Babies who are left alone, crying, may become so upset that they hurt themselves by banging against the sides of their crib. They may aspirate their own vomit (babies who cry alone for more than a few minutes sometimes become literally hysterical

and vomit). They may thrash about and become tangled in their bedclothes. A parent listening to her baby's crying from the other side of a closed nursery door or at the receiving end of a baby monitor has no way to know whether he is crying from cold, fear, or pain.

• **It dulls parental responses and instincts.** There is no sound more arresting to an attached parent than the sound of her baby's cry. Many mothers and fathers describe the sound of their little one's cry as *physically* disturbing. Ethnopediatricians and other researchers believe that this intense parental response to crying is a behavior developed over thousands of years to assure that babies are able to elicit the care they need promptly. But when parents use the "cry it out" method to try to get their children to sleep, they must force themselves to ignore their baby's wailing—usually for extended periods of time and from behind a closed door. By "turning off" their baby's crying in their heads and guts, parents risk losing their natural sensitivity. Ignoring a baby's crying "takes the edge off" of what should be a primary form of communication between parent and child. If you begin to believe that you don't need to respond to your child's plaintive wails at night, you will certainly respond to her cues with less instinctive intensity the rest of the time. You will also risk losing your ability to sense when something is truly wrong with your baby during the night.

• **It can cause parents to feel negative toward their baby.** A crying baby can be very grating on adult nerves. Some parents who set themselves up for long periods of listening to their baby cry find themselves feeling irritated or even angry with their child.

• **Prolonged crying is bad for babies.** You know what it feels like to cry in fear or distress. It feels terrible. And it's no different for your baby. When your baby cries—for whatever reason—he experiences physical changes. His blood pressure rises, his muscles become tense, and stress hormones flood his little body. Crying decreases the oxygenation in your baby's bloodstream. Crying also uses up calories and energy, things that your baby needs to grow, especially as a newborn. As Jean Liedloff notes in her book, *Continuum Concept,* "a baby's cry is precisely as serious as it sounds." Certainly there will be times when your baby's cry represents a healthy and necessary release of his pent up emotion or pain, but your job as a parent is to be *with* your baby at those times; you should not be the one actually *creating* the impetus for the crying by subjecting your baby to stressful and frightening separations. Babies who are subjected to "cry it out" sleep training do sometimes seem to sleep deeply after they finally drop off. This is because babies and young children frequently sleep deeply after experiencing trauma. This deep sleep shouldn't be viewed as proof of the efficacy of the Ferber method but rather as evidence of one of its many disturbing shortcomings.

But Do the "Cry It Out" Techniques "Work"?

▶ *"The ways that other people described the whole Ferberizing experience just didn't match mine. I am so glad that after trying it one time I said, 'This is wrong for my child or she wouldn't be acting like this.' She was mad as hell at me the next day too."*

—PEGGY, MOTHER OF TWO

▶ *"I tried Ferber on Ethan when he was about six months old. Despite the fact that Ferber implies that the method works on all babies, I discovered that it certainly didn't work on mine. Ethan screamed for three hours and only screamed more when I came into the room, not less. Supposedly when you come in the room they are reassured. It was obvious that Ethan felt incredibly betrayed*

> *not reassured in the least. I finally gave up and decided that it was the worst night of his babyhood and I would never try it again. In retrospect I see that Ethan was a very wise baby and knew how to get what he needed. I was so glad that Ethan taught me that babies are babies for a very short time and that everything else I felt I had to get done could wait. He was what I had to 'get done.' The baby will alter your life and that is a good thing. Crying serves a purpose—if they cry in pain you would never ignore it so why should you ignore it when they are in emotional pain? It is their communication tool telling you they need you."*
>
> —LAURIE, MOTHER OF TWO

If you are an exhausted parent (and all parents have occasional days or weeks when they feel overwhelmed by parenthood), or if you are being pressured by friends or grandparents to "get that baby on a schedule," or constantly asked "why isn't he sleeping through the night yet?" these arguments against the "cry it out" sleep training methods may not seem as important to you as getting a solid eight hours of sleep *right now, this very night!* You may be wondering if this method can really get your baby to immediately begin sleeping soundly from 8:00 P.M. until 8:00 A.M. If so, the method may look tempting to you, no matter what your other reservations. "So," you may be wondering, "can using one of the 'cry it out' sleep techniques really work?"

The answer to this question depends on a number of factors. Your baby's temperament and personality will certainly play a large role in determining what will happen if you leave him, awake and alone in his crib with the door to his room shut. Some very mellow babies may only fuss for a moment, without even crying, and then fall right to sleep. These babies will probably sleep through the night fairly early and easily anyway, and your application of this "method" will have had nothing to do with it. Babies with an "average" temperament—meaning neither exceptionally laid back or very intense—will most likely become frightened and upset when you leave them. Eventually, however, they may fall into an exhausted slumber from their crying and screaming, just as you would if placed in a similarly scary situation from which there was no escape. After a few nights of crying, the parents of a baby like this may come to believe that the method has indeed "worked" because their baby no longer calls to them in the night. In fact, the baby has simply learned that he is powerless to attract his parents' attention no matter how loudly he cries out for them. He has given up. Does this mean that the method has "worked"? Or does it mean that you have frightened and cowed your baby into unnatural nighttime lethargy and broken his spirit?

The babies for whom the "cry it out" techniques are most troublesome are those who have temperments usually described as "fussy," "intense," or "high-need." These babies can be very tiring for parents, especially those mothers and fathers who are operating without the benefit of attachment parenting tools. High-need babies tend to wake more frequently at night and for a longer period of their early childhood. With these babies, it is likely that a greater number of parents feel compelled to "do something" to try to get them to sleep longer at night. Parents of high-need babies are often pressured by others to stop letting the baby "manipulate" them into so much holding, nursing, and nighttime parenting. However, high-need babies truly *need* their parents to physically comfort them and help them organize their sleep-wake cycles through co-sleeping and extra loving touch at night. When a high-need baby is left to "cry it out" in order to force sleep, he can become hysterical and physically ill with fright, grief, and anger. These are the babies who will go on screaming for *hours* without dropping off to sleep. Parents of babies with an intense personality often report that "cry it out" methods *definitely* don't work . . . on any level.

▶ *"The Ferber method actually turned us into attachment parents. We tried Ferberizing our very high-need six month old after seeing the characters Paul and Jamie try it on the TV show* Mad About You. *Jenna began screaming her head off the second we left the room (after patting and reassuring her as Ferber's book suggested). She continued to cry a horrible, ear-splitting cry off and on for more than four hours. We periodically went in to tell her that we loved her and were only doing it for her own good. Every time I saw her little tear-streaked face looking up at me, begging me not to leave, I felt like dying. But the book had made it clear that as good parents, we needed to do what was 'best' for Jenna or she would never learn to sleep on her own. Well, to make a long story short, she never really went to sleep that night and I felt so wrong inside about what we were doing. For weeks afterwards she clung to me like a baby monkey and wouldn't let me out of her sight. Her throat was scratchy and sore from the crying. She actually began sleeping much worse at night because she was afraid we would leave her again. The whole awful experience set me off on a search for another way to handle her personality. I am so glad to have discovered Dr. Sears' book,* The Fussy Baby: How To Bring Out the Best in Your High-Need Child *(Signet, 1989). It has changed our lives."*

—JULIANA, MOTHER OF A ONE YEAR OLD

Of course, when deciding how to parent your baby, the question of whether a certain method "works" to produce a short term goal (like a baby who sleeps for long stretches at an early age) shouldn't be your primary consideration. Instead, you should ask whether the idea in question is *right for your child and your family in the long run.* After all, taping a preschooler's mouth shut to prevent him from constantly interrupting his parents' conversation would most likely achieve the desired effect of silencing him immediately. Obviously, however, the technical effectiveness of this idea certainly doesn't make it a desirable parenting practice, or one without long term consequences for a child's emotional health and psyche. An extreme analogy? Not really. Only a few decades ago, "sleep experts" were commonly advising parents to solve "sleep problems" in their children by literally strapping them into their beds each night. Of course, that was after parents had dutifully affixed a pediatrician-endorsed metal anti-thumbsucking device to their little-ones' hands. Get it?

CHAPTER 7

The Working Parent's Guide to Attachment Parenting

✦ **"The issue is not the working mother, the issue is *attachment* with your baby."**

—*Dr. William and Martha Sears*

PERHAPS YOU HAVE PREVIOUSLY HEARD OR READ ABOUT ATTACHMENT parenting and come away with the impression that this parenting style can only work for traditional, nonemployed, full time at-home parents. In fact, this simply isn't true. Many working mothers and fathers today are finding ways to successfully and joyfully combine the attachment parenting style with their vocational roles. Working parents usually find that the basic attachment parenting tools, such as breastfeeding, babywearing, and a family bed can all play an invaluable part in maintaining and enhancing a healthy bond with their young children, even when their work day takes them away. And as a bonus, many working parents have found that the flexibility of attachment parenting can really simplify their very busy lives.

In this chapter we won't be telling you whether you *should* or *should not* work outside your home. That's a decision only you can make in consideration of the many factors unique to your own family. Instead what we will offer is open-ended food for thought, as well as several ideas for alternative work arrangements which may make it easier for you to meet your child's attachment needs while still earning a living. Additionally, you will gain an abundance of practical, real life advice on the hows and whys of utilizing attachment parenting tools as a working parent.

Your Baby's Need for You and Your Decision Whether or Not to Work

It is important to start any honest discussion of balancing work and parenting with a recitation of one indisputable fact: your physical and emotional presence *matters* to your baby and young child. As her parent, you are not interchangeable with a substitute caregiver. This is not to say that a skilled, attuned caregiver cannot serve a complementary role to your own, but don't ever delude yourself into thinking that your baby doesn't need *you*. She does. In fact, child development experts are in agreement that psychologically healthy infants are actually "enmeshed" with their parents. In other words, they still don't know where they leave off and you begin. Whether you are a working or stay-at-home parent, you are irreplaceable to your baby. Far too many parents are under the mistaken impression that babies and young children don't really care who diapers, feeds and holds them, just as long as they are dry and their little tummies are full. In fact, babies clearly begin to prefer their own parents to other caregivers as early as the first days and weeks after birth. Even in the face of the most mediocre parenting, young children generally seek the company and attention of their parents as opposed to anyone else, especially when they feel tired, hungry, stressed, or frightened. This is a normal and healthy phenomenon of human development that says a great deal about how primal the parent-child attachment really is. Although every family's situation with regard to outside school or employment is different, young children's need for responsive, attached parenting remains constant.

So, what exactly does your baby or young child's intense need for you mean in terms of your decision as to whether, when, or how often you choose to be separated from her? There is no formulaic answer to that much-discussed question, although every expert, pundit, and next door neighbor will try to tell you that there is. Several important factors should play a featured role in determining how soon and how much you are away from your child each day, including:

• **The strength of the underlying attachment between you and your child.** Although you may find that a deep, strong bond between you and your baby makes it more difficult for you to leave her in the first place (which is a natural, healthy response on the part of an attached parent), this bond provides an emotional foundation that is *critical* to her ability to successfully deal with any necessary work-related separations from you. As we have been discussing throughout this book, a loving attachment between parent and baby grows as a result of such things as very early parent-child bonding, the biological boost of breastfeeding on cue, frequent physical contact from loving touch, co-sleeping, baby-wearing, and—perhaps most importantly—consistently responsive parental caregiving (meaning that, when she lets you know that she needs you, you respond without hesitation). In order to maximize the attachment promoting benefits of these factors before leaving your "nest" to go back to work, *employed parents should take the very longest parental leave they can possibly manage*. But don't then spend your parental leave—whatever its duration—obsessing over the day when you will return to your job. And don't buy into the idea that allowing your child to become "too attached" or "too dependent" on you now will make it more difficult for him when you return to work. By spending your time enjoying your baby and consciously fostering his attachment to you (and vice versa), you will find that when you *do* begin leaving for some or all of the workday, the strong bond you have forged keeps the two of you emotionally tied together even when you are apart. *If the time comes for you to return to or begin outside employment and you do not feel completely confident in the attachment that you share with your child, you may want to postpone regular separations from him.*

• **The quality and consistency of the substitute childcare you will be able to provide.** Study after study has attempted to make a definitive judgment concerning the effects of maternal employment on young children. Each researcher comes to a slightly different conclusion, which various interest groups then use in an attempt to prove their particular argument for or against parents leaving their young children to go to work. However, virtually everyone involved in this heated debate is able to agree on one point: *if a parent is going to be separated from her baby or young child, the quality and consistency of the substitute care to which she entrusts her little one is of critical importance.* A really terrific, preferably long-term substitute care arrangement is an absolute fundamental for working attachment parents. In an upcoming section of this chapter we will discuss how to evaluate and choose substitute care for your child. However, as you decide whether you will work at all, you should make a commitment to yourself and your child that any childcare you *do* employ will be uncompromising in its quality. For some attachment parents, the cost of childcare that meets their high standards is simply prohibitive, thus swaying their decision away from full-time employment during their child's early years.

- **Your child herself.** Different children are ready to face regular separations from their parents at different ages. These differences can be based on inborn temperament, physical well-being, unique developmental timetables, and other more intangible factors. Just because some childcare manual says that "all babies" should get over stranger anxiety at exactly fourteen months of age, or your pediatrician tells you that "all two year olds" should enjoy playing in groups with peers, doesn't mean that *your* child will. Children who are separated from their primary caregivers too early or too often can experience feelings of depression, loss, and abandonment. You should carefully consider your child's individual readiness for separations in weighing any decisions you make.

Why, you may be asking, would a chapter on combining work and parenthood start with a section on how much young children need their parents, how separations can be hard on children, and how difficult it can be to arrange and afford high quality childcare? Won't this only serve to make working parents feel stressed out and guilty? No. The point is to make parents feel *aware* when sorting through their options on this very important issue. Few discussions about balancing work and family give equal weight to the perspective of the young child. Although there are no pat answers, you won't go wrong in your own decision if you fully accept your little person's intense dependency needs and allow them to act as your guiding principle as you carefully craft a day-to-day life that works well for you and your family.

To Work or Not to Work? That Is the Question

It goes without saying that your priorities will be dramatically altered once you become a parent. Suddenly, every decision you make and every step you take must be weighed against its potential impact on your child and your ability to effectively meet his needs. That's why there are no easy answers to the now weary "should women work" question. Every parent faces a unique set of financial, emotional, and organizational circumstances in deciding what employment arrangement will best nourish her entire family. For this reason, it is critical that you take some time to mindfully reflect on what really matters to *you*—both as an individual and as a parent. For some mothers and fathers of babies and young children, the question of whether or not they will work is an easy one. For most, however, the various choices require a lot of thought and self-exploration. Here are some questions to ask yourself as a starting point in the identification of personal priorities that will shape your decision:

- **If you were employed (or in school) before your baby was born, why were you working?** Was it for money alone? Emotional connection with other adults? A strong belief in the importance and value of your job? Did your job/academic career satisfy your intellectual interests in a way that is extremely important to you?
- **What are your partner's views on employment for parents of babies and young children?** Do his/her views matter to you?
- **From where do you derive your sense of self-worth?** Is it from relationships with others? From your occupation? Something else?
- **Does the idea of "surrendering to parenthood" by either temporarily or permanently giving up the financial independence or stimulation of your work leave you feeling apprehensive?** Do you worry that you will "end up" like your mother (grandmother, aunt, sister, best friend, etc) if you aren't actively pursuing a tangible career goal?
- **What decisions have people you respect and ad-**

mire as parents made in regards to combining work and family? Can you spend some time talking with these individuals to learn more about their own choices?

Keep Your Options (and Your Mind) Open!

> ► *"I remember having a conversation with some friends while I was first pregnant about how I would put my baby in daycare at six or eight weeks and go right back to full time work. I actually argued that infants need group care to develop properly and socialize with other babies! And, at the time, I didn't even like my job that much! Instead I was just identifying myself as a 'working person.' My views have changed a lot over the past eight years. I still work and I still identify myself as a 'working mother,' but I also identify myself as a full-time parent. I have had my mind opened in so many ways by the experience of parenthood. I can't believe how rigid I was in my views before I became a mother."*
>
> —FRIEDA, MOTHER OF TWO

As an expectant or new parent, you will want to keep your options open as much as possible as you decide what employment arrangement will best suit your family. If you decide definitively that you *will* return to full-time work just as soon as your parental leave is up, you may find yourself blindsided by the strong desire to be with your baby twenty-four hours a day once he arrives. You may also come to discover that no substitute caregiver meets your criteria or that you have been blessed with a baby whose temperament or health condition clearly *requires* full-time parental care.

On the other hand, if you inform your employer too soon that you absolutely, unequivocally *will not* return to work once the baby arrives, you may miss out on an unexpected offer of very flexible scheduling, telecommuting, or part-time work that would allow you to comfortably combine parenting and work. Although it certainly isn't reasonable for you to actively mislead your employer in any way, your primary responsibility is to your child. Waiting until you are *very* sure of your decision and the reasons behind it before you burn any bridges is the most prudent course of action for anyone with interests in both her parenting and her career.

Working Parent/Attachment Parent

Some working parents make the grave mistake of physically and emotionally detaching from their baby in a misguided attempt to spare their child (and themself) from a sense of pain or loss due to their work-related separations. This detachment—which can often be unconscious—presents a real threat to your long-term relationship with your child. If, after careful deliberation of your young child's needs and your own, you make the decision in favor of outside employment or schooling, don't wallow in negative feelings about your choice. Instead, you should confidently work to create a daily environment that is most conducive to your child's optimal mental, emotional, and physical growth within the realistic context of life with you as a working parent. And whatever the specifics of your own work situation, the attachment parenting style can help you to forge and maintain a strong and secure bond with your baby, even when your days take you away. Here are some ways to successfully combine attachment parenting with working:

- **If you are gone eight hours a day, plan to spend evenings and weekends with your child.** Although you may have enjoyed frequent evenings out alone or vacations away with your partner or friends before having a baby, you will now need to rethink this aspect of your life. Although an evening out sans child may be an occasional special event for working, attachment parents, there is, quite simply, a limit to how frequently a baby or young child can be physically separated from his parents without compromising his ability to trust and bond. When you are gone from your child all day, you shouldn't then plan to be gone all evening or weekend. Additionally, breastfeeding mothers who are away eight or more hours a day really need cue-feeding and skin-to-skin contact during nonworking hours in order to keep their milk supply up. But attachment parenting families don't usually need anyone to tell them to stay close to their little ones when they aren't at work; a securely bonded parent-child pair literally craves one another's presence after a day apart. And although it may take some getting used to, parents can plan "dates" with babies and young children along. With a sling and nursing clothes, your nursling can go virtually anywhere you go with a minimum of fuss (although smoky environments are an obvious no-no). Remember that this period of intense neediness in your child's life is relatively short. The day will come all too soon when your older child will look forward to a fun evening at grandma's, a best friend's, or the sitter's while you go out to see a concert. In the meantime, you should concentrate on building a family-centered lifestyle that doesn't take you away from your child any more than necessary.

> ✦ **"I urge the working parents I see in my practice to give the family bed a try. It gives working families extra time together. If you are away for nine or ten hours at work, when do you hold the baby? Also, working moms need to get all their sleeping done at night because they don't get those wonderful afternoon naps with baby."**
>
> —*Julie Graves Moy, M.D., M.P.H.*

• **Sleep with your child at night.** The family bed is a fundamental attachment tool for families with working parents who are gone all day. It provides an easy way for parents and their young children to reconnect after a long day apart. The inevitable skin-to-skin contact of family bedding offers babies and young children tactile expressions of love from their parents, and helps to boost and maintain a working/pumping mother's milk supply. If you think about it, working parents who sleep with their little ones at night probably have more hands-on contact with their children than many parents who stay home all day.

> ▶ *"Other parents at my office are always complaining about what a hassle it is trying to get their little kids in bed for the night. The kids fight sleep and resist bedtime because, after being away from their parents all day, they don't then want to face the overnight separation. Our kids know that the whole family will be together at night, close and cozy. As a result, they don't dread bedtime."*
>
> —*Thomas, father of two*

• **Wear your baby when you are at home.** Carrying your baby or young child in a sling, frontpack, or backpack is one of the best ways to promote both his trust in you and your responsiveness to his cues. When you wear your baby, you and he become "as one." He is simultaneously stimulated by your movement and activities and soothed by your close physical presence. Naturally, all of these things are extra important for parents who must be away during the day. Also, working parents must often squeeze housework, cooking, and errands into a few short hours in the afternoon and on weekends. By wearing your baby, you can more easily keep up with all of your responsibilities while still staying close to your child.

> ▶ *"John-Mark likes to climb into the sling almost as soon as I get home. I change out of my work clothes before I leave*

my office so that I am ready for hands on mothering when I walk in the door. If I need to decompress before switching into mama mode, I stop at a coffeehouse or the gym before I get home. But when I walk in that door, I want to feel ready to mother. I don't want to put John-Mark off while I switch gears."

—*MARIE, MOTHER OF AN EIGHTEEN MONTH OLD*

Breastfeeding and the Working Mother

► *"I am a nurse and I often work ten to twelve hours shifts. Although I love my job and can't imagine giving up my work, I also wish that I didn't have to be away from my child so many hours each week. By breastfeeding him, I have kept the close connection between us despite the separations. Producing milk for him is something that only I can do. It is something that we share as mother and child. Initially my employer was very resistant to allowing me the time to pump my breasts on the job. I persisted, however, and now several other nurses and one resident are pumping as well. And to be able to reconnect with my child with a relaxing nursing session when I get home is just indescribable. It reminds him that—even though our caregiver spends almost as many hours with him as I do, I am his mother. And nursing full time when I am home and on weekends is much easier for this busy working mother than dealing with bottles and formula."*

—*DENISE, MOTHER OF AN ELEVEN MONTH OLD*

The topic of breastfeeding while working outside the home is one that could (and has!) fill a book or two all on its own. The most important thing to know about breastfeeding as a working mother is that *you can do it!* In fact, in the United States, a greater percentage of employed mothers than nonemployed mothers initiate breastfeeding with their babies. It's true that maintaining a breastfeeding relationship with your child when you must be separated during your working hours has its own challenges, but it also has innumerable rewards. Many mothers who work outside the home continue to happily breastfeed their babies well into toddlerhood or even beyond.

> ▶ *"I work full time in a very demanding job, and I have to say that breastfeeding my baby and continuing to breastfeed my toddler is the most important thing I've ever done. Breastfeeding allows me to give my baby something no one else can: liquid love and milk made just for her. Expressing in the middle of my work day gives me the opportunity to take a time out from the working world and think about my baby, which in turn makes me more productive, or at least motivated to finish what I'm doing and go home. Breastfeeding also gives us an easy way to instantly connect and relax at the end of a busy day; it makes me slow down and focus on my child."*
>
> —MAURY, MOTHER OF TWO

Working women who breastfeed rather than turning to artificial feeding are particularly pleased that their babies weren't deprived of either breastmilk or the breastfeeding relationship as a result of their employment. Additionally, working, breastfeeding mothers can feel proud of a major accomplishment. Because we live in a culture that often makes it difficult for *any* mother to succeed at breastfeeding, those who confront the added issues of pumping and storing their milk while on the job deserve support and accolades from partners, employers, family and their community.

Breastfeeding on the Job: The Basics

Working, breastfeeding mothers have various options open to them. Some mothers choose to delay their return to work until their babies are around one year old. In this case, a nursling is usually eating a sufficient quantity of other foods so that breastfeeding during the hours a mother is at work isn't strictly necessary from a nutritional standpoint. Because the milk supply is well-established, most mothers in this situation won't need to pump at all during their work hours. With a younger baby, mothers may choose a childcare provider close enough to their job site that they can go to the baby at lunchtime—or maybe even during breaktimes—in order to nurse. Other mothers have a partner or childcare provider bring the baby to them for one or more nursing sessions during the day.

The reality, however, is that many nursing mothers must return to work early in their baby's first year and don't have the opportunity to actually put their baby to breast during their working hours. If this is the case for you, pumping your breasts in order to provide milk for your little one while you are gone will become a part of your daily routine. This is because breastfeeding works on a supply and demand system, and if no one—baby or breastpump—is "demanding" milk during the hours you are at work, you may see a sharp decrease in your overall milk production. Here are some tips to introduce you to the basics of "the pumping life":

- **Try to network with other working, nursing mothers during pregnancy and maternity leave.** It is likely that you will find the support and knowledge of more experienced working/breastfeeding mothers very helpful at times when other people are trying to convince you that it would be easier to quit nursing altogether. Sadly, some working mothers who chose to turn to artificial feeding rather than deal with pumping may be the most vocal in their negative opinions regarding your own commitment to provide your breastmilk for your baby. You can locate other working/breastfeeding mothers through a local La Leche League group which has working mothers as attendees or on the Internet (try the APW e-mail list included in the resources section in the chapter, "What is Attachment Parenting" or The Pumping List in the resources section following this discussion). If you do utilize La Leche League for support, an evening group is more likely to have other working mothers involved. You might also ask your lactation consultant for information about hospital-based breastfeeding support groups in your area.

• **Take the longest maternity leave you can possibly arrange.** In one recent study by lactation consultant Kathleen Auerbach, Ph.D., reported in the *Journal of Human Lactation*, the length of maternity leave seemed to have the strongest influence on breastfeeding success for working women. In fact, the duration of a woman's maternity leave played a larger role than the number of hours a working mother was separated from her baby each day. Women who stayed home at least sixteen weeks ended up breastfeeding for more months overall than those who were back on the job sooner.

• **It takes four to eight weeks for a woman's milk supply to become well-established. During this early period, don't worry about bottle-feeding.** Just enjoy your baby and nurse on cue. If you find that you are having any difficulties in these first weeks, be sure to contact a La Leche League Leader or International Board Certified Lactation Consultant (IBCLC). The last thing you want on your already full plate is to have to go back to work without having resolved breastfeeding difficulties. And remember, paying for a consultation with an IBCLC can be a real money-saver if it allows you to successfully pump your milk instead of paying for bottles of infant formula for your baby while you are at work.

• **Purchase or rent a breastpump.** What kind of pump

should you get? Well, let's start by telling you what you should *not* buy: any breastpump manufactured or sold by one of the infant formula companies. As we mentioned earlier in the book, these cheap (generally under $50) electric/battery powered pumps—usually available at the grocery store, pharmacy or "baby superstore"—are of notoriously poor quality. Many women who try to use them experience pain and an inability to express milk, leaving them frustrated and inclined to turn to artificial feeding. You should also avoid any of the older "bicycle horn" type manual pumps that you might see around or be given as a hand-me-down, as these will give you similar results. What you *will* want is a high quality pump manufactured by one of the reputable breastfeeding supply companies such as Medela or Ameda-Egnell. Here are your options:

1. "Hospital-grade" breastpumps.

These pumps are quite expensive to purchase outright (at least $500, and up to $1,500), For this reason, most women rent them for $30–$75 per month. The rental cost can vary widely depending on what part of the country you live in and what other services (breastfeeding counseling, low-cost replacement tubing, etc.) you get with the pump itself. Of course, renting a breastpump is still a heck of a lot cheaper than a year's supply of infant formula plus the higher cost of medical care that formula-fed infants are more likely to need. You can find out where to rent a breastpump in your community from a local La Leche League Leader or lactation consultant. Hospital grade pumps are generally the most effective pumps available. Women who must pump full-time (such as for a premature or sick baby who can't latch on yet) will almost certainly need one of these. They're designed for frequent, heavy use. When renting a pump, it's necessary to purchase your own washable, reusable attachment kit (for around $50) that consists of things like collection bottles, tubing, and breastshields. Some workplaces with lactation rooms buy hospital-grade pumps for their employees and keep them on-site so that mothers need only to bring their own pump attachments and storage bottles each day.

2. Professional-grade breastpumps.

Until recently, women had to rent a hospital-grade pump to get really great pumping results. That is no longer true. Professional grade pumps are nearly as effective as hospital-grade pumps, but they're far more affordable at about $200 to $350. They're intended for individual use only, as they don't have the filtering systems that the hospital grade pumps do. As with the hospital-grade pumps, moms can single or double-pump (meaning pump one or both breasts at the same time). The attachment kits for the major brands are the same as for the hospital-grade pumps, making it convenient for moms to buy one after having first rented a pump. These pumps are made for daily use, but typically last for only a year or two. These are probably the best choice for a woman pumping during a regular, eight hour workday and nursing her baby full time during the other sixteen hours and on weekends. Currently, the two best pumps in this category are:

The Medela Pump In Style.

This pump has arguably become the number one choice of working mothers and has an excellent reputation. It comes in an attractive shoulder bag that looks just like a professional attache. The bag has room for all the pump's parts and includes a separate insulated compartment for milk storage. Women can adjust the suction level.

The Purely Yours from Ameda-Egnell.

This pump is lighter than the Pump In Style and enables women to adjust both speed and suction. The pump can be removed from its bag, which has a sportier look. This pump is a bit less expensive than the Pump In Style.

3. Small electric pumps.

These pumps are designed for very occasional, casual use (such as to leave a sippy cup of breastmilk for the sitter to give your toddler). They usually cost between $50 and $125. Remember, though, not to buy one made by an infant formula manufacturer, tempting as it may be due to their lower price. Small electric pumps tend to be very noisy to operate.

4. Manual pumps.

These vary greatly in price and quality. There are dozens of different brands and designs on the market, and the only thing they all have in common is that they operate on mother power and that they're generally only appropriate for "once in a while" uses. The very best manual pump is the Avent Isis. This newer manual pump is getting rave reviews from mothers who have tried it. Some mothers report getting as much milk using the Isis as with an electric pump. You can get the Isis with either a reusable bottle or a holder for disposable bottle bags. It sells for around $50.

- **Begin pumping your breasts several weeks before you will return to your job so that you can get the hang of your pump and begin freezing and stockpiling breastmilk.** It's a wise idea to stay a bit ahead of your baby's pumped milk needs because all pumping mothers have high production and low production days. Try pumping around the times you will be pumping on the job. You will initially need to pump every three hours or so while at work, although later in your baby's first year you may be able to cut back.
- **Freshly expressed human milk can be safely kept at room temperature for up to eight hours and in the refrigerator for up to five to seven days. If you must keep it longer than five to seven days, label the bottles with the date and store them in a home freezer.** Breastmilk will keep in the freezer for six months. Thaw frozen milk in warm water; do not microwave or boil it. You can purchase spe-

cial bags and small bottles for freezing, thawing, and feeding your milk from one of the vendors listed in the resource section on working and breastfeeding (among other places).

• **Once your milk is well-established and your baby is nursing well (at about four to eight weeks, depending on the mother-baby pair), you can introduce a bottle so that she can become accustomed to taking one while you are at work.** Introducing a bottle before about three weeks of age can lead to nipple confusion in some babies, and *don't let anyone tell you otherwise.* Some breastfed babies take easily to the bottle, some require patience and ingenuity in order to accept it (such as trying different nipple brands or letting someone other than mother offer the bottle), and some forcefully refuse it no matter what you do. Babies who refuse the bottle can present a real challenge to a working attachment parent. If you find yourself in this situation, people may advise you to let your baby cry until he "gives in" and accepts the bottle. Obviously this is incompatible with gentle, responsive attachment parenting, but you do have alternatives. You should consult one of the books on working and breastfeeding listed later in this chapter and/or a Board Certified lactation consultant who has experience in assisting working mothers. Through either of these resources you can learn about alternatives to the bottle, such as early cup feeding.

• **Use a double-pumping kit with your electric breastpump.** By emptying both breasts simultaneously, most mothers can complete a pumping session in just ten to fifteen minutes, meaning that only about thirty minutes to one hour of your total workday will be spent pumping. Many experienced pumping moms are even able to easily pump while eating lunch or conferencing on the phone! Additionally, double-pumping stimulates your breasts—and thus the hormonal support for breastfeeding—more thoroughly.

• **Plan to return to your job mid-week and work an**

abbreviated schedule for a few weeks as you and your baby adjust to pumping and separations.

• **Plan to nurse your baby as soon as you can after you return home or reach your childcare provider's, and also as often as possible during the evening, early morning, and on weekends.**

• **If your employer does not make a special room available for mothers who are breastpumping, find a spot that is as private and comfortable as possible.** Many women use their own or a friend's office and lock the door. Others use a women's lounge or (least desirable of all) the bathroom.

• **You can store the milk you pump each day so that it is available for your baby the following day while you are at work.** If a refrigerator is not available on site, use a small carry-cooler with blue ice. Some electric breastpumps (such as the Medela Pump In Style) come with a discreet, built in cooler system to store and transport your fresh milk home each day.

Creating a Breastfeeding-Friendly Workplace

A growing number of employers are discovering the many benefits of supporting breastfeeding on the job. Workplace lactation programs are now widely recognized as an innovative, family-friendly employer benefit. Breastfeeding-friendly workplaces may offer a range of benefits to their employees, from a comfortable private room for pumping and adequate breaks in which to do it, to on site professional grade breastpumps and milk storage facilities. The most cutting edge breastfeeding-friendly employers even offer free or reduced rate consultations with lactation consultants for employees and their partners. In return, employers are able to recruit and retain top employees, and see lower rates of absenteeism. In fact, research presented in the *American Journal of Health Promotion* in December, 1995 examined absenteeism and infant illness among breastfeeding vs. nonbreastfeeding mothers in two large U.S. corporations. It found that employee absenteeism was twenty-seven percent lower and health care claims were thirty-five percent lower among employees who breastfed.

Many women are pleased and surprised to find their employers very accommodating in providing a place and time to pump or feed a baby on the job. (Usually, legally mandated break time should be sufficient for this purpose. Breastfeeding mothers don't need any more "free time" than other employees who stop for a few cups of coffee during the day or some watercooler gossip.) And in some states—including Florida and Texas—state law actively encourages employers to accommodate the needs of their employees who are breastfeeding. On the federal level, in 1998 Representative Carolyn B. Maloney of New York introduced H.R. 3531, the *"New Mothers' Breastfeeding Promotion and Protection Act."* This bill addresses the harassment and discrimination that has been directed toward some women who choose to breastfeed or pump their milk on the job. It will ensure that breastfeeding mothers cannot be fired, discriminated against, or treated differently from other employees, as is already the case for pregnant women through the federal Pregnancy Discrimination Act. H.R. 3531 will mandate that free lunchtimes or breaks can be used for the expression of breastmilk, and ensure that additional unpaid breaks could be taken if breaks are not currently offered. It will also ask the Food and Drug Administration to develop minimum standards for breastpumps. (Currently, breastpumps constitute a completely unregulated type of medical equipment. This is one reason why the quality can vary so widely from manufacturer to manufacturer.) Lastly, H.R. 3531 will offer a tax credit to employers who offer lactation facilities to their employees.

Some women find that they must act as trailblazers in informing their employer as to the importance of providing a breastfeeding-friendly workplace. In many cases, other breastfeeding colleagues have had similar concerns but were unsure how to approach the issue with management. Here is one sample letter that was actually used by an employee who was successful in encouraging her own employer to adopt breastfeeding-friendly workplace policies. You can use it as a template for writing your own letter. You should direct your letter to whomever handles your company's healthcare and other employee benefits, and be sure to CC a copy to your supervisor:

Dear [Human Resources Manager],

This is a letter to address an important issue and to propose a viable solution. Currently, there is no facility in our building appropriate for breastfeeding employees who need to pump their breastmilk. In fact, the only alternative for those employees without private offices are the bathrooms. Obviously, the restrooms are not adequate or appropriate for this purpose for the following reasons:

- *Unsanitary conditions for infant food preparation*
- *Lack of privacy for pumping*
- *Practical problems (in order to operate a breastpump, at minimum one needs somewhere to set up the pump and collection bottles, as well as a place to sit down while pumping).*

I propose that our company set aside one office with several private areas partitioned off to be used by nursing mothers. This will provide not only the obvious benefits to new mothers/employees and their babies, but some well-documented benefits to the company as well. Studies have shown that breastfed babies are healthier. Healthier babies mean fewer medical expenses for the company's insurance carrier and fewer lost workdays for parents. Lastly, new mothers who are aware that their breastfeeding relationship with their child will be supported on the job are more likely to return to the workforce after maternity leave. (See attached supporting references.)

In order to set up a very basic on site lactation program, the following things will be required:

- *A private room with a lock on the door.*
- *Partitions or curtains to make two or three privacy areas.*
- *A chair and small table for each privacy area. In addition, it would be helpful to have a small sink and refrigerator (for breastmilk storage) in the room, as well as an electrical outlet in each privacy area for operation of electric breastpumps.*

I would like to see our company stay on the cutting edge of providing a healthy work environment and excellent benefits for employees. I believe the process of becoming more breastfeeding-friendly would be a step in that direction. Please see the attached documentation for examples of how other highly competitive companies across the country are working to support their breastfeeding employees.

Do not hesitate to let me know if I can answer any questions regarding this issue, or if this proposal is more appropriately directed to another department. I look forward to hearing from you.

Sincerely,

[employee's name here]

If you or your employer are interested in learning more about the documented benefits of workplace lactation programs or how to create a more breastfeeding-friendly workplace, you can contact:

DCC® Inc.
P.O. Box 2783
Westport, CT 06880
Phone: (203) 226–2680
Fax: (203) 291–3571
http://www.momsatwork.com
E-mail: info@dcclifecare.com

DCC® is a company which offers interested employers an individualized workplace lactation program package which can help organizations support their breastfeeding employees.

The Very Best Resources for Working, Breastfeeding Mothers

HOW-TO BOOKS

Nursing Mother, Working Mother: The Essential Guide for Breastfeeding and Staying Close to Your Baby After You Return to Work. Pryor, Gale. Boston: Harvard Common Press 1997.

So That's What They're For: Breastfeeding Basics. Tamaro-Natt, Janet. Holbrook, MA: Adams Media, 1998.

Although Tamaro's fun, lighthearted book addresses all aspects of breastfeeding, as a working, breastfeeding mother herself, she covers this particular topic very thoroughly. Her information on breast pumps is extremely up to date and understandable.

The Nursing Mother's Companion. 3rd. rev. ed. Huggins, Kathleen. Boston: Harvard Common Press, 1995.

A nationally known lactation consultant's complete and reassuring guide to every aspect of breastfeeding. Always completely up-to-date. The section on working and breastfeeding is excellent.

Motherwear's Guide to Breastfeeding and Returning to Work. Order from The Motherwear Catalog at: (800) 950–2500 or http://www.motherwear.com

Breastfeeding and the Working Mother. rev. ed. Mason, Diane, and Diane Ingersoll. New York: St. Martin's Press, 1997.

SELECTED RETAIL RESOURCES FOR BUYING BREASTPUMPS

Note: Be sure to ask your baby's doctor to prescribe your breastmilk for your baby. This way, the cost of buying or renting your breastpump will sometimes be covered by your health insurance. (If it isn't, you should make a case to your insuror that it ***should*** *be.) This is one instance when taking the time to find a truly breastfeeding-friendly health care provider for your baby can prove very valuable. And if, after pumping for a while, you discover that you have stockpiled much more breastmilk in your freezer than you will ever be able to use, you might consider contacting the Human Milk Banking Association of North America (see page 86) to donate your extra milk for other mothers and babies.*

Mother's Nature
703 Main Street
Watertown, CT 06795
Phone: (888) 8SLINGS (toll free for US) or (203) 945–3431 (outside the U.S.)
http://www.babyholder.com
E-mail: danie@babyholder.com

Breastpumps, etc
210 Green Lake Road
Hayneville, AL 36040
Phone: (334) 220–1039
http://breastpumps-etc.com
E-mail: michelle@breastpumps–etc.com

Nursing Mother Supplies
Phone: (800) 688–6545
http://www.nursingmothersupplies.com
E-mail:wendy@nursingmothersupplies.com

The Motherwear Catalog
Phone: (800) 950–2500
http://www.motherwear.com
Authors' Note: Motherwear has the best selection of career clothing with discreet nursing access.

Slightly Crunchy
37 West Street
Cromwell, CT 06416
Phone: (860) 635–5662 or (877) CRUNCHIES
http:// www.crunchmail.com
E-mail:slightlycrunchy@aol.com

Little Koala
PO Box 9102
Pittsburgh, PA 15224–9102
Phone: (412) 687–1239
http://www.littlekoala.com
E-mail: sales@littlekoala.com

WEB SITES

Cecilia Mitchell Miller's Breastfeeding and the Working Mother Page
http://www.kjsl.com/~cee/working.htm

Breastfeeding and Returning to Work
http://www.promom.org/bf_work.html

Breastfeeding Solutions from Medela (a leading manufacturer of breastpumps)

http://www.medela.com

WABA: The World Alliance for Breastfeeding Action

http://www.elogica.com.br/waba/working.htm

Laura's Pumping Page

http://www.deleons.com/pumping_page.htm

The Pumping Moms' Information Exchange

http://www.enscript.com/pump/index.html

The Working Cow

http://www.geocities.com/Wellesley/4092

Author's note: Love the site; hate *the name! After all, breastfeeding women don't need to be compared to cows. We are lactating mammals in our own right. Comparing us to cows reinforces the idea that there is something unusual about* humans *producing milk for our own babies.*

Breastfeeding: A Feminist Issue, by Penny Van Esterik

http://www.elogica.com.br/waba/acsh4.htm

Breastfeeding in the Workplace at Zelda's Feminist Mom Center of the Universe

http://www.geocities.com/Athens/5262/bfwork.htm

INTERNET E-MAIL LISTS

The Pumping List *This group discusses pumping and related topics (ie: lactation problems, supply boosters). You can reach them on their Web page* http://www.enscript.com/pump. *Upon subscribing please introduce yourself. Also, they have compiled a list of frequently asked questions (FAQs) that may be helpful. To subscribe (single post version), send a message to:* listbot@interlink-bbs.com with 'subscribe pump' in the **body** of the message.

NEWSGROUPS

misc.kids.breastfeeding

The Attachment Parent's Guide to Childcare

Authors' Note: *In organizing the following information, we are proceeding under the assumption that readers are* ***already*** *aware of the absolute fundamentals of any quality childcare setting: safety, background checks for caregivers, universal health precautions, CPR certification, cleanliness, etc. Therefore, the following discussion deals* ***only*** *with childcare issues specific to attachment parenting and isn't meant to provide an exhaustive checklist for evaluating childcare. The organizations listed in the resources at the end of this section can provide any parent with a list of* ***all*** *the things that should be considered in choosing a safe, appropriate caregiver for your child.*

If you spend time talking with working parents, you will soon discover that quality childcare is a topic constantly on their minds: how to find it, how to evaluate it, how to keep it, and how to pay for it. Working attachment parents, with their deep respect for their young children's developmental timetables and intense dependency needs, are often even more acutely aware of childcare issues. And when it comes time to find the perfect caregiver for their own breastfed, co-sleeping, sling-worn little one, they want to entrust him to someone who shares their parenting values. Finding that perfect someone *is* possible. But you have to know what to look for.

The Attachment Parenting–Friendly Caregiver

> ▶ *"Our nanny is from Honduras and she grew up with a number of younger brothers and sisters. She says that she always had a baby riding on her hip or back after she was a teenager. She hates using the stroller and keeps Kyle in the sling most of each day. I gave her her own sling within a few weeks of her starting work with us. She loves using it for him and looks forward to using it with her own baby when she has one. Kyle is very happy riding in the sling and the two of them are very close. It's very cute to see Rosa carrying Kyle in the sling at the park alongside all the other nannies and moms pushing strollers."*
>
> —*PAULA, MOTHER OF AN EIGHT MONTH OLD*

Ideally, you will be able to find a caregiver who shares your parenting style. You want someone who will understand the importance of offering your pumped breastmilk to your baby, who will hold or wear your baby during your working hours, and who will respond swiftly and attentively to his cues. The best place to look for such a person is among other families who also believe in the benefits of attachment parenting. Start by talking to playgroup friends, parents in your neighborhood, your midwife or doula, and other mothers at La Leche League meetings. Maybe you have a friend from your childbirth class who gave birth at around the same time you did and who would now like to provide childcare in order to stay home with her own child. If you know that you will be returning to work after a few months, you should begin putting out feelers for childcare while you are still pregnant. Mention your search to everyone you can think of.

If you are unable to find a suitable childcare provider for your child through personal referral, you may need to place an ad in the newspaper or a notice up at the food co-op, grocery store, bookstore, coffee house, etc. *Mothering Magazine* (listed in the resource section in chapter one) also features frequent classified ads from attachment parenting families searching nationally for live-in help. Here is what one attachment parenting family wrote in their local newspaper ad. They were so successful that they were able to choose among several terrific applicants who told them that they really appreciated the highly descriptive nature of their ad:

Childcare Provider Needed

We are searching for a loving, responsive full-time caregiver for our six month old son. We are a vegetarian family committed to breastfeeding, natural weaning, gentle guidance, and deep respect for children. We are seeking someone who also embraces these values and who would like to become a trusted, long-term member of our family. No spankers, Ferberizers, or yellers need apply! Competitive salary with some benefits. Rigorous background check required.

Once you have narrowed down your applicant pool (or list of daycare centers or family daycare homes) over the phone, you can begin interviewing the potential caregivers in person. It is best to ask open-ended questions (again, these will be in addition to very specific questions regarding such things as work history, knowledge base, education, and references) so that you can get a real feel for the person's views on chidren and parenting. Here are some suggestions for questions to ask:

- What are your views on breastfeeding?
- What do you think babies and young children need in order to thrive?
- How will you get my child to sleep for naps?
- What are your views on discipline for babies and young children? School-age children?
- Why do you want to care for my child?
- Imagine an ideal day caring for my child. How would it go?
- How much or how little do you think babies and toddlers should be held or carried?
- How will you respond if my child cries?
- Do you have a favorite childcare guide?
- What are your views on how to develop independence in a child?
- Do you have children of your own? (Sadly, many women who work as nannies are forced to leave their own babies and young children in order to earn a living by caring for the children of more affluent families. The painful ironies of this arrangement are clear. As an individual with respect for the special and important bond that exists between parent and child, you should obviously approach a situation such as this with sensitivity. If you find a caregiver for your own child who has a baby of her own, you might consider offering her the option of bringing her little one with her to your home.)

Creating Community for Your Child

Attachment parenting is about respecting the uniquely sensitive bond that families share. Working attachment parents have both the opportunity and the responsibility to create a larger community of caring for their child which honors that bond, while at the same time offers one or more additional people with whom a child can become bonded. When a childcare arrangement works as it should, your child will grow to care deeply for his caregiver and his caregiver will support and celebrate your attachment with your child. Keep this ideal in mind as you seek and evaluate potential caregivers.

When you do find the right caregiver for your child—whether it's a daycare teacher, family daycare provider, or nanny—you should work hard to include her in your circle of family and community. Get to know her as a person. Invite her to your home for the occasional meal. Remember her birthdays and special holidays. Meet her own children and have them over to play with yours. She will let you know the level of familiarity with which she is comfortable, but make every effort to let her know that you value her and the complementary role she plays to your own. You might buy a sling or baby backpack just for her use and you can offer to share your favorite parenting books and articles with her.

The Critical Importance of Consistency in Caregiving

Perhaps no other factor is as important to attachment parents in evaluating the suitability of an otherwise safe and appropriate childcare situation as the consistency of care. Just as we should be sensitive to the bond between a parent and child, we should also be sensitive to the meaningful bonds that can develop between young children and their parent substitutes. Babies and young children simply don't have the ability to understand or deal with repeated changes in caregivers.

Many daycare centers—even fancy, high priced ones—have a very high turnover rate. This is because childcare workers tend to be underpaid, underappreciated, and overworked. A baby or young child who is in a daycare center may have two daycare teachers, plus aides, plus substitutes caring for him over the course of any given week. It can be difficult for a little person to grow close to anyone (or for them to grow close to him) in a situation like this. Additionally, most daycare centers move children from class to class as they grow. Thus, an eleven month old baby who has developed a deep, trusting relationship with one or two teachers (with whom he has spent forty hours a week since he was eight weeks old) may suddenly find himself "promoted" to the "toddler class"—and into the arms of adults he doesn't know from Adam—the day after his first birthday. This is confusing and upsetting for a young child. A child under three who is shuffled around in this way doesn't care whether the toys in his new daycare classroom are more colorful and age appropriate, or whether the other children in the group share his chronological age, so much as he does that he has just lost the sound, smell, and touch of the people he has come to depend on in his parents' absence.

When evaluating a potential childcare situation, strive to find a caregiver for your infant or toddler who is likely to remain "on the job" for as long as possible. If you are considering a daycare center, ask them about their turnover rate and how they handle class promotions (a very gradual, sensitive approach is best). If you are interviewing a nanny, au pair, or family daycare provider, inquire about their plans for three months, six months, and one year down the road. Find out how long the person has stayed in her last several positions. If she has a history of brief employment stints, you will probably want to avoid her. Obviously, there are never any guarantees when you hire someone that she won't suddenly decide to leave in the future, but finding out whether a potential caregiver understands and appreciates the value of caregiving consistency in a young child's life is vital.

Child-Caregiver Ratio

The ratio of children to caregivers in a childcare setting is also very important. As an attachment parent, you understand the importance of plenty of hands-on, responsive care for your baby or young child. You want your child held and rocked when she is given her bottle at daycare, and talked to and massaged when her diaper is changed. And you know how time-consuming it is to offer that kind of special care to even one or two of your own little ones. Therefore, you should be aware that many otherwise attractive daycare centers and family daycare homes have a ratio of four or more *infants* per caregiver! In fact, in many states this is considered the low end/most attractive infant-to-caregiver ratio! It is highly unlikely that one person can give high quality, attentive care to more than three infants at a time. With even three babies per adult, the simple fact is that your child will have to spend a good portion of her day sitting alone in a bouncy seat or swing, or on a blanket on the floor. If several babies are fussing at once, a caregiver in this situation will be forced to leave one or more of them to soothe themselves.

Because a nanny or au pair generally cares for only one or two children in the same family at a time (and if there are more, they aren't all infants unless you are the parent of higher order multiples), they can often provide more responsive care while your child is an infant. Many working, attachment parents hire a nanny to provide one-on-one care for their infant, but begin adding part-time nursery school or daycare into their caregiving mix after their child becomes verbal and can handle larger groups of children. If you are the mother of one baby and feel that you can't afford a nanny, you might look into splitting her salary with one other single baby, attachment parenting family. In this way, your child will get highly personalized care and a very low child-to-caregiver ratio at a cost more comparable to group care. Another option is to choose a small, *licensed* family daycare home with only two or three children in which your child would be the only infant in the group.

Attachment Grandparenting

One sometimes overlooked possibility for one-on-one care for your child is a grandparent. Grandparents often care for a grandchild while parents work, at least through the first year or two. If you get along with your parents and they live nearby, you might consider asking them to give your child this special gift of themselves. Even if their parenting views aren't in perfect alignment with your own, this arrangement can work beautifully as long as both parents and grandparents are able to be honest and respectful with one another regarding differences in parenting style. In other words, your child's grandparents must be willing to accept that *you* are your child's parent and handle the caregiving "biggies" (like feeding, discipline, toilet training and sleep) in the way that *you* choose. You, on the other hand, might need to be more relaxed about smaller things like what books your parents choose to read to the baby or how they play pat-a-cake. In many cases, the intense love of a grandparent who provides childcare for her grandchild more than makes up for any minor differences in childcare practices or philosophies.

► *"When my first child was born only eleven months after I was married, I was still warily getting to know my new in-laws (and vice versa!). Because our finances required me to return to work when the baby was only eight weeks old, I was understandably very nervous about who could care for such a tiny baby. We couldn't afford a nanny and even the best daycare centers seemed so impersonal and institutional. My husband was thrilled when his parents unexpectedly offered to care for Sara while we worked. They didn't want her in daycare at that age and neither did we, but I wasn't so sure about their offer. I could see that they were so very different from me and I wanted to do everything my way with the baby. But in hindsight, allowing them to provide childcare for Sara for her first two years was one of the best decisions I ever made. Although I was gone forty hours per week, Sara was tenderly rocked and sung to and loved by her grandparents. They learned a lot about breastfeeding from me (my mother-in-law never considered breastfeeding her own children) and have become real breastfeeding boosters. My father-in-law has even tried the sling with Sara a few times! I had to be flexible on some issues though. For example, I didn't want her in disposable diapers at all and they refuse to deal with cloth. But the frustrations of the arrangement were minor compared to the payoff. It brought us all closer together as a family. Now Sara goes to a daycare center, but she is still very attached to both her parents and her grandparents."*

—CARRIE, MOTHER OF A THREE YEAR OLD

Don't Settle

Many times, working parents have a very difficult time finding and keeping suitable childcare for their baby or young child. If you live in a rural area or small town, your choices may be severely limited. If you are on a very tight budget, you may have trouble affording the type of substitute care you know your child needs. And even parents with lots of choices and the income to pay for a live-in nanny can find themselves repeatedly left in the lurch when their caregivers suddenly and unexpectedly quit. At times like these, you may be left feeling desperate and inclined to settle for less than ideal childcare just so you can get to work each day.

If you find yourself feeling that you have no choice but to settle for what you know in your heart to be suboptimal childcare, we encourage you to step back, take a deep breath, and reevaluate your entire situation. You know that your child's first three years are critical to his long-term development and emotional well-being. Now is not the time to settle for less than the best when it comes to his care. If you simply cannot find, afford or retain attachment parenting friendly childcare, you may want to consider some of the following work alternatives (such as sequencing and working from home) that we will discuss later in the chapter. Maybe your partner could even take a second job or later shift for a year or two so that you can be home during the day. Although these measures may sound extreme, the investment you will be making in your child by honoring the special needs of his infancy and early childhood will pay dividends for the rest of his life. Don't settle for less than your child needs and deserves from the adults in his life.

The Very Best Childcare Resources for Attachment Parents

The National Association for the Education of Young Children (NAEYC)

National Association for the Education of Young Children
1509 16th Street, N.W.
Washington, DC 20036
Phone: (202) 232–8777 or (800) 424–2460
Fax: (202) 328–1846
http://www.naeyc.org
E-Mail: naeyc@naeyc.org

The NAEYC is the nation's foremost organization of early childhood specialists and professionals. They provide a rigorous accreditation process for child care centers and preschools, as well as information for parents on how to find and evaluate child care providers.

The Child Care Action Campaign
330 Seventh Avenue, 17th Floor
New York, NY 10001
Phone: (212) 239–0138
E-mail: hn5746@handsnet.org

The Child Care Action Campaign (CCAC) is a national, nonprofit coalition of individuals, organizations and businesses. CCAC focuses most of its efforts on defining good child care, spurring cooperation among business, government and private agencies, and assisting grassroots community efforts to expand the availability of good child care.

Child Welfare League of America (CWLA)
440 First Street, NW, Third Floor
Washington, DC 20001-2085
Phone: (202) 638–2952
Fax: (202) 638–4004
http://www.cwla.org

Children's Defense Fund (CDF)
25 E Street, NW
Washington, DC 20001
Phone: (202) 628–8787
Fax: (202) 234–0217
http://www.childrensdefense.org

Both CWLA and CDF advocate at the legislative, grassroots, and personal level for quality, affordable child care. Parents can contact either organization for information on how to find, evaluate, and pay for child care.

Money, Money, Money

Many parents, when asked why they work, will tell you that they do it "for the money," meaning that, although in some cases, they really don't even *like* their jobs that much and would prefer to be at home with their children, their family simply couldn't survive without their income. In some instances, this is literally true; if the parent in question didn't go to work each day, the family would be without shelter or food on the table. For many others, however, the issue of money is one that *can* be dealt with creatively if a parent feels that this is the only thing preventing her from being at home. When deciding whether you can afford to stay home with your child, here are some points to consider:

• **Take a hard look at your budget and separate "needs" from "wants."** This may seem like a ridiculously simplistic bit of advice, but it's amazing how many parents driving brand-new sport utility vehicles (with attendant car and insurance payments) believe that they "can't afford" to stay home with their children. Car payments, cable television, magazines, dry cleaning, take-out pizza, lawn maintenance costs . . . these can all add up to a second salary for many middle-class families. Additionally, a growing number of families today are finding that curing their "affluenza" by paring down and cutting the fat out of their budgets (and lives) yields many great rewards in addition to allowing one parent to be at home. Excellent resources on this topic include:

Your Money or Your Life: Transforming Your Relationship with Money and Achieving Financial Independence. Dominguez, Joe, and Vicki Robin. New York: Penguin Viking, 1993.

Financial Peace: Restoring Financial Hope to You and Your Family. Ramsey, Dave, and Sharon Ramsey. New York: Viking Penguin, 1997.

• **Ask yourself how much you are actually earning at your job.** Unless you have a higher-than-average income, it may not make much financial sense for you to work full-time while paying for childcare. Why? Because once you deduct the cost of highest quality childcare (which, in some areas of the country costs more than half of many middle-class workers' take home pay), taxes, transportation, extra clothing, etc, you may discover that you are working for almost zero net gain. With more than one child in childcare, you may end up actually *losing* money by working outside the home.

- **Are there alternative sources of income that you could tap into in order to invest in a year or more at home (or at home part-time) with your child?** Some parents decide to liquidate an investment, sell a piece of property or a valuable possession (like a second car), or even take out a loan in order to fund one parent's ability to stay home with a baby or young child. After all, if providing your child with a college education is an investment commonly seen to be worth borrowing for, providing your child with a secure base of love and attachment in early childhood should certainly be as well. If staying home is a priority for you, this option may be worthy of your serious consideration.
- **Some parents decide to take the admittedly extreme measure of applying for public assistance of some sort to cover or supplement their income in order for them to spend at least their child's infancy at home.** Although the idea of relying on public assistance, including WIC or food stamps, is harshly judged by many in the United States, other countries' governments consider supporting new parents' at-home care for their babies a wise investment.

Paradigm Busting: New Ways to Work for Attachment Parents

► *"My partner and I are working hard to create a family-based way of life. We want home, parenting, work and our relationship to all be part of a seamless web, not separate and compartmentalized boxes. It's exciting!"*

—*MARY ALICE, MOTHER OF TWO*

In the past, parents—and mothers in particular—were labeled as either "working" or "stay-at-home." Increasingly, however, these labels aren't nearly as clear cut. A growing number of parents are refusing to accept the traditional "either/or" mentality of the work-family decision. Instead they are seeking out or creating a variety of new ways to work that meet the intense attachment needs of their young children, while still offering them the chance to remain active in their career or academic pursuits. These include:

- **Sequencing.** Sequencing is a concept that allows parents to have it all . . . but not all at the same time. Instead, parents recognize that their lives will have a series of "sequences" during which they will devote more time to career (before having children and as their children mature) or family (during their children's early years). Sequencing parents wisely recognize that a life path can do some zigging and zagging while still generally heading in a chosen direction. In other words, you don't necessarily have to stay on an unflappably straight and narrow path toward your career goals. You might choose to leave your career for several years in order to parent from home, while fully expecting to return to your job at a particular point in the future. In the meantime, you can stay up-to-date in your field with Internet e-mail lists or newsgroups or occasional consulting or part-time work. For more information on the sequencing concept, check out:

Sequencing. Cardozo, Arlene R. Reprint edition. Minneapolis, MN: Brownstone Books, 1996.

- **Part-time work.** Although part-time work was once viewed as the province of those who couldn't get a "real job," this is most assuredly no longer the case. A growing number of parents seeking satisfaction on both the home and work fronts are finding or creating part-time work situations for themselves. Because separations of a few hours at a time are easier on young children and breastfeeding mothers, part-time work is very appealing to many working attachment parents. Some people approach their current employers with proposals for reconfiguring their jobs temporarily (while children are young) or permanently, so that they work less than the forty hour per week standard. Other working parents make a complete career change in order to facilitate their desire for part-time employment. Creative part-time solutions such as job-sharing, in which one full-time job is split between two part-time employees (which can sometimes be two parents in the same family), are also becoming increasingly popular and well-accepted by all types of employers. In today's competitive business climate, savvy employers know that making reasonable accomodations in order to retain a valuable employee (like you) makes good financial sense. There are many excellent resources available for parents seeking to find or create part-time employment. The best include:

Going Part-Time: The Insider's Guide for Professional Women Who Want a Career and a Life. Tolliver, Cindy, and Nancy Chambers. New York: Avon Books, 1997.

The Part Time Solution: The New Strategy for Managing Your Career While Managing Motherhood by Canape, Charlene (1991)

• **Working from home.** The era of the work-at-home employee has arrived. With the advent of the modern home office, including dual telephone lines, modems and fax machines, more and more jobs can be relocated to an extra corner of your house. Economic forecasters predict that working from home—as an employee or a self-employed individual—will be the hottest trend of the next several decades. Attachment parents who wish to minimize separation from their children while still earning a living often find this an extremely attractive option, albeit one with its own challenges. Most work-at-home parents discover it necessary to trade off primary child care with their partner or employ some in-home childcare in order to maximize their own productivity.

In other cases, work-at-home parents perform some or all of their work after their child is in bed for the night.

> ► *"I have really enjoyed working from my home office for the past several years. My publisher acquired this book when Elliot, my third baby, was only a few months old. As a result, I wrote a good bit of the first half of the book, as well as conducting telephone interviews and Internet research for my other freelance writing assignments, while Elliot was happily breastfeeding or snoozing in the baby sling on my chest. He was happy and so was I. Although I work at least twenty hours per week, I never once had to bother with a breastpump or bottles (I'm lazy, so I really appreciate that aspect of staying close to my babies!). As Elliot has become more mobile and wants to get down on the floor and explore, and sometimes on days when my three year old is home from preschool and my seven year old is home from first grade, I employ a college student to care for the children in our home while I work at my desk. When one of my younger two wants to nurse, my mother's helper just lets me know and I take a very pleasant snuggle break from what I'm doing."*
>
> —KATIE, MOTHER OF THREE

Resources for learning more about the work-at-home option and for networking with other parents making the same choice include:

BOOKS

How to Raise a Family and a Career Under One Roof: A Personal Guide to Home Business for Parents. Roberts, Lisa M. Edited by Maria Olson. Moon Township, PA: Bookhaven Press, 1997.

Mompreneurs: A Mother's Step-By-Step Guide to Work-At-Home Success. Parlapiano, Ellen H., and Patricia Cobe. New York: Berkley Publishing Group, 1996.

WEB SITES

The AP-BIZ Network of attachment parents in business.

http://www.apbiz.com/

AP-BIZ is an Internet community of families who are self-employed, freelancers, home-based workers, business owners, and entrepreneurs with a commitment to attachment parenting. You can also subscribe to the AP-Biz e-mail list at http://www.apbiz.com/charter.html

The *iVillage* Work-from-Home

http://www.ivillage.com/work

This page contains perhaps the best collection of resources on the Internet for anyone contemplating working from home.

The Entrepeneurial Parent

http://www.en-parent.com

Brings you essays, links and resources for the work-at-home family. This site also includes a related Web site and message board specifically for work-at-home fathers.

Moms Network Exchange

http://www.momsnetwork.com/

WAHMZ

http://www.wahm.com/business.html

Both of these sites provide a wealth of support and useful information for work-at-home parents.

• **Taking Your Child to Work With You.** All over the world, women go about their daily lives with their babies and young children along for the ride. In many cases, you can do the same, especially during your child's first year. With a baby sling or backpack, your child can stay physically close to you without impeding your ability to perform many tasks, such as gardening, shelving books, working behind a counter, or cooking. Office workers and other professionals can set up a baby area in one corner of their work space. As a nursing mother, you have everything your baby needs (ok, except for diapers . . .) conveniently on hand. As your baby becomes more mobile and less interested in always being physically attached to your body, you might consider bringing your child care provider with you to your place of employment so that you can do your job and still remain available to your child. And of course, a growing number of employers are developing on-site childcare options for their employees in order to maximize both productivity and company loyalty. Both work-at-home parents and those who bring their child along with them have the special benefit of knowing that their child sees the work that they do each day. This is an experience generally lost to modern families in which each family member disappears in a different, wholly separate direction—to the office, daycare or school—each morning.

▶ *"I took Benjamin with me to teach and advise students, and to my own classes. He was most content to breastfeed often, and wasn't easily comforted by others when he was a baby. I couldn't bring myself to leave him with a bottle that I knew he was unlikely to accept, and wonder whether he was desperately crying for me. I think that's a normal maternal feeling, and I'm really glad I honored it. I think the greatest benefit was to me and him, in that we were able to stay close the way a mother and baby were meant to be. I was able to finish my graduate work and earn the money we needed at that time in our life. And I consider it a nice bonus that hundreds of young people saw a mother caring for her child while going about her professional life—that having children and caring for them without daycare is possible and empowering."*

—*Amy, mother of two*

▶ *"When N, my older son, was born, we decided for many reasons, including the fact that we didn't want to abdicate his care to others any more than we had to and also for financial reasons, to try to keep him with us as much as possible. My husband was managing a used bookstore at the time and was able to flex his schedule some. I was teaching at a state university and had some flexibility as well. So, as much as possible, we tried to work alternate schedules. When I was at work and my husband also had to work, he took N to the store with him, bottle of breastmilk and sling in tow. I would finish teaching and pick N up. This worked very well for us until N got to be about 12 months. Then a bookstore was just not an appropriate place for a walking and running toddler. So, we hired a friend who hung out in the store anyway to help out with him there. Later, that arrangement morphed into her taking care of him at our home. As a university instructor, I have taken the children to work with me many times. When I only had one child and he was a baby, I took him to faculty meetings, staff meetings, and to classes. This arrangment became more challenging with more than one child. But I've brought mother's helpers to many a meeting, setting them and the kids up in empty classrooms or out on the university's lawn. We load up with lots of snacks, drinks, and toys and we try to arrive early so the kids get a chance to acclimate before I have to start teaching, and it usually works really well. I also have loads of toys in my office, and I've noticed that several other of my colleagues do as well. It is important for me that my children have a part in our lives outside of the home."*

—DAWN, *MOTHER OF TWO*

Perhaps the best resource for parents seeking new ways to effectively combine good parenting with earning a living is *The Families and Work Institute*. Founded in 1989, FWI seeks to "identify and address the pressing questions around how to create stronger families, more supportive communities, and more effective workplaces." Interested parents can contact FWI to obtain one of their many publications on such topics as developing on site childcare, negotiating parental leaves, or proposing job sharing arrangements at:

Families and Work Institute
330 Seventh Avenue, 14th Floor
New York, NY 10001
Phone: (212) 465–2044
Fax: (212) 465–8637
http://www.familiesandwork.org/index.html

CHAPTER 8

To Have and to Hold

✦ **"One Sunday, at an outdoor festival in Florida, I did a casual count of how infants under one year of age were transported. Babes in arms totalled five, one carried by mother, and four carried by father. Babies in buggies numbered thirty, divided equally between mother propelling and father propelling. This indicates that even on Sunday, when both mother and father can share carrying, babies are primarily wheeled. In other words, not carrying our babies goes beyond our lack of helping hands. If Florida is at all representative, it has become a national habit."**

—*Sharon Heller, Ph.D. in*
The Vital Touch: How Intimate Contact With Your Baby Leads to Happier, Healthier Development

► *"Once I became accustomed to actually carrying my child on my body in the frontpack and later, the backpack, it began to look really strange to me to see tiny babies in carriages. It seems very artificial and bizarre to wheel around at arm's length a fifteen pound bundle of baby human who longs to snuggle in close to your body warmth."*

—Cindy, mother of an eighteen month old

IN THE MINDS OF MANY MODERN PARENTS, THE STROLLER AND carriage are truly essential items of baby equipment. New models are released every season, and each one is more colorful, feature-laden, and costly than the year before. Nowadays, parents can buy strollers made of space-age titanium, "sport-utility" strollers, or even baby carriages that will coordinate with the color and theme of their diaper bag and nursery bedding. In recent years, a veritable smorgasbord of other expensive baby-holding gadgets such as vibrating bouncy seats, "exersaucers," rolling bassinets, automatic swings, portable playpens, reclining high chairs, and feeding seats have also come to be seen as necessary items to have on hand when a new baby arrives. In fact, navigating through a new parent's house these days can often be tricky, as one attempts to avoid stumbling over the vast array of brightly colored baby-containers that litter every room. Entire households appear to be organized around figuring out how the new parent can escape from actually holding and carrying her baby. And it's a common sight to see a parent lugging her baby around town by the handle of an unwieldy, heavy, plastic "baby bucket" (carrier/carseat)—often weighing as much or more than the baby himself—rather than simply transporting the baby in her arms. Of course, the companies who manufacture, market, and sell these products, as well as the glossy parenting magazines which advertise them on virtually every page, have a strong interest in promoting the idea that parents really *shouldn't* carry or hold their babies excessively. But the fact is that human infants, like most mammal babies, are happiest, most comfortable, and develop best when they are kept physically close to a warm body much of the time. And parents who hold, carry, or "wear" their babies on their bodies find themselves better able to read and respond to their babies' cues, as well as to more easily go about their own regular daily routine while staying physically close to their little one. For these reasons and more, "babywearing"—a term coined by Dr. William Sears—is one of the basic (and most enjoyable!) attachment parenting tools.

Baby-Carrying Around the Globe

> ✦ **"From a baby's point of view, the hunter-and-gatherer life is better because it supplies all the necessary ingredients and opportunities for a symbiotic parent-infant dyad. The point is not that we need to re-create the dynamics of hunter/gatherer societies, but rather that we recognize those parts of other lifestyles that are beneficial to infants and figure out those ways to incorporate those lessons into the parent-infant tradition in our own culture, if we choose to do so."**
>
> —*Anthropologist Meredith F. Small*

As with so many of our parenting practices, our excessive reliance on baby containers differs markedly from the way families all over the globe handle the issue of where the baby will "be" as a parent goes about her day. Many other cultures assume that a parent/infant pair *simply belong together*, comprising two parts of the same whole, for at least the first year or so. Additionally, these busy parents have things they need to accomplish and they need a way to keep their child close by and safe without being unreasonably tied down themselves. They also need to be able to breastfeed easily and on the go. For these reasons, in a wide variety of cultures, babies and young children spend the greatest part of each day riding comfortably in a cloth sling of some type that is worn on an adult caregiver's front, back, or side. In some instances, women even create slings out of the same fabric as a favorite item of clothing so that her carried baby literally becomes a part of her "outfit."

Why Don't We Carry and Hold Our Babies?

In the United States, our views on baby-holding and carrying are at the other end of the spectrum. Prior to the advent of the male dominated "scientific" childcare guidance that began to flood the American marketplace at the end of the nineteenth century, our babies were probably carried and held much more often. But once the pediatric advice industry began strongly influencing new parents, many mothers and fathers became convinced that too much holding or carrying of a baby was actually a *Bad Thing.* Today, lingering fallout from this outdated and unsupported point of view can still be found in many childcare guides and pediatric offices, which advise that carrying, holding, or wearing a baby can hinder a child's progress toward independence, tie a parent down, and even (according to one well-known childcare advisor) cause "developmental damage" in children. Of course, none of this is true, and a rapidly growing number of modern, western parents are discovering the ease and advantages of holding, carrying, and wearing their own babies and young children.

Our Untouched Babies

> ✦ **"Essentially, first touch—not only the first moment of physical touch, but the touch that the infant receives at the beginning of his or her life—is the single most influential factor that will determine a future life of love, or one of unlove. . . . First touch is that important."**
>
> —*Mariana Caplan, author of* Untouched: The Need for Genuine Affection in an Impersonal World

Not coincidentally, but as a direct result of popular mainstream parenting styles, American babies are among the least touched on the planet, according to researchers. In fact, the average American baby is in physical contact with a caregiver only twenty-five percent or less of the time, with touch-time down to below twenty percent by a baby's ninth month. These percentages represent a significant deficit compared to the rest of the world. Korean babies, for example, spend *more than ninety percent of their time* "in touch" with another human.

Why does this low-touch approach to babycare matter? Because a wide and well-respected variety of research from a number of different fields of study—including child development, psychiatry, neonatology, and anthropology—has revealed that human infants literally *require* sufficient physical touch in order to develop to their optimal potential. Premature babies have been shown to gain weight and strength better the more they are touched by their parents. But even full term babies who do not receive sufficient physical contact grow more slowly and can experience developmental delays. New imaging technology has allowed scientists to see that the brains of untouched babies are demonstrably different than those who are cuddled and stroked regularly.

How much touch is enough? No one knows for sure. And different babies likely have different needs. But the fact that cross-cultural analysis reveals that our babies are getting *significantly* less physical contact each day than other babies around the world should serve as a wake-up call. Sure, babies can *survive* with the mainstream, low-touch approach; but as caring parents, we want more than that for our infants, we want them to *thrive*. Carrying or holding our babies instead of abandoning them to plastic baby-containers provides them this touch that they crave and deserve. Plus, nothing feels better to an attached parent than cradling an adorable baby in her arms and breathing in his delicious baby smell. We should indulge ourselves in this—one of life's great pleasures—as often as possible because in the blink of an eye, our babies and toddlers will be seventy-five pound, tree-climbing ten-year olds!

► *"As your children grow, you aren't aware until much later of the very last time you carried, rocked, or held them. It's such a gradual process as they grow out of your arms and venture out into the wider world. I like to think of it in terms of a gentle weaning from the safety of my arms. But my children are secure and independent because they had their needs met fully and unquestioningly as babies and toddlers. Plus, they knew that I would never push them away before they were ready to stand on their own."*

—*Bill, father of three teenagers*

Artificial Baby-Containers

✦ **"Infant seats . . . do nothing to promote attachment between mother and baby. The mother's body draws the baby into a pulsing circle of warmth, softness and roundness that contains and cushions his shape in supple, receptive contours; that adjusts and adapts in sync with his turns, squirms and stretches; that massages him in slow fluid motions that vary his day and give rhythm to his existence. This cements the connection between mother and child; plastic containers do none of this. As such, they dramatically change the baby's sense of life and human relationships."**

—*Sharon Heller, Ph.D., in*
The Vital Touch: How Intimate Contact With Your Baby Leads to Happier, Healthier Development

Used in moderation, strollers can obviously be a wonderful help to a parent, as can swings, bouncy seats, high chairs, and other similar products. Once a baby is old enough to sit up and look around, he may really enjoy a brisk stroll around the neighborhood. Parents who run or walk for exercise can include their older babies and toddlers in their daily routine with the use of "baby joggers"—which are sturdy strollers made just for this purpose. And many parents of intense or high needs infants are grateful for the relief that an automatic swing or vibrating seat can sometimes provide their fussing babies. The newer stationary walkers (the older, rolling walkers are no longer recommended by most child safety experts), such as "exersaucers," can entertain an older baby for short periods and give him a sense of accomplishment as he stands and bounces.

However, parents are often *overly* reliant on all this baby gadgetry to the exclusion of actually *holding* and *touching* their babies. Increasing numbers of infants are moved from baby-container to baby-container all day long with a bare minimum of real physical human contact. With the advent of the carseat/carrier combos, buckets full of baby—encased in heavy plastic and colorful canvas—are simply toted around by their handle from car to shopping cart to tables at restaurants, rarely being removed from their carrier for more than a diaper change. When one of these babies-in-a-bucket needs to eat, many parents or caregivers place a plastic bottle full of artificial baby milk in his mouth without even taking him out of his seat. Fussy, bucketed babies are too often plugged into lethargy with the use of a pacifier.

> ✦ **"Plastic infant seats are stiff. Babies' soft, flexible bodies are suited to fold into the crook of an arm, nuzzle into a neck, enfold into a breast, not to press against rigid, solid, unyielding surfaces."**
>
> —*Sharon Heller, Ph.D.*

The best advice is to utilize the modern baby-containers *in moderation*. Watch your child's cues to determine how much time he is comfortable sitting in one position in a rigid plastic seat or strapped into a carriage. If he seems fussy or malcontent, respect what he is trying to tell you. If your baby is very placid and accepting by nature, don't take advantage of his calm disposition by overusing the baby-containers. Remember that newborns and young infants have a special need for almost constant physical closeness with another human. And consider the alternatives: in this chapter you will be introduced to a variety of baby carriers that will allow you to conveniently transport your baby wherever you need to go while still keeping him "in-touch" with you. Additionally, you can employ siblings, partners, friends, and grandparents as substitutes when you feel that your own arms need a break from baby-holding. The smiling face of a sister or cousin or neighbor will offer your baby much more in the way of emotional sustenance and brain food than any colorful plastic mobile fastened to the side of a playpen.

Can a Baby Be Held or Carried "Too Much"?

> ✦ **"On the most basic, instinctual level, physical contact is essential to sustain all human life . . . On a deeper level, the intimacy that is created through touch is what creates a feeling of 'aliveness' in the individual—for touch brings us to life."**
>
> —*Mariana Caplan, author of* Untouched: The Need for Genuine Affection in an Impersonal World

You may worry that carrying or holding your baby or toddler a great deal will inhibit his emerging independence or even prevent him from learning to walk. If this were the case, babies all over the world—many of whom are carried for most of their waking hours for their entire first year or so—would never learn to crawl, walk, run, or play with other children! But these babies *do* learn to do these things—and your own (securely attached, touch-nourished) baby will too. Try to let go of your preconceived notions of how a baby *should* spend his day—perhaps contentedly stacking blocks behind the mesh fence of his playpen or lying in his crib gazing up at a mobile or strapped into a bouncy seat while the rest of the family watches TV. Instead, think of those times as temporary interruptions in a different sort of daily routine—one in which your baby is in contact with your body or that of another caregiver much of the time.

With a newborn and young infant, you will likely find that he is blissfully content as long as you are holding him, wearing him in a carrier, or sleeping beside him.* Instead of feeling that you *should* put him down, rest assured that he is *exactly* where he needs to be. Once you find the right baby carrier for you, you will be able to do much of your baby-holding *hands-free* (and that is something your carriage-pushing pals can't say!). As your baby becomes older and more mobile, he will let you know when he wants to get down to kick, stretch, roll, practice his crawl, and eventually, his first steps. In the meantime, consider baby-holding your "default" setting as a parent. Don't worry about holding or carrying your baby or toddler too much. Instead, you should worry about all those young children who don't get held or carried enough.

> ✦ **"In counseling parents of fussy babies, we strive for two goals: to mellow the temperament of the baby and to increase the sensitivity of the parents. Babywearing helps foster both of these goals. By creating an organized, womblike environment, wearing lessens a baby's need to cry. Even when a baby does cry,**

---

*Even those babies who—no matter what you do or try—seem naturally predisposed to cry a great deal in the early months of their lives, need a parent close by to empathize with them.

> **babywearing teaches her to 'cry better.' Parents, please remember that it is not your fault that your baby cries, nor is it your job to keep baby from crying. The best you can do is not to let baby cry *alone*, and create a secure environment that lessens baby's need to cry. Babywearing helps you do this."**
>
> —*DR. WILLIAM AND MARTHA SEARS FROM* THE BABY BOOK

Wonderful resources for attachment parents of a fussy, high-needs, or colicky child include:

BOOKS

Parenting the High-Need Child. Sears, William, and Martha Sears. New York: Little, Brown & Co., 1996.

Raising Your Spirited Child. Kurcinka, Mary S. New York: HarperCollins, 1998.

The Many Benefits of Wearing Your Baby

- *"When I am carrying my son in the sling, I feel like we are whole, complete and connected. I can't describe how 'just-right' having him nestled against my body feels."*

  —*STEPHANIE, MOTHER OF A FIVE MONTH OLD*

- *"When I need to get her to sleep, I just put her in the sling at around bedtime and we go for a walk around the neighborhood. She nods right out."*

  —*MICHELLE, MOTHER OF A ONE YEAR OLD*

- *"I wear Margaret in the backpack while I cook dinner, browse at the bookstore, or walk for exercise. She loves it up there. She feels close to me and has a great view. I have my hands free and don't have to worry that she is into something. The backpack is definitely a dad's best friend."*

—JONATHAN, FATHER OF FOUR

► *"My very fussy baby simply would not allow us to put him down . . . ever. I was going crazy thinking something was wrong with him and that a baby should want to be put down sometimes. Then a friend loaned me her sling and voila! We were both happier. He is much more content being worn in the sling and I feel much freer. My hands are actually available now to get things done, but I still am able to offer my baby the extra nurturing that his personality clearly requires."*

—BETH, MOTHER OF A SIX MONTH OLD

✦ **"Both clinging to the mother and having the mother move around while the baby is attached are important experiences for all higher primates, including humans. Just like breastfeeding and co-sleeping, these are suites of behaviors that have evolved over many millions of years. None of the higher primates leave their babies in nests—they all carry them on their bodies for many months/years."**

—KATHERINE DETTWYLER, PH.D.,
ASSOCIATE PROFESSOR OF ANTHROPOLOGY AND NUTRITION
AT TEXAS A&M UNIVERSITY

The benefits of wearing your baby are numerous and profound, and include the following:

• **Carried babies cry less.** Published scientific studies, as well as a wide variety of anthropological and anecdotal evidence, have revealed that babies who are frequently carried, worn, or held cry significantly less than babies who are not. In fact, researchers observing cultures in which baby wearing is the norm have reported that prolonged bouts of crying among infants in these societies are virtually nonexistent.

• **Wearing a baby frees a new parent.** Many new parents report feeling housebound. By wearing her baby, however, a parent can easily take her child almost anywhere she needs or wants to go. As a baby-wearing parent, you will avoid the hassles of folding and unfolding a stroller, and of maneuvering it in and out of cars and public transportation. There is also no heavy, unwieldy plastic carrier for you to lug around. A sling-worn baby who is out with his parent has his own cozy environment in which he can easily sit up or lie down or nap or nurse, all while comfortably nestled against his parent's warm body.

• **Wearing a young infant protects him from overstimulation.** Many newborns become irritable and distressed when bombarded with too much noise, sound, color, or light. When he is cradled snugly against his parent's body in a secure, cozy carrier, a baby's "womb with a view" lets in only as much stimulation as he can handle. Alone in a wide open stroller or carriage, however, a tiny baby is completely vulnerable to overstimulation.

• **The movement of babywearing encourages a tired baby to wind down and go to sleep.** Wearing your baby works as a wonderful alternative to the tried and true bedtime tricks such as a rocking chair or a ride in the car. Many parents choose to make babywearing a part of their evening routine by taking a stroll at bedtime while wearing their baby or toddler.

• **Carrying your baby promotes his language and social development.** Babies who are worn by their parents are up at eye and voice level. They see and are engaged in their parents' conversations with others. They are able to closely observe how people interact with one another and they can begin eliciting their own responses from the people their parents encounter. This has the obvious benefit of encouraging a baby's developing language skills. Babies in a bucket or a stroller, on the other hand, are placed far away from their parents' interactions with other people.

• **A baby who is held, carried, and worn frequently and joyfully is less clingy as he grows.** He doesn't develop the feeling that he has to whine or beg to be picked up.

• **Wearing your baby promotes your attachment to him.** The close physical contact of carrying, holding, and wearing a baby stimulates the attachment promoting hormones in a nursing mother's body. Plus, both fathers and mothers who wear their babies say that they are able to actually *sense* their babies' changing moods, needs, states of mind, and hunger when they are held close, as opposed to at arm's length and separated by a physical barrier of plastic. The baby sling, in particular, serves as a type of "external womb" which allows a parent to maintain a close bond and a feeling of being "as one" with her baby as he gradually seeks more and more individual autonomy at his own healthy pace.

• **Wearing a baby allows a parent to more easily spend time with her older children.** With your baby in a carrier, you can have your hands free to pull your toddler in a wagon, push your preschooler on the swingset, hold your twins' hands while crossing the street, or kick a soccer ball around the yard with your teenager.

• **Babywearing helps to get breastfeeding off to a good start.** Newborns who are frequently carried, held, or worn by their mothers are stimulated to breastfeed more often and are better able to coordinate the physical aspects of breastfeeding.

• **Wearing a baby stimulates his developing nervous system in just the right way.** Babies who do not receive enough rhythmic touching and movement from their caregivers sometimes develop anxious, nervous traits such as self-rocking, head banging, excessive thumb sucking or general fussiness.

Which Baby Carrier Is Right for You?

> ▶ *"When I see parents clumsily wheeling carriages and strollers up and down narrow aisles in stores, or over rough, bumpy patches of sidewalk that shake their baby, or when they can't figure out where to stash the stroller on the subway or an airplane or even in a restaurant, I just look down at my baby, contently resting against my chest in my soft, cloth sling and smile. I now give a sling as a baby shower gift every time."*
>
> —JODI, MOTHER OF TWO

As more and more modern parents are discovering the benefits of wearing their little one around town in a baby carrier of some sort, the variety and quality of carriers available has increased. Now parents can choose from scores of styles, brands, colors, fabrics, and features in a baby carrier. However, in this veritable sea of baby carrying options, parents can simplify the decision if they first realize that carriers come in three basic styles, each with its own pros and cons:

The Frontpack

The frontpack is a style of infant carrier that parents in the west have used for several decades. Although there are many frontpack styles available today, they all have the same basic design consisting of a padded pouch that is strapped onto a parent's chest. The baby is then placed upright in the pouch, with his legs dangling through the legholes at the bottom. In his early months, the baby has his face nestled into a parent's warm chest, and as he grows, he can be turned outward—with his back then facing the baby-wearer—so that he can look around.

PROS:

- Most parents find a good frontpack very easy to use.
- They are widely available.

CONS:

- Although some models claim that the pouch can be adjusted so that you can nurse your baby in it, most parents generally find nursing in a frontpack to be difficult at best. Thus, the upright position is really the only one available to your baby.
- Some parents find that even well-made, more expensive models are hard on their own backs.
- Small babies usually need a parent to support their heads with one hand while in the pack.
- Some parents and pediatricians worry that the frontpack's upright design can be damaging to a new baby's developing spine and pelvis.
- Even the most enthusiastic users of the frontpack style of carrier agree that it is usually only comfortable to use with a baby under about six or eight months of age. Many parents use the frontpack until the baby can sit up well and hold his head steady, and then they switch to a backpack.

WHAT TO LOOK FOR IN A FRONTPACK

Look for very wide, thickly padded shoulder straps, as well as one-handed adjustability and access to the buckles and straps *while you are wearing the baby.* Thin, under-padded straps will dig into your shoulders and back, and if you can't get the baby in and out of the carrier without help from another person, it won't be of much use to you. Also look for a well-padded pouch and plenty of firm head support for the baby. Better models will allow you to adjust the snugness of the pouch so that it cradles a tiny baby more firmly. Choose a frontpack that says it can be used with babies up to at least twenty pounds. If you get one with a lower weigh limit, a fast-growing baby may not be able to use it very long. Lastly, look for a model that can be used with the baby front- or rear-facing. The top vote-getter by a mile in a poll of attachment parents who use and enjoy a frontpack was the *Baby-Björn* brand frontpack, available through better baby stores and catalogs. For information on a distributor near you, contact Baby-Björn at:

REGAL+LAGER INC.
1990 Delk Industrial Blvd., Suite 105
Marietta, GA 30067
Phone: (800) 593–5522 or (770) 955–5060
Fax: (770) 955–1997
http://www.babybjorn.com
E-mail: babybjorn@regallager.com

The Backpack

The backpack is another style of infant carrier that has been popular for a number of years now. But recent advances in strong, lightweight materials and comfortable, durable fabrics have made today's baby backpacks vastly improved over older models. With a backpack, a parent wears the baby or toddler strapped into a secure seat on her back. As with the frontpack, the baby's legs dangle down through legholes at the bottom of the seat. Better backpacks have a kickstand device as a part of the supporting frame that allows a parent to get the pack on and off without assistance (although this can take a little practice). This kickstand feature can also allow the backpack to serve as a stand-alone "high chair" while camping or picnicking.

► *"I wear Annie in the backpack most of the day as I do my cleaning, shopping, and walking with other mothers at the mall. I can't imagine getting along without it. She actually goes and gets it out of the coat closet, drags it into the living room and tries to climb in it when she is ready for a ride!"*

—LEEANNE, MOTHER OF A TWO YEAR OLD

PROS:

• A well-designed baby backpack provides a very secure and comfortable ride for a child. Most babies and young children enjoy the vantage point that a backpack's "catbird seat" provides.

• A well-fitting, well-constructed backpack allows a parent to briskly and comfortably hike or walk for exercise while carrying her child.

• A backpack is great for keeping your baby close while doing work that requires the baby to be truly "out of the way" and a parent's hands to be free, such as chopping vegetables, certain shopping, or vacuuming.

• Many backpacks include a convenient attached pouch that can carry extra diapers, snacks or parent's keys.

CONS:

• The backpack can't be used until a baby is old enough to sit up easily on his own and consistently hold his head upright (a very young infant should *never* be carried in a backpack).

• Some parents with lower back problems find that the backpack aggravates their condition.

• Some babies develop an annoying habit of grabbing at a parent's neck, hair, or earrings while riding in the backpack.

• Obviously, a parent has to remove the backpack and take the baby out in order to nurse.

• Sitting while wearing a backpack is possible, but usually not terribly comfortable.

WHAT TO LOOK FOR IN A BACKPACK

Look for the same things you would look for in a good camping/hiking backpack: a lightweight frame, well-padded shoulder straps, easy adjustability, and a comfortable fit. Make sure that the model you get can be fitted to your particular height. The cheaper (under $100 models) usually lack the adjustability and support of more expensive models ($100–$200), which are found at outdoor stores and in catalogs such as REI and L.L. Bean. Many parents—particularly those who don't plan to do any extensive city walking or weekend hiking in their baby backpack—find the less-expensive models perfectly adequate. If you do plan to use the backpack in the great outdoors, you may want to look for a model with a sun/rain guard for the baby's protection. Be sure that the backpack includes a safety harness (not just a waist strap) for your baby to keep him securely situated in his seat even if you should stumble while carrying him. And whatever model you choose, make sure that the edges of the baby's seat are thickly padded so that he won't accidentally bump his face and so that he can comfortably rest his head against the sides of the seat when he wants to fall asleep.

The Baby Sling

The baby sling is a relatively recent addition to the modern, western pantheon of baby carrying options, but it is the one growing in popularity most quickly. It is also the type of carrier which most closely resembles the various cloth carriers that women in other cultures use to transport their babies on their bodies. Baby slings—which come in a variety of slightly different designs—commonly consist of several yards of soft cotton cloth, with padded "rails" of fabric on either side. A fabric tail is threaded through interlocking plastic rings which allows the sling to be adjusted easily with one hand. The sling is supported by looping it over one of the parent's shoulders. *Slings are by far the most versatile, useful, comfortable type of baby carrier and one which no attachment parent should be without.* Once you begin using a sling regularly, you will truly wonder how sling-less parents get along.

Many parents report that having a sling is sort of like having a third arm for helping to take care of their baby or young child! Some parents mistakenly worry that a newborn baby in particular is "too scrunched up" when nestled in the sling. But you should remember that babies generally *like* being balled up and gently supported in a position similar to being back in the womb.

PROS:

- A sling can be used in a wide variety of positions, allowing the baby to sit upright, face outward, or fully recline for a comfortable sleep.
- The soft contours of the sling mold to the baby's shape and take the weight off the baby's spine and pelvis.
- Used properly, a sling provides plenty of head support for a young infant.
- A sling is less expensive than most other baby carriers (usually retailing between $25 and $45, depending on the brand).
- Unlike other carriers which are only useful in early infancy or only after the baby can sit up, the sling can be comfortably worn from the day you give birth until well into your baby's toddlerhood.
- With a sling, there are no straps to cut into a parent's shoulders or back. A sling has only one wide, soft, contoured pad for your shoulder.
- Once you get the hang of it, a sling takes only a few seconds to put on and get a baby into. Because it is less complicated to put on, you are far more likely to use it.
- A sling can be easily adjusted with only one hand. There are no belts, buckles, snaps, straps, or zippers.
- The soft sling conforms perfectly to any wearer's torso.
- Again, once you get the hang of it, it's easy to quickly adjust your baby's position in the sling for his maximum comfort. If he

falls asleep upright in the sling, you can gently ease him into a reclining position without waking him up.

• A sleeping baby in a sling can be easily put down without being awakened.

• Parents with back pain/injuries are often able to use the sling with no problem.

• Slings come in a vast array of colors and fabric prints. Anyone—male or female, young or old—can find a sling fabric that suits her sense of style.

• You can wear two slings at once—one on each side—with twins.

• An all-cotton sling is much cooler than other baby carriers made of nylon, canvas, or corduroy.

• You can easily nurse in your sling, including while walking around. There is no need to remove your nursling in order to feed him.

• The sling can be positioned so that you are able to nurse very discreetly.

• A parent can comfortably stand up *or* sit down while wearing a sling. You can easily eat while seated at a table.

• When you carry a new baby close to your body and deep in the folds of the sling, strangers and well-wishers are less likely to place their germy and uninvited hands all over your baby. Your baby remains in *your own* personal space, which other people are less likely to intrude upon.

• Some slings come in sizes for petite, average and tall babywearers.

• A sling is easily machine washable with the rest of your regular laundry. In fact, the more you wash it, the softer and easier to adjust it will become.

• A sling can be folded up easily and stuffed into a diaper bag or purse.

CONS:

• A sling usually isn't the best choice for times when parents want to walk or hike very briskly for exercise (the backpack is best for this).

• Slings can take some practice in order to get the hang of using them and to feel comfortable wearing them. Some parents, without guidance, give up on a sling too soon because they can't figure out how to use the various sling holds and thus, they don't feel confident that the baby is secure in the sling. *The Baby Book* by Dr. William and Martha Sears contains a number of excellent diagrams and explanations of the various sling holds. Several sling brands, such as the Over the Shoulder Baby Holder, also come with very helpful photographs and descriptions of how to wear a sling. Although these written instructions can be really useful and are highly recommended, many parents find that the best way to learn to use a sling is to watch other sling-wearing parents and to get some hands-on assistance. If you have a friend or acquaintance who uses a sling for her child, ask her to help you get started with yours. Many La Leche League members use baby slings, so you might try a meeting or call a local Leader for some sling guidance.

• Slings vary in both features and quality. Many parents say that—even within the same sling brand—the consistency in design and quality among slings can range from wonderful to almost useless. If a sling has too much or too little padding, or a tail that is too short, or fabric that is too thick or rough to slide smoothly through the plastic hoops, or is the wrong size for the wearer, it won't work well. When you buy your sling, hang onto the sales receipt so that you can exchange it if you find that it is poorly made or doesn't feel right to you. And if you are having trouble getting your sling to work properly, you might try another brand or another sling of the same brand but made of a different fabric to see if that solves the problem. Don't give up though, because once you settle on the sling that works well for you, you will find it a truly indispensable item.

• Not all babies like all the holds that are available with the sling, and some babies require a little adjustment time to begin enjoying riding in the sling at all. If your baby seems fussy, try a different sling hold. And if he doesn't seem to like it at all, put the sling away for a few weeks and try again later. The vast majority of babies *love* the sling, especially when they have been introduced to it in the first month or two after birth. A parent's confidence and comfort in using it also encourages babies to relax and enjoy a ride in the sling. If you are tentative while carrying the baby in the sling and constantly shifting and adjusting him, he will probably fuss.

Where to Get Your Baby Sling

There are a number of different brands and styles of baby slings available today. Here are some of the best resources for choosing your own baby sling, as well as advice and support on exactly how to use it:

Wears the Baby
Phone: (800) 527–8985
http://www.wearsthebaby.com/
E-mail: wtb@wearsthebaby.com

Mother's Nature
703 Main Street
Watertown, CT, 06795
Phone: (888) 8slings
http://www.babyholder.com
E-mail: products@mothersnature.com

Maya Wrap, Inc.
1541 S. 109th St.
Omaha, NE 68144

Phone: (888) MAYA–WRAP
http://www.mayawrap.com/
E-mail: mayawrap@mayawrap.com

Parenting Concepts
P.O. Box 1437
Lake Arrowhead, CA 92352
(Shipping) 29109 Hook Creek Rd.
Cedar Glen, CA 92321
Phone: (800) 727–3683
Fax: (909) 337–0969
http://www.parentingconcepts.com
E-mail: moms@parentingconcepts.com

The Original Babysling by NoJo
22942 Arroyo Vista,
Rancho Santa Margarita, CA 92688
Phone: (800) 541–5711
http://www.NOJO.com
E-mail: info@NoJo.com

New Native Baby Carriers
P.O. Box 247
Davenport, CA 95017
Phone: (800) 646–1682
http://gate.cruzio.com/ newnativ/
E-mail: newnativ@aol.com

Slings 'n' Things
3312 Corona del Mar Dr.
Las Vegas, NV 89108–4828
http://www.slingsnthings.com
E-mail:slingsetc@aol.com

Heart to Heart Designs for Mothering
33 Glassco Avenue North
Hamilton, Ontario
Canada L8H 5Z7
http://www.heart2heart.on.ca/index.html
E-mail: sales@heart2hearton.ca

Breastfeeding.com
2171 Dailey Street
Superior, CO 80027
http://www.breastfeeding.com
E-Mail: order@nursingmother.com

In addition to the retail sources listed above, many individual parents offer baby slings as a part-time, home-based business. You might ask a La Leche League Leader or other sling-wearing friends or neighbors if they know of anyone in your community who sells slings.

Safety Tips for Baby-Wearing Parents

As with all items designed for infants and small children, baby carriers require common sense attention to safety by parents. Here are some things to keep in mind when using the various types of baby carriers:

- Always be sure that a frontpack or backpack is securely fastened to your own body, with all buckles, snaps, and zippers in place.
- Always buckle your child securely into a backpack's seat by fastening the safety harness.
- Don't allow your young infant's head to flop or jerk around while riding in a baby carrier; support his little head with one hand if necessary. Never carry babies in a backpack before they have good head control.

- Be sure that your baby's legs are in their proper place. You don't want them to become uncomfortably twisted in a carrier.
- Make sure that your baby doesn't become overheated in the summertime while riding in a carrier. Remember that a carrier provides at least one extra layer of warmth against your baby, and your own body heat will warm your baby as well.
- Don't run or jog with your baby in a carrier. They aren't designed for this purpose.
- Never use a carrier of any type as a substitute for a carseat.
- Never mow the lawn or ride a bike while wearing your baby or young child.
- Never use a frontpack or sling while cooking at the stove, around an open flame, while eating or drinking very hot items, or near machinery in which the carrier could become caught.
- Bend at the knees when stooping over or reaching down while wearing a baby carrier.
- Realize that the baby on your back or hip may be able to grab (and eat) leaves off the trees or touch hot or sharp objects that you might pass as you walk by. Be aware of all that is in the space around you when you are wearing your baby.

CHAPTER 9

Breastfeeding Past the First Year

▶ *"I want to nurse my boys long enough so that they'll have some memory of it. You know how you have early memories that are comforting—whether a smell or sensation? I want their comforting memory to be the warmth of my arms and the sound of my heart and the smell of my skin."*

—*LEE ANNE, MOTHER OF NINE MONTH OLD TWINS*

IT IS LIKELY THAT ALMOST AS SOON AS YOU GOT SETTLED INTO A comfortable routine breastfeeding your baby, you began hearing other people's thoughts on when you should *stop* breastfeeding. As with so many other aspects of parenting, however, the only opinions that ultimately matter on this important topic are yours and your child's. In this chapter we will provide you with solid, reliable information—as well as words of wisdom from other parents—that will assist you in your decision about how long you will continue nursing your child. Many attachment parents choose to nurse well beyond the first year and find great joy in a long-term breastfeeding relationship, culminating in child-respectful weaning. For these families, sustained breastfeeding—with its many and varied benefits—is an integral part of their nurturing parenting style.

I've Never Seen a Nursing Toddler; Is It "Normal" to Breastfeed Past the First Year?

> ✦**"In the 1800s, more than 95% of infants in the United States were breastfed by their mothers, and children were not weaned until they were two to four years old."**
>
> —*Anthropologist Meredith F. Small*, Our Babies, Ourselves

Currently, the *average* duration of breastfeeding in the United States is very, very brief: approximately four months. Only slightly more than half of all American mothers even try breastfeeding their newborns at all; about forty percent go straight to the bottle. By six months of age, approximately seventy-five percent of all U.S. babies are *not* being breastfed, and this number rises to an astonishing ninety percent by babies' first birthday. These numbers become even more dismal when you calculate the number of mothers who are exclusively breastfeeding, without formula supplementation.

As we mentioned in the chapter entitled "Breastfeeding Matters," better educated and higher-income mothers are far more likely to breastfeed their babies—and to breastfeed them for a longer duration—than other mothers. Additionally, breastfeeding rates vary quite a bit from region to region, with the Pacific Northwest and Rocky Mountain regions having the highest breastfeeding rates and the Midwest and Southeast having the lowest. As a group, African-American mothers are less likely to breastfeed than are White and Hispanic mothers (U.S. DHHS statistics). Considering all these factors, and depending on where you live and the socioeconomic makeup of your community, you may find that either everyone you know—or perhaps no one at all among your friends and colleagues—is choosing to breastfeed past the first month, six months, or first year. Your idea of the "normal" duration for breastfeeding has very likely been strongly influenced by your exposure to the mothers in your immediate circle and the choices they have made. If you have never seen or heard of a baby nursing into toddlerhood or beyond, the concept may seem unusual to you. Be assured that it is not. Lactation specialists, infant-maternal health advocates, anthropologists, informed physicians, and many, many experienced breastfeeding families will tell you that breastfeeding a child well past his first birthday is a normal, healthy and *positive* parenting choice.

► *"The first time I saw a mother nursing her toddler, I was taken aback—not in a negative sense—I actually thought it was neat. But I had never seen a talking child nursing before."*

—SHAWN, MOTHER OF A THREE YEAR OLD NURSLING

► *"Very old women at church, like over age eighty, are the ones who most often say something sweet when they see me nursing Zane. They either fondly remember their own mothers nursing them—which means they were breastfed a pretty long time to be able to recall the experience—or else they remember happily nursing their own toddler when they were young mothers themselves."*

—KAREN, MOTHER OF A TWO YEAR OLD NURSLING

Breastfeeding Duration Around the World

> ✦**" . . . only in the West are infants weaned before one year of age."**
>
> —*Anthropologist Meredith F. Small*

All over the world, mothers routinely breastfeed their babies well into early childhood. In Nepal, the average duration of breastfeeding is two and a half years. In Thailand, it is eighteen months. As a group, Guatemalan mothers breastfeed their babies for twenty months. And in Indonesia, a baby can expect to receive mother's milk for about two years (WHO statistics). Many subcultures within various nationalities, including the Kung San of Africa, breastfeed for three or more years. Of course, these numbers factor in the mothers who breastfeed for only a very short time, so within these groups, there are also lots of mothers nursing for much *longer* than the average durations cited here. Although there are places other than our own little corner of the planet in which babies are routinely weaned before one year of age, these are clearly the *marked* exceptions rather than the rule. It is safe to say that worldwide, the expected duration of breastfeeding is much closer to two or even three years than the paltry few months of breastfeeding that the average American, Canadian, British or French baby receives. Unfortunately, but rather predictably, global weaning ages seem to be inching downward as infant formula manufacturers continue to make aggressive inroads into many traditional breastfeeding cultures.

A Natural Duration for Breastfeeding?

> ✦**"In all cases, this hominid blueprint of the way babies were fed for ninety-nine percent of human history indicates breast milk as the primary or sole food until two years of age or so, and nursing commonly continuing for several more years."**
>
> —*Anthropologist Meredith F. Small*

Leaving cultural and family influences aside, how long does *nature* intend for human beings to nurse their young? According to Katherine Dettwyler, Ph.D., Associate Professor of Anthropology and Nutrition at Texas A & M University—and the world's foremost authority on this topic—there are several ways to approach this question:

> ✦**"My research has looked at the various 'life-history' variables—such as length of gestation, birth weight, growth rate, age at sexual maturity, age at eruption of teeth, and lifespan in nonhuman primates, and then looked at how these variables correlate with age at weaning in these animals. These are our closest relatives in the animal kingdom, especially gorillas and chimpanzees. I came up with a number of predictions for when humans would 'naturally' wean their children if they didn't have a lot of cultural rules about it. This interest stemmed from a reading of the cross-cultural literature on age at weaning, which shows that cultures have very different beliefs about when children should be weaned—from very early in the U.S. to very late in some places. A survey of sixty-four 'traditional' societies done prior to the 1940s showed a median duration of breastfeeding of about 2.8 years, but with some societies breastfeeding for much**

shorter, and some for much longer. It is meaningless, statistically, to speak of an average age of weaning worldwide, as so many children never nurse at all, or their mothers give up in the first few days, or at six weeks when they go back to work. It is true that there are still many societies in the world where children are routinely breastfed until the age of four or five years or older, and even in the United States, some children are nursed for this long and longer. In societies where children are allowed to nurse 'as long as they want,' they usually self-wean, with no arguments or emotional trauma, between three and five years of age. Other animals also have 'natural' ages of weaning—for example at around 8 weeks for dogs and eleven to twelve months for horses in the wild. Presumably these animals don't have cultural beliefs about when it would be appropriate to discontinue breastfeeding.

Here are some data points to consider when thinking about a natural duration of breastfeeding in humans:

- In a study by Holly Smith of twenty-one species of nonhuman primates (monkeys and apes), it was found that offspring were weaned at the same time they were getting their first permanent molars. In humans, that would be 5.5–6.0 years.
- It has been common for pediatricians to claim that length of gestation is approximately equal to length of nursing in many species, suggesting a weaning age of nine months for humans. However, this relationship turns out to be affected by how large the adult animals are–the larger the adults, the longer the length of breastfeeding relative to gestation. For chimpanzees and gorillas, the two primates closest in size to humans and also the most closely genetically related, the relationship is six to one. That is to say, they nurse their offspring for approximately six times the length of gestation. So for humans, that would translate into 4.5 years of nursing (six times our nine months of gestation).

- It has also been common for some pediatricians to claim that most mammals wean their offspring when they have tripled their birth weight, suggesting a weaning age of one year in humans. Again though, this is affected by body weight, with larger mammals nursing their offspring until they have quadrupled their birth weight. In humans, quadrupling of birth weight generally occurs between 2.5 and 3.5 years of age.
- One study of primates showed that the offspring were weaned when they had reached about one-third of their adult weight. This happens in humans between 5.0–7.0 years of age.
- Studies have shown that some aspects of a child's immune system don't completely mature until about 6 years of age, and it is well established that breastmilk helps develop the immune system and augment it with maternal antibodies.

So, taking these factors, among others, into account, the minimum predicted age for natural weaning in humans is 2.5 years, with a maximum of 7.0 years."

Dr. Dettwyler's research on this topic is covered in her chapter, "A Time to Wean" in the book, *Breastfeeding: Biocultural Perspectives* (Aldine de Gruyter, 1995).

The Growing Popularity of Sustained Breastfeeding

> ✦**"The American Academy of Pediatrics says that babies should be breastfed until age one. It's the lucky baby, I feel, who continues to nurse until he is two."**
>
> —*Dr. Antonia Novello, former U.S. Surgeon General*

A great deal of anecdotal evidence suggests that a growing number of women in this country are now choosing to breastfeed into their nursling's toddler years and beyond. La Leche League International offers "toddler meetings," and the amount of print and Internet resource material directed specifically at mothers of older nurslings is increasing. It made a significant impact on women's decision how long they should breastfeed when the American Academy of Pediatrics (AAP) revised its breastfeeding guidelines in 1998 to better reflect the newest research on breastfeeding. Today, the AAP's statement on Breastfeeding and the Use of Human Milk reads:

"It is recommended that breastfeeding continue for at least 12 months, and thereafter for as long as mutually desired."

This recognition of the normalcy and desirability of breastfeeding past a baby's first birthday represented a change on the part of the AAP that was slow in coming, relative to the assembled evidence in favor of sustained breastfeeding. The World Health Organization, on the other hand, has recommended breastfeeding for *at least two years* for some time now. So, if you haven't yet met anyone who is breastfeeding a child past the first year, it's likely that you soon will, as more and more mothers make the decision to sustain their breastfeeding relationship past their child's first, second, or third year . . . or beyond.

> ▶ *"When I had my first child, fifteen years ago, I was definitely the only person I had ever met who was breastfeeding a toddler. People really thought it was strange. Now, with my fourth baby, all my friends are breastfeeding for at least a year. It is considered very odd if you don't. If someone I know is no longer breastfeeding her sixteen month old, for example, her friends quietly wonder what might have precipitated such an early weaning. There is a lot more good information readily available to support breastfeeding mothers today than there was even five years ago."*
>
> —JACKIE, MOTHER OF FOUR

Sustained Breastfeeding and Your Child's Health

For an infant, breastfeeding is indisputably *critically* important. It protects him as his immature immune system develops and it provides unmatched nutritional excellence for optimal physical and cognitive development. Infants *need* breastmilk. However, after about the first birthday, the picture becomes a bit more complex, but no less convincing in favor of continued breastfeeding. Most one or two year olds *can* get along without breastmilk in their diet . . . but should they?

Although no research has yet been done specifically to measure the composition or nutritional value of breastmilk after the somewhat arbitrary cutoff of twenty-four months postpartum, a significant amount of research *has* been done on the value of breastfeeding with children up to two years of age. In a wide variety of studies—including those looking at gastrointestinal illness, upper respiratory illness, multiple sclerosis, diabetes, heart disease, and SIDS—the results were clear: *the longer the child was breastfed, the lower his risk became for the disorder under review*. In the case of breastfeeding's impact on I.Q., studies indicate that—even after adjusting for socioeconomic variables—the longer a child is breastfed, the higher his IQ score will be. There is absolutely no reason to believe that the health promoting benefits of breastmilk suddenly—or even gradually—disappear at one year or two years postpartum. After all, banked breastmilk is now sometimes prescribed to adults and older children suffering from immune dysfunction.

Sustained Breastfeeding and Your Health

The World Health Organization concerns itself with the health of both children *and* their parents. Part of the reason behind WHO's recommendation of breastfeeding for at least two years is the fact that *sustained breastfeeding also benefits nursing mothers.* As we have already discussed in earlier chapters, the longer and more frequently you breastfeed your baby, the longer you will likely go before resuming your pre-pregnancy state of fertility (although individual variations in patterns of fertility should be expected). Lactational amenorrhea—the time during which you are period-free as a result of breastfeeding—has positive ramifications for your health, as well as providing a nice break from the hassle of having your period.

For starters, it can serve as one element in your family planning bag of tricks. Most women who are in a state of lactational amenorrhea remain infertile until the months immediately preceding the resumption of their periods. Some lactating women remain anovulatory even *after* resuming menstruation, until they are no longer breastfeeding. In areas of the world where artificial methods of birth control are hard to come by, or for women in the developed world who are uncomfortable with the use of artificial methods, sustained breastfeeding can play a valuable role in making sure that children are not spaced too closely. It has also been theorized that the fewer periods a woman has in her lifetime, the lower her risk is for certain diseases. That may explain the research showing that a woman's risks for premenopausal breast cancer and ovarian cancer are related to duration of breastfeeding. The more months during her lifetime that a woman breastfeeds, the less likely she is to develop one of these illnesses. The same appears to be true for development of osteoporosis.

► *"I loved being without a period for more than a year while breastfeeding. When you add in pregnancy, I didn't have to deal with a period for two years."*

—MARCIE, MOTHER OF TWO

Two excellent resources for women who wish to learn more about sustained breastfeeding and its effect on their fertility are:

Taking Charge of Your Fertility: The Definitive Guide to Natural Birth Control and Pregnancy Achievement. Weschler, Toni. New York: HarperCollins, 1995.

The Art of Natural Family Planning. Kippley, John F. and Sheila. (May 1997) Couple to Couple League.

Mothering Your Older Nursling

✦**"We have a sign in our office: 'Early Weaning Not Recommended for Babies.' If you view parenting as a long term investment, why sell your options short?"**

—DR. WILLIAM AND MARTHA SEARS

► *"What do mothers who don't breastfeed do when their child needs to nurse? When he falls or feels anxious or sleepy? It's pretty obvious to me what a one year old in one of those situations wants from his mother, even if he was never breastfed in his life and can't quite figure out himself what it is he is lacking."*

—JON, FATHER OF A NINETEEN MONTH OLD NURSLING

Most mothers who have breastfed their children through the toddler or preschool years can't *imagine* trying to parent their newly dynamic little people without the benefit of the nursing relationship. All of the emotional and relational benefits of breastfeeding an infant remain in place for the older nursling, but a mother's ability to utilize breastfeeding to calm, relax, soothe, and parent-to-sleep her growing child becomes even more helpful. Once you have breastfed a one, two, or three year old, you will really feel for the nonnursing mothers you see at the park or at preschool who are struggling to meet the changing needs of their rapidly developing little people without the benefit of breastfeeding. After all, most toddlers have not yet lost their biological *need* to suck for comfort and security. That's why you see so many prematurely weaned toddlers or preschoolers—or those who never got to breastfeed at all—clinging with all their heart and soul to a beloved pacifier, bottle, blankie, or thumb. These walking, talking babies still want and need to nurse.

✦ **"Suckling plays an enormous role in a child's ability to grow up. Some children, unless their mothers nurse them or help them find substitutes, may never completely overcome the anxieties and confusion they experience through the changes of their early years. Some seek ineffective substitutes, either in behavior or objects. Unlike suckling, however, which will cease all by itself once it has done its job, the dependence upon less effective behaviors or upon objects may not go away nearly so easily or reliably."**

—*Norma Jane Bumgarner,*
Author of Mothering Your Nursing Toddler

As your newly independent young nursling explores the world around him, he will also remain securely attached to you and confident that when his expanding universe becomes overwhelming—when a dog barks too loudly, or another child takes his favorite truck at playgroup, or he is frustrated by his inability to get a certain word out of his mouth—he can return to the comfort of the breastfeeding relationship he shares with you for recharging before venturing forth again.

What's It Really Like to Breastfeed Past the First Year?

Sharing a breastfeeding relationship, no matter what a child's age, does require a commitment on the part of a mother to remain available to her child. (Optimally, the same should be true for parenting the nonbreastfed child.) During a nursing baby's first year, that commitment can sometimes be quite time consuming, due to the fact that breastmilk is the major portion of a baby's healthy diet, and because a securely bonded, cue-fed infant does usually ask to nurse at minimum every few hours. In most cases, cue-fed one year olds will continue to nurse fairly frequently, though usually not with the intensity of a six month old. However, there are some breastfed one year olds who take eagerly to solids and cups, and become happily engaged with learning to walk, talk, climb and interact with people. These busy young toddlers often ask to nurse only a few times a day and tend to become early self-weaners. After about the second birthday, the nursing patterns of cue-fed toddlers seem to vary quite widely from child to child, with some toddlers quickly initiating the process of self-weaning, while others continue to depend heavily on the nursing relationship for both nutrition and comfort. Either variation—and everything in between—is normal. After a child's third birthday or so, very few mothers continue to nurse entirely on cue. Most begin to set some gentle limits on nursing, ranging from only nursing at home to only nursing a set number of times per day—or even just at bedtime. There are, however, some mothers who choose to continue to nurse entirely on cue for the duration of their nursing relationship, whatever its length.

Dealing with the Opinions of Others

> ► *"Most of the comments I get regarding nursing Melody are quite positive. Either that or people have questions. They wonder if the milk is still any good or how often she nurses. But once or twice friends have said something I thought was pretty negative. One of my husband's friends told him that breastfeeding a toddler is 'perverse.' I feel sorry for people like that. They are just jealous that they never had this kind of relationship with their own mother. They know that there is a truly special love between a mother and a nursing child."*
>
> —MARY ELIZABETH, MOTHER OF A THREE YEAR OLD NURSLING

Because sustained breastfeeding is still fairly uncommon in many segments of U.S. society, your decision to continue breastfeeding your child past the first year may be the area of your parenting style about which you receive the most unsolicited commentary. Although you will find many people full of admiration for your commitment to meeting your child's needs, and others who are congenially inquisitive about you and your older nursling, you may also encounter some annoying or even negative feedback from people who are simply ignorant about breastfeeding. Sadly, many health care providers are completely uninformed about sustained breastfeeding. Although antibreastfeeding individuals may grudgingly tolerate an *infant's* need to nurse, the sight—or even the thought—of your toddler or preschooler being mothered at the breast may send them into a tizzy. Although the greatest part of any negative reaction you may get will be due to simple ignorance, many mothers of older nurslings have observed that men in particular seem to become very testy about the idea of walking, talking children continuing to nurse. This is probably due in large part to the sexualization of the breast in western culture. Although the primary purpose of women's breasts is to feed and nurture their children, many men have been raised to believe that breasts actually "belong" to men in general. The concept of a sustained breastfeeding relationship with a child—as opposed to an infant—challenges that sexist world view. Other negative feedback might come from women who have simply never experienced nursing a child past the first year—or at all—or those who were raised to believe that breastfeeding is "indecent" under virtually any circumstance.

So how do mothers of older nurslings handle this issue? Here are some real life examples:

- *"It is absolutely none of anyone's business how long I decide to breastfeed. Although I have personally only received positive feedback from people, they would certainly get an earful if they ever dared make a peep about there being something wrong with us still nursing."*

  —CATHY, MOTHER OF TWO NURSLINGS, AGES THREE AND SIX MONTHS

- *"After he turned about two and a half, I made the decision to limit nursing to home and to public places where we know everyone and feel comfortable, like La Leche League meetings. I am mindful that I have a responsibility to protect him from people's potential for saying hurtful things to children regarding something they know nothing about."*

  —BARB, MOTHER OF A FIVE YEAR OLD NURSLING

- *"I have slowly built a community of like-minded friends for myself so that we tend to mostly hang around with other families who also believe in child-led weaning."*

  —JOANNE, MOTHER OF A THREE YEAR OLD NURSLING

- ▶ *"When my father or mother continually asks me how long I plan to keep nursing, I try to keep it light and say something like 'Until she's had enough to eat.' or 'Until you quit bugging me about it!' "*

  —SHELLY, MOTHER OF A TWO YEAR OLD NURSLING

- ▶ *"We just tell anyone who asks that we're 'in the process of weaning.' It seems to satisfy their nosiness."*

  —KURT, FATHER OF A FOUR YEAR OLD NURSLING

- ▶ *"I think the few people who have said anything to me ended up being really sorry because I turned the issue around and educated them for a good long time on the importance of breastfeeding."*

  —PIETRA, MOTHER OF A TWENTY-ONE MONTH OLD NURSLING

- ▶ *"We finally changed doctors because, even though he was conveniently located, I got so sick of listening to his ridiculous views on breastfeeding a toddler. He seemed really supportive of nursing until Max's first birthday and then he suddenly began browbeating me every time we went in for either of the kids, telling us that we needed to wean 'cold turkey.' I just finally had had enough."*

  —LISA, MOTHER OF TWO FORMER OLDER NURSLINGS

- ▶ *"I enjoy nursing the two of them around other people and making friendly eye contact. People need to see that breastfeeding beyond one year and breastfeeding more than one child is natural."*

  —PATTIE, MOTHER OF TWO NURSLINGS, AGES ONE AND FOUR

The Very Best Resources for Parents of Older Nurslings

As one of the parents quoted above mentioned, many mothers of older nurslings find it especially helpful and enriching to connect with other attachment parents who are also nursing past the first year. Reading about sustained breastfeeding can also help you feel confident and supported in your parenting style. Here are the best resources available on this topic:

BOOKS

Mothering Your Nursing Toddler. Bumgarner, Norma J. Schaumburg, IL: La Leche League Intl., 1982.

This is the book every mother nursing a baby past the first year will want to read. Warm and informative, the book takes a realistic look at the many joys—and the challenges—of mothering an older nursling.

The Nursing Mother's Guide to Weaning. Huggins, Kathleen. Linda Ziedrich. Boston: Harvard Common Press, 1994.

Although this book is ostensibly about weaning, it is also a wonderful guide for any mother nursing past the first year.

PERIODICALS

Beyond One Year
P.O. Box 54492
Irvine, California 92619
http://www.kjsl.com/ boynews/intro.html
E-mail:korlinsk@pacbell.net

A terrific newsletter for parents interested in all topics related to parenting the breastfed child past his first birthday.

WEB SITES

Dr. Katherine Dettwyler's Thoughts on Breastfeeding
http://www.prairienet.org/community/health/laleche/dettwyler.html

Parent-L Breastfeeding Resources Page
http://www.greatstar.com/lois/parent-l.html

The Parent-L Frequently Asked Questions (FAQ) on Extended Breastfeeding
http://www.greatstar.com/lois/extend.html

INTERNET E-MAIL LISTS

Parent-L *is the best known e-mail list for parents who currently are or who plan to nurse past the first year. To subscribe, send the following command to* majordomo@uts.edu.au: "subscribe parent-l-digest" or "subscribe parent-l" (no quotes)

Great Big Kids (GBK) *is a list specifically for women who are nursing children aged 3.5 or older. To subscribe, send an essay to* bfandhs@juno.com *explaining who you are and why you want to join GBK. Mention where you heard about the list and expect at least one week for processing of your application.*

Nursing Through Pregnancy

Although breastfeeding provides protection against pregnancy, its contraceptive effect lessens over time as your nursling grows and nurses less frequently, and a few women see the resumption of their fertility within only a few months after giving birth, despite cue-breastfeeding their baby. This means that some mothers will—by choice or by circumstance—find themselves pregnant while still nursing another child.

- **Can you continue to nurse through a pregnancy?**

Yes, most of the time. In cases in which a pregnant mother is at demonstrated risk for or begins to show signs of premature labor, breastfeeding during pregnancy may be inadvisable. If you find yourself pregnant while still breastfeeding, you should consult a midwife or physician with experience and knowledge of all aspects of breastfeeding (take another look at the section in Chapter Two on finding a breastfeeding-friendly physician). This health care professional can consult with you on the advisability of continuing to breastfeed based on your individual obstetrical history. Much more likely than not, however, there will be no reason whatsoever that you will have to stop breastfeeding while pregnant.

• ***Should you* breastfeed through a pregnancy?** This is a highly individual decision. Many women who nurse through pregnancy enjoy every minute of it and are pleased to be able to retain the close bond that they share with their older child. They enjoy the fact that they can grab a nap in the afternoon by simply nursing their older child to sleep. They look forward to the fact that their child will get to enjoy nursing alongside his new sibling. Other women who choose to continue to breastfeed during pregnancy experience some minor nipple soreness or irritability, but still find the experience a pleasant one overall.

However, a significant minority of pregnant, breastfeeding mothers suddenly or gradually find themselves intensely physically and emotionally "turned off" to the idea of further breastfeeding with their older child. This is probably due to a combination of hormonal and psychological factors brought about by the pregnancy. Some women who have this experience choose to work through their discomfort with a variety of coping mechanisms so that they can continue to breastfeed. Other pregnant women make the choice to wean. If you decide to discontinue breastfeeding during your pregnancy, your nursling's feelings should always be taken into account. After all, he didn't ask you to become pregnant before he had satisfied his own nursing needs. It isn't fair to abruptly wean a child in this circumstance. Gentle, gradual weaning is best (as it is in virtually every weaning situation). Because many women find themselves unwilling to breastfeed through a pregnancy—including women who never imagined that they would find the experience anything but wonderful—you should think long and hard before purposely becoming pregnant before your older child has had his need for breastfeeding completely satisfied.

Tandem Nursing

✦"Tandem nursing is not particularly common cross-culturally, because the older child is often weaned before the next pregnancy, or weaned during the pregnancy. It does occur in some societies—usually in cases where the mother got pregnant again very early. And women may nurse their grandchildren along with their children, or their co-wives' or sister-in-law's babies along with their own, depending on local cultural beliefs. I think that tandem nursing occurs most frequently in well-nourished Western women who are breastfeeding relatively infrequently (every 3–4 hours) and maybe even less at night, meaning that their fertility returns quickly. Because these women are dedicated to long-term breastfeeding and child-led weaning, in these cases, we find women giving birth to children every two to three years, but nursing each child for three, four, or five years, which means tandem nursing. There are also some women who breastfeed three children of different ages at one time. In my survey research on women in the United States who breastfeed longer than three years, the record holder is a woman who was breastfeeding a five year old and a three year old when she gave birth to twins. For a short while, she was breastfeeding four children, until the oldest weaned. I have several children in the sample who breastfed for four years or

more, first with an older sibling, and then with a younger sibling, but never by themselves!"

—ANTHROPOLOGIST KATHERINE DETTWYLER, PH.D.

Tandem nursing in the context of sustained breastfeeding describes the experience of nursing different age siblings at the same time (the term is also sometimes used to describe breastfeeding twins or triplets). Although it isn't a statistically common occurrence—here or anywhere else in the world—that doesn't mean that it can't be a uniquely pleasant and special one for both mother and nurslings. Many nurslings, particularly those aged three or older when their mother became pregnant, gradually self-wean during the pregnancy as their mother's milk supply changes. On the other hand, some nurslings who appear to have completely weaned during a pregnancy begin eagerly and happily nursing again when the gush of new milk appears with the birth of the baby.

Mothers who tandem nurse discover that there are many positives to breastfeeding an older child while also nursing a new baby. Some find that it lessens the older child's potential resentment of his new sibling. Others say that they are pleased to be able to continue to share intimate one-on-one time with their "former baby." In the case of healthy breastfeeding women, the principle of lactational supply and demand means that there should be plenty of milk for one, two, or more children, as long as the tandem nursing mother is completely responsive to her youngest nursling's need-to-nurse cues.

► *"Tandem nursing has been a mixed bag for me. I personally don't believe that nature intended women to do it. But I also realize that as a human being, I have the ability to make the* ***choices*** *that are best for my children. I freely chose to continue nursing my older child when I became pregnant before her second birthday. She still* *needed to nurse and I didn't feel right about depriving her. And there certainly have been some special moments while nursing both children that I wouldn't trade for the world."*

—Katie, mother of three, including nurslings ages three and one

There *are* some challenges that can come with tandem nursing. When a mother is nursing two or more children, she may come to feel "touched out" and "used" by the constant attention of little hands and mouths. Some women find the very different sucking patterns of an infant and an older child difficult to tolerate. Because of this, some tandem nursing mothers avoid nursing both children at the same time. In other instances, one or the other of a mother's nurslings becomes upset when his sibling—usually the younger child—"gets to nurse first." No mother can be completely sure how she will feel about tandem nursing before she actually has the experience. As with nursing through pregnancy, it is wise to carefully consider your older nursling's needs when planning your child spacing. Every human being deserves the opportunity to enjoy the fullness of his own babyhood.

Weaning: Upward and Onward!

The concept of weaning is widely misunderstood in our bottle-feeding culture. Many parents who have been offering an infant both breast and bottle will report that their baby "weaned himself" at three, six, or nine months. "He just completely gave nursing up all on his own," they will proudly report. In this instance, the baby has developed a nipple preference for the bottle. He has indeed weaned, but it was most assuredly something that was done *to* the baby by his parents, as opposed to something done *by* the baby himself. It is extremely unusual for a responsively cue-fed nursling to freely give up breastfeeding before about eighteen months of age. In fact, most cue-fed children who are not offered excessive bottle or pacifier use, or pressured to wean will continue nursing for three to five years.

Attachment parents usually strive for something called "child-led weaning," in which the child himself has the largest say in when he ends his nursing relationship and moves on to the next phase of his life. Child-led weaning is an ideal which few parents manage to completely achieve. In most families, gentle limits such as when, where, and how often *are* eventually placed on an older nursling's breastfeeding habits. This means that even the most gradual weaning of a four year old child isn't truly "child-led." For this reason, a better term for this concept is probably "child-respectful weaning" (CRW, for purposes of brevity). CRW provides a fitting culmination to the loving, responsive breastfeeding relationship between a cue-fed nursling and his attachment parenting mother. Children who are lucky enough to experience CRW usually wean quite gradually. First the child might quit asking to nurse during the daytime. Then, six months later, he might give up his bedtime nursing. One day a parent will realize that her child hasn't nursed in a week. The next gap may be two to three weeks before he suddenly asks to nurse again. Finally, she will find herself having gone months without mothering her child through breastfeeding. With CRW, parents don't worry about when a child will completely stop breastfeeding. They trust the child himself to decide when he no longer needs nursing in his life.